ESCAPE FROM ST-VALERY-EN-CAUX

To the lasting memory of all who fought with the 51st Highland Division in 1939–1940 and in North Africa and North-Western Europe in 1942–1945. So many gave their lives, more were injured, many lost their freedom for years and all gave us peace.

Also to those brave French men and women who helped escaping prisoners in France and North Africa.

Finally, to the memory of the most courageous and modest man I have ever known.

Bill Bradford's medals:
From left: 1) DSO and Bar; 2) MBE (Military); 3) MC;
4) The 1939–1945 Star; 5) The Africa Star with 8th Army clasp;
6) The Italy Star; 7) The France and Germany Star;
8) The Defence Medal; 9) The 1939–45 War Medal, with Mention in Despatches; 10) The Coronation Medal, 1953

ESCAPE FROM ST-VALERY-EN-CAUX

THE ADVENTURES OF CAPTAIN B.C. BRADFORD

ANDREW BRADFORD

The
History
Press

Cover illustrations: Detail from Bradford's US Foreign Service ID; Envelope provided by the French to their British prisoners-of-war at Depot 602, Montferran-Saves; Lt-Col Bradford, 1944.

First published 2009
This paperback edition first published 2024

The History Press
97 St George's Place, Cheltenham,
Gloucestershire, GL50 3QB
www.thehistorypress.co.uk

British Library Cataloguing in Publication Data.
A catalogue record for this book is available from the British Library.

ISBN 978 1 80399 592 2

Typesetting and origination by The History Press
Printed and bound in Great Britain by TJ Books Limited, Padstow, Cornwall.

Trees for LΥfe

Contents

List of Maps		7
Principal Officers of the 1st Battalion		
The Black Watch in June 1940		9
Foreword		12
Introduction		15
1	The Phoney War: October 1939–May 1940	27
2	One Day in the Saar: May 1940	52
3	From the Maginot Line to St-Valery-en-Caux:	
	May–12 June 1940	61
4	A Prisoner of War: 12 June–19 June 1940	94
5	On the Home Front (1)	107
6	Alone: 19 June–25 June 1940	113
7	Travelling in Company: 25 June–2 July 1940	123
8	Alone Once More in Occupied France:	
	2 July–10 July 1940	143
9	From Châteauroux to Spain: 10 July–4 August 1940	165
10	Spain to Marseilles: 4 August–November 1940	188
11	On the Home Front (2)	239

12 Marseilles and North Africa:
       November 1940–May 1941   257
13 On the Home Front (3)   291
14 From Algiers to Gibraltar: June 1941   313

    Post Script: July 1941–June 1945   330

    Appendix 1   355
    Appendix 2   357
    Notes and Sources   364
    Glossary   368
    Index   371

List of Maps

The Maginot Line: May 1940
From the Maginot Line to Picardy: May 1940
Retreat from the Somme: 28 May–9 June 1940
Retreat from the Somme: 9–11 June 1940
Encirclement by 7th Panzer Division: 5–10 June 1940
The German Advance: 8–10 June 1940
St-Pierre-le-Viger: 11 June 1940
St-Valery-en-Caux: 12 June 1940
A Prisoner of War: 12–19 June 1940
Escape: 19–21 June 1940
Escape: 21–25 June 1940
Escape: 26–27 June 1940
Escape: 28–29 June 1940
Escape: 30 June–1 July 1940
Escape: 1–2 July 1940
Escape: 3–4 July 1940
Escape: 5–8 July 1940
Escape: 7–9 July 1940
Escape: 7–27 July 1940

Escape: 27–31 July 1940
Escape: 31 July–22 October 1940
Escape in the Pyrenees: 2–11 August 1940
Escape in the Mediterranean: 23 October 1940–21 June 1941
The Whole Route Home

Principal Officers of the 1st Battalion The Black Watch in June 1940

Commanding Officer	Lt-Col G.E.B. Honeyman (Honey) who had replaced Lt-Col C.G. Stephen (Steve) owing to sickness.
Second in Command	Maj. W.F. Dundas (Nogi)
Adjutant	Capt. B.C. Bradford (Bill)
Signal Officer	Lt R.N. Jardine-Paterson (Noel)
Intelligence Officer	Lt R.U.E. A. Sandford (Roger) Lt J.R.P. Moon (John)
Quarter Master	Lt S.H. Allison (Stan)

OC A Company	Maj. N. Noble (Johnnie) [evacuated sick 7 June 1940] Capt. D.H. Walker (David)
OC B Company	Maj. G.H. Milne (Geoffrey)
OC C Company	Capt. N.A.M. Grant-Duff (Neill)
OC D Company	Capt. G.P. Campbell-Preston (Patrick or Pat)
OC HQ Company	Maj. O.G.H. Russell (Odo)
Carrier Platoon	Lt A.D.H. Irwin (Angus)
Anti-Tank Platoon	Lt A.D. Telfer-Smollett (Alastair)

The 51st Highland Division in May 1940 included three infantry brigades:

| General Officer Commanding | Maj.-Gen. Victor Fortune, DSO |

152 Brigade
Brig. M.W.V. Stewart DSO   Seaforth Highlanders
2nd Battalion The Seaforth Highlanders
4th Battalion The Seaforth Highlanders
4th Battalion The Queen's Own Cameron Highlanders

153 Brigade
Brig. G.T. Burney   Gordon Highlanders
4th Battalion The Black Watch
1st Battalion The Gordon Highlanders
5th Battalion The Gordon Highlanders

154 Brigade
Brig. A.C.L. Stanley Clarke   Royal Scots Fusiliers
1st Battalion The Black Watch
7th Battalion The Argyll and Sutherland Highlanders
8th Battalion The Argyll and Sutherland Highlanders

Note: During the campaign in the Somme in late May 1940, 1st Battalion Black Watch changed places with 4th Battalion Black Watch and remained in 153 Brigade until St-Valery-en-Caux.

Foreword

This story leaves me with irreconcilable regrets that are probably familiar to anyone who has lost a parent. Why on earth didn't I take my father to France to retrace his steps in the 1980s? It would all have been so much easier. However, I must satisfy myself that at that time my father didn't want to talk of his adventures. In tackling this work a decade after his death I have had the added challenge and entertainment of discovering parts of the story for myself.

This book contains my father's full account from May 1940 until June 1941. Towards the end of his life he added a certain amount of background information. The only changes I have made to his writings are to expand some abbreviations to make the record more readable for those from a non-military background. I have completed the full names of villages where they are first mentioned. In most, but not all, instances I have been able to insert the name of individuals or places left blank at the time of writing for reasons of security.

In providing the background to his story I have drawn on numerous conversations with my father, mostly during the last few years of his life. Additional sources include a report submitted to Military Intelligence and one written by my grandfather Lt-Col E.A. Bradford in 1941, and archives at the Black Watch Museum. I have also taken material from a recorded interview between Saul David, my father and me in 1992 and from an interview with Air Chief Marshal Sir Lewis Hodges in 2005. I have included extracts from the diary of another escapee, Major Naps Brinckman, who was in North Africa with my father during 1941.

Frustratingly there is no surviving 1st Battalion Black Watch War Diary covering this period of their history. I suspect that my father was responsible for this, as he describes the burning of documents on 12 June 1940. I have drawn on a box of wartime papers collected by my grandparents which only came to light after my father's death. This includes those of his letters which reached home, together with some of his parents' correspondence. The box also contained my father's original notebook and identity papers and food coupons from Algiers and Marseilles. All have suffered somewhat from the effects of seawater, the reason for which will become apparent.

The maps that I have prepared are intended to give a picture of events. From these and with reference to 1:200,000 maps the actual route of my father's escape across France can easily be identified.

In 2002 my wife Nicky and I re-traced the route, by car, from St-Valery-en-Caux, to the point of escape near Billy-Berclau and thence to Nanteuil; we concluded that we were on the actual route for at least 95 per cent of the time. Owing to the fact that the route avoids nearly all large towns and major roads it led us through a largely unspoiled rural France.

In 2005, together with our daughter Louisa, we continued with the route from Nanteuil to Spain and thence to

Monferran-Savès. I can think of no finer excuse for wandering about the less populated parts of France.

I have not attempted to cover, in any detail, events after July 1941. My father's full correspondence exists and may yet shed an interesting light on the heroic deeds of the 51st Highland Division as they fought their way from El Alamein to final victory in Germany. That history is well documented elsewhere.

I am grateful for the assistance given by Piers Mackesy who kindly read an early draft of this work and made some useful suggestions. Also to my niece Lucy Johnston, Julia Chambers and my brother Robert for keeping me right with Latin, French and German translation respectively. Thanks also to Liam Harvey for his constructive comments and to Yvonne Taite for her patient work in typing all the historic correspondence. The encyclopaedic knowledge of Thomas Smyth, Archivist at the Black Watch Museum in Perth, deserves special mention. I am indebted also to Andrew Jardine-Paterson and Sir Theodore Brinckman who let me have access to their fathers' records. To Ed Howker and John Leigh-Pemberton for encouraging me to publish, and David Hawson deserves a special mention. Finally I don't think this work would have happened had it not been for the support of my dear wife Nicky.

Andrew Bradford

Introduction

Born on 15 October 1912, Berenger Colborne Bradford followed his father to Eton College. The family home was Empshott Lodge, Liss, Hampshire. Holidays away from home were spent mostly in the Isle of Man or in Scotland, where they often stayed with his aunt at Corsindae in Aberdeenshire. Little did he know that thirty years later marriage would bring him to Kincardine, which is less than a dozen miles from Corsindae. In a break to routine in 1927 the family went to Brittany for a holiday and, along with days spent on the beaches, visits were made to châteaux. The interest in old castles lasted a lifetime.

After leaving Eton, Bradford spent a few months during 1930 at Château de Nanteuil near Blois on the Loire. There Billy Gardnor-Beard and his French wife Anne-Marie, affectionately known as Souris, ran a finishing school for young British gentlemen. They improved their French and learned the manners and customs of the French gentry. As it happened this visit was to have considerable significance to both Bradford and Souris a decade later, but that part of the story must wait its turn.

Late in 1931 he went to the Royal Military College, Sandhurst, and on 26 September 1932 joined 2nd Battalion (Bn) The Black Watch. I am often asked why my father joined that illustrious regiment. Although he had Scottish blood in him he was essentially brought up as an Englishman in the heart of Hampshire. This was his explanation.

His uncle, Col Sir Evelyn Bradford Bt., Seaforth Highlanders, was killed while commanding 2nd Seaforth in the early days of the First World War and was revered by the family; this inspired young Bradford. Sir Evelyn was decapitated by a shell explosion at the Battle of Aisne on 14 September 1914. Bradford's own father Lt-Col Edward Austen Bradford (1879–1958) of the King's Royal Rifle Corps had fought in the Boer War and won a DSO in the First World War (1917).

Soldiering was clearly his destiny. Sir Evelyn's son, Sir Edward Montagu Andrew Bradford, who was two years older than Bradford, was not accepted by the Seaforth Highlanders and instead commissioned into the Cameron Highlanders. Bradford felt that if he then joined the Seaforths it could lead to tension between them and instead sought a commission in the Black Watch. He was delighted to join them as he had always thought that they were the best regiment in the world. Cordiality was maintained with his cousin Edward and they met several times in France during 1939–40, one meeting including a curious wartime experience involving a small pack of beagles.

Another great influence was a second uncle, Capt. Ronnie Hardy of the Rifle Brigade. He was 'The Beloved Captain', described as such in the great pen-portrait on leadership written by Donald Hankey in his book 'A Student in Arms'. Ronnie Hardy was killed in action in 1915 and his name is one of over 54,000 inscribed on the Menin Gate in Ypres, of those who have no known grave. Hankey's essay is appended to this book.

Bradford's initial posting was in England. While stationed at Colchester in the summer of 1933 he went for his first ever day's dinghy sailing with fellow Black Watch subalterns Bernard Fergusson, Mick Baker-Baker and Michael Young. They may not have been great sailors but they had successful military careers. In the coming war these four young officers were to win five DSOs and two MCs between them; three were to retire as brigadiers and one as a lieutenant-colonel; and two were to become colonels of the Regiment. Though they were just 'mucking about on the water' this limited introduction to sailing clearly struck a chord, for in September 1934 while on leave in Dumfriesshire, Bradford spent a day boating with his sister Felicity on Loch Ken. He rigged the rowing boat with an improvised mast and laced a bed-sheet sail to even more makeshift spars to form a gaff rig. Judging from the photograph of this event it seems that the wind was light which, given the state of the rig, is perhaps just as well. Although he had been a wet-bob (rower) at Eton, these two days formed the sum total of Bradford's pre-war sailing experience – but that limited experience proved handy some years later.

Shortly after that period of leave in Dumfriesshire, on 13 November 1934, a draft from the 2nd Black Watch embarked for India where the regiment's 1st Battalion was stationed. The family was no stranger to India. Bradford's grandfather Col Sir Edward Ridley Colborne Bradford, Bart., GCB, GCVO, KCSI (1836–1911) had served in the sub-continent for thirty years. First, as an officer in the Indian Army, he served with distinction in the Mutiny and elsewhere. He suffered the loss of an arm to a tiger in a hunting accident[1] and, moving to the political service, rose in 1879 to become agent to the governor general for Rajputana and Central India. On leaving India Sir Edward survived the shipwreck of SS *Tasmania*, off Corsica. He and fellow passengers and crew spent the night fighting for survival on the stern of the storm-swept deck of the half-sunk ship before being rescued the following day. Thirty-four souls lost their lives and all Sir Edward's possessions, including numerous splendid gifts from many Maharajahs, were lost. Sir Edward served for two years in the India Office, during which time he conducted Prince Albert Victor on a tour of India. In 1890 he was offered the Governorship of the Cape Colony which he declined because, according to family legend, he felt he couldn't afford to live like an Earl, which honour came with the job. In June the same year he became chief commissioner of the London Metropolitan Police at a difficult time for the force; three commissioners having resigned in the previous two years. Sir Edward held the position for the next fourteen years until 1904. He was ADC to Queen Victoria and extra equerry to both King Edward VII and King George V.[2]

Sir Edward's children were all raised in India and on reaching school age the surviving ones – for two small boys lie in graves out there – were left behind, after home leave, to be educated in England. There they were looked after by their uncle, Montagu Knight of Chawton Park in Hampshire. Montagu was the grandson of Jane Austen's brother Edward, who had changed his name on being given, by his cousin Thomas Knight, the two estates of Chawton, and of Godmersham in Kent. The extended family was very close and became closer still, for Sir Edward and his wife Lizzie's (*née* Knight) youngest son, Edward Austen Bradford, subsequently married his own first cousin Maggie Hardy. Maggie was the daughter of Lizzie's sister Louisa. They had four children, Adela (Ad), Berenger (Ben), Cassandra (known as Felicity or Cit) and Diana (Di). One can speculate as to whether they were trying for the whole alphabet!

Confusion exists about my father's name. Called Ben by his family, he was known, for no reason ever admitted to me, as Bill by everyone else. At no time was he ever called William. Towards the end of his life, when he had to go into hospital, I made the error of entering his given name in a registration form with the result that all the young nurses referred to him as Berenger which offended him; first because of the attempt at familiarity which grated with him and, secondly, he had almost never been called Berenger. Too late I realised that I should have entered 'Brigadier' as his Christian name on the form and everyone would have been content. One lives and learns.

During his time in India Sir Edward Bradford governed with considerable success. He had high respect for the Indian people who did not forget this. In consequence of his grandfather's reputation Bradford, as a young officer now stationed in India, received invitations to stay and hunt with many of the princely Indian rulers. Being only a young subaltern and an impecunious one at that, he had little opportunity to accept. However, he did manage to get away occasionally.

Once, while entraining at Calcutta station when leaving on a hunting expedition, one of the bearers dropped a case full of annas, tiny coins of little worth. Apparently the bearers and other servants preferred to be paid in these rather than rupees as they received more coins for their work. The mayhem and a frantically scrabbling horde can easily be imagined. His chief bearer took the matter in hand and made everybody freeze at gunpoint and most, but not all, of the coins were recovered.

He paid a visit to Kolhapur where the stables held over four hundred horses and hunting for black buck consisted of a 'stalk' by stealthy approach in an open Rolls Royce and the 'shot' made by the release of a pair of cheetahs from a wagon behind. The cheetahs, having a limited range of around 300 yards, either killed or lay down and were collected by their handlers.

A fresh pair was then brought forward and the process repeated many times during the day until, finally, the supply of cheetahs (fourteen pairs on this occasion) was exhausted. In these dreadful days of a ban in the UK on hunting with dogs, is this perhaps a legal option for the dedicated sportsman?

In 1937 Bradford was cross-posted to the 1st Bn Black Watch which moved to the Sudan before returning home in March 1938 when they made Dover their home station. There then ensued a period of frantic training, for by then the political situation was such that war was a very distinct threat to which the battalion was not ready to respond. Bradford's CO, Lt-Col C.G. Stephen, described the situation:

> *The unit was under strength and like all units returning from abroad immediately discharged to the reserve a large number of men, and a party of over 120 men were sent on vocational training to complete the last 6 months of their service. There was a great shortage of officers owing to the fact that nine had been dropped on the way home at Suez to join the 2nd Bn, then stationed in Palestine.*[3]

The aftermath of the First World War had left Britain ill-prepared for future military action. Initially this stemmed from the very strong antipathy towards war among a British public exhausted by the 1914–18 conflict. In trying to meet the cost of the First World War and the subsequent economic depression military budgets were cut, cut and cut again. By 1931 even the politicians accepted that this situation could no longer continue. Nevertheless, five more years were to pass before real action was taken.

Despite frantic preparations in the years since rearmament had been declared a priority in 1936, the British Army was still by 1939 ill-equipped for war.

Saul David reports a regular officer recalling the following:

I remember going on manoeuvres in 1938 in Suffolk. As soon as the date was announced, all the field officers, bar one, and most of senior captains, found that they were unavoidably unable to attend because of engagements elsewhere and all took their leave. I found myself, as a very junior lieutenant, commanding C Company, consisting of myself, the company sergeant major, the company quartermaster sergeant, one other sergeant, four corporals, and about ten jocks. The ridiculous sight which has always stuck in my mind, as it must have done in the minds of the locals, is of the company in column route-marching along a main road with me at the front, followed by the CSM and a platoon consisting of a sergeant and a jock carrying a flag, then a long gap filled by the length of a tape held at the other end by another jock. That was a platoon. As the new light machine gun, the Bren gun, had not arrived yet, we had wooden silhouettes and wooden rattles to simulate the sound of them being fired. It's amazing to think that, only 15 months before hostilities broke out, a Regular battalion was in this state.[4]

Things weren't quite as bad as that in the 1st Bn Black Watch but nevertheless a parade in August of 1938 showed a strength of only 279 men.[5] Normal peacetime battalion strength was around 600, rising in war to nearer 1,000 men. Lt-Col Stephen wrote:

The equipment was quite pathetic; there were twenty-two Bren guns in the unit, no mortars, no anti-tank guns; anti-tank rifles were represented by gas piping stuck into a piece of wood and Bren-gun carriers by 15cwt trucks carrying blue flags. Despite it all a considerable amount of training took place, to the amusement of the German, Italian, Turkish and Egyptian Military Attachés who could not make out whether we were bluffing or in quite such a parlous condition as was apparent.

Bradford's own comment was that by 1938 it seemed to him that war was inevitable, not because of the political situation, but because of the state of the equipment. He said that when German officers visited manoeuvres they genuinely thought that the British were trying to fool them with their wooden machine guns, and horse-drawn camp cookers with metal rimmed wheels.

Territorial battalions, such as those which originally made up the 51st Highland Division, were still using horse-drawn transport in 1938 and only received their first Bren-gun carriers in the summer of 1939. These were planned to form the basis for the infantry's new role as a mobile force, but their late arrival gave little time to develop tactics or for training. It should also be noted that the Germans used horse-drawn transport in their standard infantry divisions throughout the coming war.[6]

The standard firearm for the infantry was the First World War .303 Short Lee-Enfield rifle – which fired single rounds from its magazine of ten bullets. The infantryman was also equipped with a long bayonet for this rifle and Mills hand grenades. Infantry platoons were equipped with 2in mortars for use both as weapons and smoke-projectors. There were two types of machine gun – the Vickers .303, also a First World War model, and the new and lighter Bren gun (also .303 calibre). Mortar platoons were equipped with 3in mortars while anti-tank platoons had both 25mm anti-tank guns and the Boys .55 anti-tank rifle. The British anti-tank guns were unable to deal with the more heavily armed German tanks.

Not only was the equipment scarce but also the ammunition for these weapons was in such short supply that it was often impossible for the infantry to train adequately with live firing of weapons.

A clear distinction must be made between the regular soldiers and territorials. The regular 1st Bn Black Watch was posted to France shortly after the outbreak of war and later in the spring of 1940 joined the largely territorial 51st Highland Division, which itself had only been mobilised on 1 September 1939.

On 1 January 1939 Bradford became Adjutant to the 1st Bn Black Watch.

In February 1939 the government formulated a policy to send a British Expeditionary Force to France in the event of the outbreak of war. It had been realised, belatedly, that it would become very difficult to protect British interests if France was in enemy hands. Lt-Col Stephen describes the mood:

The winter of 1938/9 and the spring of 1939 were spent in train-ing on the new weapons as they gradually appeared, but with the appeasement of Munich, where Mr Chamberlain went on bended knee to Hitler, the powers that be gradually woke up to the fact that the only outcome was war, thus on the 15 June the unit received about 190 reservists, who left on 15 August after most valuable training. The same day a further 190 reservists arrived for train-ing and these were still with the unit on general mobilisation. On 22 August the code word was received placing the battalion in a state of emergency. It was quite obvious that a state of war was imminent and, although no order to mobilise had yet been received, certain matters connected with mobilisation were gone into and the wheels started for that purpose. On 24 August all anti-aircraft posts were manned by L.M.Gs (light machine-gunners) and on the next day the battalion was put on 8 hours notice to move. There was now a period of 5 or 6 days of restless waiting and the unit went ahead with its mobilisation arrangements, and the famous docu-ment 'The Short Sea Passage' was extracted from the safe and very

> *carefully read. The first news of reservists being called up appeared*
> *in the evening papers of 31 August but the next day at 2 a.m. this*
> *was confirmed by telegram and the draft conducting party was des-*
> *patched to the depot by the train leaving Dover at 6.26 a.m..*[7]

Early on 1 September 1939, fifty-six divisions crossed the border from Germany into Poland. By noon on 3 September, the British ultimatum to withdraw having been ignored, Britain had declared war. Some 6 hours later France too joined the alliance against Germany.

At the outbreak of war the 1st Bn Black Watch was stationed at the Castle Barracks, Dover. Orders for General Mobilisation were not received until 4 September. The pace of events quickened and comings and goings to and from the battalion intensified. Two drafts of reservists marched into the barracks: 'a fine sight with the pipe band and they all wore the kilt with the kilt apron' recorded Noel Jardine-Paterson who also noted changes among the officers: 'Arrive David Campbell, Roger Sandford, John Moon, Brian Madden, John Graham, Pat Douglas and Timothy Bowes Lyon. They arrived on 7 September. To the Depot went Dopey, Robert Orr-Ewing, Ian Cochrane, John Glenorchy and Drummond Dunbar.'[8]

There was much to think about and apart from the preparations for war there was also the matter of personal belongings to consider for, with the battalion leaving Dover on active service, surplus goods and chattels had to be dealt with. Jardine-Paterson recorded his solution:

> *I had a great piece of luck here as John Cochran was suddenly*
> *ordered to Perth. I at once thought of my car and so asked him to*
> *drive it up complete with all my luggage, call in at home, collect a*
> *chauffeur who would go with him to Perth and bring the car back*

home. It was a great relief to thus be able to get off all my moveable kit and also my car. This plan was approved by the CO and worked perfectly. The remainder of my stuff I stored with Henry Hart in Dover. This consisted of all my furniture and a box of oddments.[9]

There were changes too in the Officers' Mess, where Jardine-Paterson noted the arrival of females, members of the ATS, to take over the work of the mess staff. He recorded: 'The two officers, "Furious" and "Glorious", became great friends of "Uncle Charles"and managed under great difficulties to put up a very good show.'[10]

On Friday 8 September the battalion moved a few miles out of Dover to Waldeshare Park and remained there under canvas while they carried out further training. On 25 September they marched back to the Marine Station at Dover and entrained for Aldershot and took up residence in Salamanca Barracks. The following day they were inspected by their corps commander, Lt-Gen. Alan Brooke.

A day later the CO, Lt-Col C.G. Stephen, was ordered by GOC 4th Division (Maj.-Gen. D.G. Johnson VC, CB, DSO, MC) to meet him on the barrack square within the next ten minutes. There he was told, in confidence, that the King and Queen were arriving at Aldershot that afternoon and that Their Majesties would inspect the 1st Bn Black Watch in drill order with full pipes and drums and brass band. Her Majesty the Queen was colonel-in-chief of the Black Watch. This order caused some degree of activity as can be imagined. The surplus pipes, drums and brass had already been packed up for dispatch by train to the regimental depot for safe keeping and had to be retrieved at short notice. After the parade they had to be taken to France as, by then, the baggage train for Scotland had already left.[11] In the early afternoon Their Majesties arrived and took the royal salute. The King said to the Queen: 'This is your regiment, you inspect it.' Jardine-Paterson noted that the parade 'went off all right except for a slight muddle at the end, when instead of the expected "Order Arms" we got "Left Turn" a command which only the front two companies managed to hear and execute, the remainder doing a somewhat complicated "order arms, turn left, slope arms" all in one.'

On 27 September the depressing order was received to wear battledress, not the kilt, effective the following day. This was said to be on the grounds that the Regiment might be recognised. CSM MacGregor summed up the general mood: 'but damn it, we want to be identified.'[12] In truth, with the changes in warfare and mechanisation and with the dreadful experiences wearing the kilt in the trenches during the First World War, the kilt was probably a most impractical garment – but nevertheless its passing was sorely missed.[13]

On 5 October the 1st Bn Black Watch embarked for France.

★★★

My father's diary and his later comments are printed in full column width; excerpts from his letters are indented; and my own comments and additions from other sources are in italics.

Mention is made of money on numerous occasions. In 1939 Bradford reported that the exchange rate was 175 Frs to the pound with Champagne costing 30–40 Frs and Vin Ordinaire 5 Frs a bottle.

1

The Phoney War:
October 1939–May 1940

The 1st Bn The Black Watch had crossed to France with the 4th Division early in October 1939, and in due course reached its area near Lens, where it remained for 2 months.

10 October 1939

I am not allowed to say where I am which is a pity. We had a simply awful voyage – rougher than anything since the war began. We were all terribly ill – very miserable and not so happy when we landed.

We are in a very nice village here, in pretty country. Chris Melville and I are billeted with M. le Notaire, and are very comfortable. There is a beautiful Château just outside the village where Bde [Brigade] is, and we all live at the inn, where they feed us very well.

I had a bath yesterday in a little tub in the laundry. There are no baths at all in the village.

Bradford's brief diary entry of the journey was economical in detail. His letter said a little more but in truth the journey had been frightful.

In peacetime their ship, RMS Mona's Queen, 2,756 tons, carried trippers to the Isle of Man. For the crossing from Southampton to Cherbourg, on the night of 5/6 October, she carried 1,940 soldiers in such a small space that a large number of men had to stand up all the rough night. Many were very sea-sick on the journey. Bradford managed to survive the crossing without succumbing but, the moment he set foot on land, was sick at the feet of his Commanding Officer to the great amusement of others.

On arrival in France there was little organisation or even provision of food. The battalion had brought, against orders, cookers, rations, blankets and ammunition and the first of these came into immediate use. Late in the evening on 6 October they entrained and made an overnight journey to Noyen-sur-Sarthe, near Le Mans. From there a 10-mile route-march took them to billets in Parcé-sur-Sarthe where the villagers were most welcoming. Col Stephen reported: 'One of the officers went so far as to sing the Marseillaise at a small dinner party. This did not go quite with the bang intended as the inhabitants of Parcé were Royalists.'

To overcome strict censorship Bradford had arranged a simple method of communication with his father. The phrase 'I am not allowed to say where I am' was the sign that he was going to tell them exactly where he was! In the next two sentences, if one knows what to look for, can clearly be read 'Parce near Le Mans' [see underlined letters]. While not necessarily included in the extracts used in this book, several of Bradford's letters contain similar hidden messages and there is no doubt his parents were able to trace his moves. Later on, this simple mechanism was to prove rather more useful.

On 9 October an advance party left by road for the Belgian border while the rest of the men, after a route-march in which all got soaked, entrained at Noyen and after a 23-hour journey arrived at Henin-Leitard and marched to billets throughout the town. Stephen noted: 'It was difficult to believe that a town could exist with such a lack of sanitation.' [14]

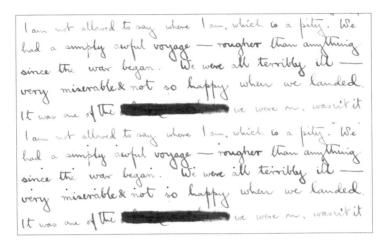

Section of letter of 10 October 1939 containing a concealed message.
I am not allowed to say where I am is the signal that the message is
concealed. The dots under the 'p' of '*simply*' and the 's' of '*so*' indicate
the beginning and end of the message. The writing has been heavily
inked with the exception of the relevant letters conveying the message
– see the black dots over the letters in the lower version.

No preparations seemed to have been put in place for any military advance and, as Stephen recorded, 'apart from a certain amount
of excitement among the civilian population at the arrival of British
troops, with the obvious hope of making a bit of money, all was peace
and quiet.'

The French border with Belgium was largely undefended which was
a considerable contrast to the heavily defended Maginot Line covering
the Franco-German border to the east. On 15 October they began,
in heavy rain, to prepare defensive positions on the canal to the north
of Dourges. The first day's work collapsed owing to lack of revetting
material. Officers cut trees in the vicinity for that purpose but this was
promptly made a court-martial offence by the French. One Guards
officer bought a whole plantation and, when the French authorities

*tried to stop him, was able to see them off by advising that the wood was
his and he could do with it what he liked. Stephen records, 'such was
the conduct of war in 1939'.*[15]

Some requests for items from home were rather prescient:

16 October 1939
My French is improving slightly. Can you send me 'Brush
up your French'?

*The battalion was put to work constructing defences over a distance of
3,000 yards on the canal-bank between Beauvin and La Bassée. This
was a large task for one battalion, especially when they had to send one
company daily to Attiches to construct an Anti-Tank obstacle around
a château in which some of the few British tanks were parked. Stephen
reported, 'it is understood that the obstacle was so complete that some of
the tanks never succeeded in getting out'. Clearly the command organisation was lacking in direction.*

*One new duty which the officers had to carry out was the censor-
ing of letters. Noel Jardine-Paterson noted: 'It was unbelievable how
many letters the men wrote and usually 1½ to 2 hours a day had to
be spent in doing this. It was not a nice job having to read the letters
through and sign them at the bottom and on the envelope but we got
used to it in time.'*[16]

*At home Bradford's parents were battening down for the war.
Clearly they'd hoarded some petrol and were having to revise their
domestic arrangements as staff were called-up:*

23 October 1939
Is your petrol lasting out well? I wonder if you have used
the bottles yet. How are those two new maids doing?

*While the battalion did not move during this time there seemed to be
frequent changes in the billeting arrangements:*

1 November 1939
We had to move our Bn HQ and HQ Company Officers' Mess, as the owner of our previous house [*a M. Sixe, Notaire*] was demobbed, and wanted his house. We have got another house, which does quite well but isn't half as nice or big. This is some way off, and so I have moved out of my banker's to be nearer it, and now live with Pat C-P [*Campbell-Preston*] in a large and comfortable mansion belonging to a mine owner. It is modern, and our rooms are papered with dark, ornate paper, but they are huge rooms, with central heating, hot and cold water, and really well furnished. We have a bathroom and everything, and it is a great improvement, except that Madame loathes having us and shows it in every way she can. She looks a typical Victorian, tall, erect, and very severe. Monsieur is very nice, about 70, with a big beard. I think we shall soon thaw Madame, as she has quite a kind face.

But it was not to be:

16 November 1939
I am afraid I have made no impression on my hostess yet, and she still disregards us completely.

Although 'at war' the quest for social life amongst at least the younger officers did not cease altogether. Jardine-Paterson reported:

We didn't dine in Mess much but usually went to Douai, the Café de Paris, or Lens, the Hotel du Monde, or to the Café du Centre. During the day we used to wear battledress but in the evening we changed into jacket and trews which was a good thing and much more comfortable. We had one regrettable incident when we went to Lens one night in trucks and a drunken Pole was run over on the way back.

However the matter was hushed up and the only result was that trucks were not allowed to be taken out for pleasure parties in the evening. This brought a new character into our ken, Pompe Finnebre, as we called him. He was a red-faced boozy old man who drove a hearse by day and a taxi by night. We travelled many miles with him, he was a great character and never seemed to mind how late we were or how far we went but he would drive on the wrong side of the road most of the time and he had a habit of turning out all his lights when we reached maximum speed. However we never crashed and without him we should have been completely at a loss. Several times we met Jim Melville and Ted Snowball, also Ian Murray, Father Clark and many others and we had many good parties together. Besides this we used to dine in each others' messes within the battalion quite a lot.

Bradford's letters are obviously sketchy in their detail about military activities but it is clear that preparations for war are ongoing.

1 November 1939
I went and watched our first go at firing 2in mortars today, which went off quite well, though the men were very slow at it.

The 2in mortar was, in theory, issued to all infantry platoons but often there were too few and there was little or no ammunition available for training. This letter shows that front line regular infantry had, until November 1939, not fired these weapons in practice. It turned out that only smoke ammunition could be used as there was no HE [High Explosive] within the whole of the British Expeditionary Force [BEF].

A letter to his youngest sister Diana starts with a rebuke.

6 November 1939
You mustn't address me as 2nd Lieut as I have been a Lieut since 1935! And shall be a captain soon I hope.

We get off to ------ near here, and have a really good dinner about once a week – champagne, oysters and everything you can think of. As quite good champagne is only about 4s 6d a bottle, it doesn't cost you much to be out for the evening. In between we get filthy and wet digging trenches in water-logged ground.

A letter to his middle sister Felicity [Cit] mentions action for the first time. Cassandra Felicity Bradford, MBE, also served in the Second World War. She gained the rank of captain in the service of the Air Transport Auxiliary. Her main duties were the delivery of aircraft from the factories to the front-line airfields. As a schoolboy it was always quite something to have had an aunt that flew Spitfires and Hurricanes in the war. She later attained the rank of captain in 1947 in the service of the Women's Auxiliary Air Force [Volunteer Reserve] [Flying] Corps.

6 November 1939
Two aeroplanes were shot down near here the other day. We saw the shells of the AA guns bursting but none of them looked very near the aeroplanes which were miles up.

10 November 1939
I wish that bomb had got Hitler the other day. I think he must be getting fairly desperate, and they seem to think he is going to try and come through Holland. We have got another air-raid alarm in progress at the moment. I hope we see something!

The bomb, to which he refers, was Elser's assassination attempt in Munich. Every 8 November Hitler went to Munich's Burger-braukeller to honour the old-time Nazis who participated in his failed

*uprising against the Weimar Republic. George Elser, a Swiss clock-
maker, attempted to kill Hitler with a time-bomb set inside a wooden
pillar which he had painstakingly hollowed out. Having made his
speech Hitler left the building a little earlier than usual and eight minutes later the bomb exploded. It would undoubtedly have killed him
had he still been on the podium.*

30 November 1939

We have been doing a certain amount of training lately,
such as digging and wiring by night, and occupying
trenches for 24 hours, and then being relieved by other
units. I suppose it is a good thing, though it has been so
wet and the ground is so sodden, that I sometimes have me
doots [*sic*]. It is very difficult for the men to get clean again
with only one pair of boots and one suit [*of battle-dress*].

We are not doing anything special for St Andrew's Day
– they have, however, let us off our night-digging, and we
are going to have a piper in our Mess, and a haggis I believe.

The Queen sent twenty-four pairs of socks out among
our Comforts and I have got a pair, with the enclosed label
on them. Don't send me anything quite as thick as I can't
get into my Newmarket boots in them!

4 December 1939

When I next send a post-card, you will know that I have
been under fire, and haven't got time to write. I don't think
I shall be sending one for some time though! Yesterday
Pat C-P, Noel J-P and I visited a lady about 12 miles from
here who had the 9th Bn quartered in her farm before the
Battle of ------, and again after it when there were only
ninety-eight survivors out of 900. She was a great friend
of the regiment's – Mlle. Henriette. You will find all about
her in Vol.3 of my regimental history which is written

by Sir Arthur [*Wauchope*], by the way. [*This was a reference to Mlle. Henriette Hennequet at the farm known as 'The Black Watch Farm' which had been held by 9th Black Watch before and after the Battle of Loos.*]

There then followed a spell in the Saar, on attachment to the French 12th Brigade, to gain battle experience. The battalion arrived on 9 December and was billeted in a French cavalry barracks, Quartier des Vallières at Woippy just north of Metz, and in a nearby hospital. Initially the barracks were in a filthy condition which took 24 hours to clean. By now the weather had got much colder.

18 December 1939

Can you send me at once a bottle of Regesan Chilblain Liniment, which I gave Cit and she had in her bedroom. I found it very good last year, and as my feet are frozen all day, I am starting chilblains again – an awful bore. We have been having bitter weather during our march up with snow and frost. We slept the first night in a small village after 13 miles – I came with CO in advance by car – and it was freezing. I have never been colder. I slept in a little cottage with a midden a foot off my window and a pig in a barn which led off my room. I was in a built-in bed and they kindly gave me coarse linen sheets which were sopping wet.

The 1st Black Watch moved from Quartier des Vallières on 16 December for its spell of duty on the front line. This was in front of the Maginot Line.

On 18 December the CO went from the fortress area to meet the Prime Minister, Neville Chamberlain and General Gamelin. Chamberlain inspected a French battalion. Their soldiers were a sorry sight but had been issued with new great coats and steel helmets especially for the occasion.

The Bn was in the line from 16 December until Hogmanay, but experienced little more than some odd shelling and active patrolling. It was bitterly cold and some men suffered from frost-bite. We were not allowed sufficient anti-freeze for the Motor Transport, and had to keep fires going under vehicles which were required to be at instant readiness. [*It was reportedly the most severe winter that anyone could remember since the turn of the century.*]

Boxing Day 1939

I have been in hospital since Friday evening with a sort of flu, which three officers have got. David Campbell, Nigel Noble and self. I felt rotten to begin with and worse with the tablets they gave me, which made me so sick that they knocked them off and now I have got better. There are no facilities of any sort here, and you get a bit of cold bacon & bread & margarine which has been carried 200 yards for a meal when you are feeling awful. No one did anything for us, but somehow we've recovered! It was a blessing us three being together. It has been a really white Christmas here & the country looks lovely with every twig covered in snow or frost. I sent the Post Card for the reason I told you.

Hogmanay 1939

It is bitterly cold here, and we have had 34°[F] of frost, which is frightful when most of the men are in positions day and night. I live in a house with some stoves and we keep fairly warm. Even so the passage in the house was like an ice slide from drips from the pump, which is in the middle of the house. Most of our trucks were frozen solid in spite of anti-freeze mixture, but not many have cracked yet. We now run the engines for 15 mins every hour, which seems an awful waste of petrol. We have to do this by day and night.

I shall be telling Mummie some interesting news about what I have been doing in about 5 days' time, but cannot say much at present. We hope to celebrate a somewhat belated New Year's Day in due course as we have been unable to have any festivities where we are. I hope we shall soon settle down 'into winter quarters' like Hannibal, as I'm sure it would be better than fighting in this weather.

There were no cases of frost-bite in the battalion despite the intense cold. The French battalion immediately to the right in the line had 156 cases in the space of 5 days.

The battalion was relieved by the 1st Norfolk Regiment on 31 December and after one night in Metz entrained for Tourcoing, north of Lille. Jardine-Paterson takes up the story:

The Bn arrived by train on 3 January to find the Advance Party had done its stuff more or less. Companies all had billets allotted to which they marched and started settling in. HQ Coy was in the buildings of a socialist organisation which was quite a good billet. There were no officers' messes definitely fixed so we all messed together the first day in the station restaurant.

The officers' billets were all fixed but I found that I had been given a room attached to a Catholic Church, a sort of priest's flat. It wasn't a bad room but the entrance to it was by way of the side door of the church and somehow I didn't feel it was quite suitable for me or for Chris [Melville] who was to be in the next door flat. So we decided to refuse the offer. We saw the priest in charge and said the officers had not arrived and so the accommodation would not be wanted. Then we set off to find new billets. I found David [Campbell] had two beds in his room so went in with him until something else should turn up. He was in a house just along the street from Bn HQ. A largish French family was in residence, Mr & Mrs, some daughters and a nurse. There was running water in the room we had but the basin had a great hole in it. On the whole we felt it wasn't too good a billet and decided to look for another the next day. Next day was spent in settling in and finding out where two companies were and what was going to be necessary in the way of telephones. Also our billets question had to be settled. I set off and spent some time trying to find a place. Eventually I came to No 73 Rue National which was a large well-furnished house. Here I found two old women, housekeeper and cook to a French couple who were living in Paris. They said that a nephew of the owner lived in Tourcoing and that if I saw him matters could probably be arranged. So I went off to his office, saw him, and fixed that David and I would live in his uncle's house with our servants. We had a largish room each on the first floor with a bathroom and geyser that worked. We also arranged that the central heating should be started up for which we agreed to pay a bit. Our servants lived upstairs in a room together – on the whole it was a first class set-up and not too near Bn HQ. A feature which struck us was that between our bedroom doors on the landing there was a fair-sized altar – not quite the usual form. We moved in that day and having got a latch-key each which meant that we could come and go as we pleased we set up house. Here we stayed the whole time were at Tourcoing. We were very warm and comfortable, the two old servants were very pleasant if somewhat retiring and seemed quite happy to have us living with them.

While on the subject of billets mention must be made of the house in which Bill Bradford and Pat C-P lived. It was a longish way from Bn HQ but was a truly magnificent place. The owner, a woman, lived there but Pat and Bill had a self-contained flat on the second floor consisting of a hall, two bedrooms, and a splendid bathroom. We saw over the rest of the house during our stay and it was all extremely pleasant if somewhat eccentric especially Madame's bedroom. In fact as a billet no one could ask for better.

Bradford described his rather un-macho billet in a letter home:

5 January
Pat and I are in a billet together. It is a really luxurious one.
We each have a lovely bedroom – mine has two lovely pink
beds with pink chintz covers and curtains. In between our
bedrooms and connecting with both is a bathroom in black
marble with a white bath and 2 basins.

Jardine-Paterson continues:

*Bn HQ Officers' Mess was in another large but not very pleas-
ant house about two houses away from Bn HQ, here Col Steve
was installed. We fed fairly well but I wasn't often in during the
evening. Roger Sandford was usually about though and had a large
supply of fondants and marons glacées always at hand! Companies
had Coy [Company] Messes, B Coy being well placed in a large
house standing in its own grounds. Altogether billets for the officers
were exceptionally good and by the time the men had fixed things
up they were very well off too. We had cold frosty weather most of
the time and so were unable to dig which seemed to be the main job
allotted to us. However positions were reconnoitred and Coys were
all set for the thaw to come.*

*This was undoubtedly the most pleasant time we spent in
France although by no stretch of imagination could it be said to
have been good training for the fighting which we all supposed
would happen in the not far distant future. Still it was a case of
'make hay while the sun shines' and everyone found plenty to do
in one way or another. We worked until tea-time and then after
tea changed into trews, and had a bath and either had dinner in
mess or, more usually, went out and had a party in Lille or some
other place.*[17]

5 January 1940

At last I am allowed to tell you what I have been doing. We were up in front of the Maginot Line for over 2 weeks – 10 days in second line and five in the front line, where we were about 1,000 yards from the Germans. They patrol right through to the second line, and we patrol a bit too. You could see them wandering about, or digging, and also their O.Ps [*Observation Posts*] but no one seemed to do much about it. Occasionally we shelled each other, but no shells must land near villages by mutual agreement. Bn HQ and Coy HQs are all in deserted villages, which have been left with furniture but fairly well looted by the French. The men were bitterly cold, as most of them were actually in positions. The maximum frost was 36°F [*-20°C*], which is very severe. People at the different HQs were fairly comfortable as they had stoves and wood was plentiful. I had, in B.O.R. [*Battalion Operations Room*] a very old kitchen range, which only had an oven with two doors, and rings at the bottom which could be taken away to boil things on. Underneath you slid in logs of wood a yard long. With the door open it gave out a tremendous heat. Bdes are being sent to the line in turn for training and propaganda.

Meanwhile the 51st Highland Division had landed in France towards the end of January 1940 and by the end of March had taken over, from the 21st French Division, the line from Mailleul to Armentières.

On arrival in France the 51st Highland Division was posted to the same general area as the 1st Bn Black Watch. Lille had become more crowded and as Jardine-Paterson reported, 'every other officer seemed to be wearing a kilt or trews. With the arrival of all these people things became rather crowded and prices soared.' He also went on to observe that 'British Officers in a crowd in a foreign country are not very pleasant. It is odd how any nation, en masse, seems rather unattractive while individually, more often than not, they are very charming.'[18]

The cold weather which had continued throughout January gave way to warmer conditions in February and the digging of defences resumed in earnest.

Having been in France since the previous October a short spell of leave was in prospect.

9 February 1940
I think I shall be arriving home on 19 February: Isn't it lovely! I have just got a new suit of battle-dress as my original one has absolutely worn out. The cloth, which they're made of, is not very good.

Early in 1939 Britain's military and political planners had realised that, in order to defend Britain, it would be necessary to have an outer defensive line on French soil and when, on 1 September 1939, the 51st Highland Division was called-up, training commenced to serve that purpose. The 51st was, at this stage, entirely a territorial division comprised of battalions from all five Highland Infantry Regiments. Initially, equipment and even uniform was in very short supply, but gradually this situation improved and by January 1940 the Highland Division arrived at Le Havre to reinforce the BEF which, by the end of January, numbered in excess of 220,000 men. In the first instance the 51st was stationed in the rear.

By the end of February General Gort, Commander-in-Chief of the BEF, wished to strengthen the 51st Highland Division through the introduction of professional soldiers. Consequently, among other changes, one of the original territorial battalions in each of the three Infantry Brigades was replaced by their regiment's regular battalions. So it was that the 1st Bn Black Watch replaced the 6th Black Watch and joined the 51st Highland Division's 154 Brigade. At the same time the

2nd Seaforth Highlanders replaced the 6th Seaforth in 152 Brigade; and the 1st Gordon Highlanders replaced the 6th Gordons in 153 Brigade. In addition the regular 17th and 23rd Field Regiments, Royal Artillery, replaced the 76th and 77th and the 238th Field Company, Royal Engineers was replaced by the regular 26th Field Company. Having been stationed in France since the previous autumn, the 1st Black Watch, as the preceding pages recount, had already spent some weeks on the front in the Saar over Christmas, being attached to a French Division.

Since the declaration of war there had been a stand-off at the front. This situation continued through the spring of 1940 with only active patrolling being carried out by both sides. There were occasional armed engagements mostly between patrolling groups.

9 March 1940

Last Monday we changed over with the 6th Bn and are now in Victor's [*Maj.-Gen. Victor Fortune's*] Division, which is rather fun. We had a 17-mile route march but it was a nice bright day for marching. Both Bns halted together for dinners [*at the Place de la Citadelle, Lille*]. The Royal Fusiliers gave us a farewell cocktail party, and the P.W.V.'s [*Prince of Wales' Volunteers*] sent their band to march us off, and one of the Argyll Bns sent their Pipes and Drums to march us in the last two miles. We are in a dirty little village and haven't got at all good billets, but even so I am glad we have changed over. It is great fun having all our own kith and kin round us. If only we were all in the kilt, what a fine show we would make.

Some days later Bradford's first cousin Capt. Sir Edward Montagu Andrew Bradford, Cameron Highlanders, who had been stationed nearby, lent him a small pack of beagles. This unlikely interlude indicates that a long stand-off was thought to be a possibility. Bradford, like so many British officers, was clearly expecting a war much like that

*fought in Europe in 1914–18. At this stage they were not anticipating
a highly mobile conflict.*

16 March 1940

Isn't it miser [*sic*] – Edward appeared this evening, and has
taken his beagles back again, as his move is cancelled. I am
disappointed.

I had great fun yesterday and today. Yesterday, I went
out with Stephen Russell my servant and one Barrie, my
kennelman! We meant to exercise quietly, but as I was
the only one with a crop, it was difficult. I got all their
names off, and all went well for about 40 mins. Then two
of them strayed away a few yards, and got on the line of a
hare. Away they went, followed by the others. After about
500 yards, they checked, and I managed to stop back all of
them except two. I told the others to look after the main
lot (only six) and went off after the two. Just as I had got
them, a hare jumped up just in front of the others and
away they all went again. Again they checked and after a
bit some semblance of order was restored, as we weren't
trying to hunt. We moved on along a road, when Vanity
saw a hare about 400 yards away. Edward said she had
amazing eyesight and was a perfect nuisance. Again we all
went off, through a bit of the village, and over a road. By
the time we got over the houses, there wasn't a hound in
sight, although you could see for about 1½ miles. We plod-
ded on. The country was awful for running – over your
boots in very gluey mud. We gradually began to collect
odd hounds, but when you got one – two would go off
after something else, till at last we got them all. Today, Pat
Douglas and I and my servant and Barrie went out – again
for a quiet exercise. They went very well with us two. Till
Vanity again saw a hare, which we couldn't, and we were

off again. After we had lost it, we saw another, and drew for it on purpose! We had the hounds coupled up and at the second check, saw Forager had broken his couple and was limping – the spring hook having gone into his pad. So we had to stop and carry him home. We got it out after some time, at home, and he wasn't cut at all, though we tried to cut the hook with a saw and a file.

Isn't it a sad end to my first pack! Can you try and find out if anyone is anxious to draft any beagles as I want to start another pack for next winter in case we are still out here. I have written to the Eton Beagles, and the Ashley Beagles at Dover. I am quite ready to take them now, and keep them through the summer as I shall get to know them.

I haven't had such fun or such good exercise for ages and feel much better for it – so does my servant. I find it a bit hard to fit it all in with my duties as Adjutant, but luckily our Brigadier *(Stanley-Clarke)* is very keen on beagling and every form of sport.

Bradford was full of advice to his parents:

20 March 1940
I see that Whiteways are advertising a 'light sherry-type wine' at 3s a bottle, which they say you can't tell from a real light dry sherry. Do try it. I expect it will be awful.

On 20 March Édouard Daladier's government in France was overthrown and Paul Reynaud became the new Prime Minister. By mid-April, despite the diversions and the fact that on 9 April Germany had invaded Denmark and Norway, frustration about the inaction crept into Bradford's letters.

14 April 1940

How awfully well the Navy have done round Norway, haven't they? [*The destruction of an entire flotilla of ten German destroyers in the Vestfjord on 10 and 13 April.*]

I suppose the next thing the Boche will do is to walk into Holland. I really think it will be best if they do so now, as we may be able to finish off the war, instead of dragging on interminably.

Until mobilisation in 1939 the 1st Bn had very little Motor Transport – just a few 3-tonners and 15cwt and 8cwt trucks. The 8cwt trucks were the smallest vehicles we had, and they were as wide as the others and were quite unsuitable for getting past convoys or for command purposes. On mobilisation the Bn was issued with an assortment of impressed vehicles – ordinary civilian lorries painted army green, all different shapes, sizes and makes.

Troop trains were the accepted way of moving about over distances longer than troops could march. Such trains were made up of a few ancient Third Class carriages for officers and old covered wagons labelled '40 HOMMES, 8 CHEVAUX' for the men. A party of men went to the station in advance to draw straw and distribute it among the wagons, sweeping them out if the previous occupants had been horses.

There were no wireless sets within the battalion. Instead we had to rely on field telephones and cable which the Signal Platoon laid soon after we stopped anywhere. We also had signalling lights and flags. There were three wireless sets per brigade; enough for Brigade HQ and two infantry battalions.

I wrote this diary soon after the various events took place and have not altered it or edited it since. In the part about fighting in France I do not know why I have sometimes described officers formally with their ranks, and at other times referred to them by their Christian names.

All our maps of Northern France had been handed in to the Corps Map Office when we moved down to the Maginot Line. Divisional HQ was cut off from the Map Office and could not supply us with any maps at all. We bought five Michelin road maps and they were all we had for the whole battalion.

In April it was decided that the British Army should take over a Divisional Sector on the Saar front, and the first and only Division to be nominated for this duty was the 51st Highland Division. In the third week in April the Division started to move by train to the Saar, and by 1 May had taken over the Hornburg – Budange sector, some 18 miles north-east of Metz. It stayed there for about three weeks.

This front-line position was parallel with, and only a few miles from, the France–Luxembourg border. The move was primarily to try and give divisions of the BEF some front-line experience while affairs were still fairly static militarily. With the 1st Black Watch having spent three weeks there around Christmas and others in the Division having been attached to the existing British brigade in that sector for five-day tours, this area was not unknown to all. Consequently the 1st Black Watch was the first battalion to be sent into the front line.

By this time the 51st was a considerably stronger division than normal. Attached to it were two machine gun battalions (7th Bn The Royal Northumberland Fusiliers and 1st Bn Princess Louise's Kensington Regiment), two pioneer battalions (6th Bn The Royal Scots Fusiliers and 7th Bn The Royal Norfolk Regiment), together with additional artillery and engineers. The total strength was now some 21,000 men. Normally divisional strength would be around 12,000 men.[19]

The Maginot Line was not a solid line of defence but a series of underground fortified observation posts and gun emplacements, and anti-tank obstacles. *The fortresses were state of the art. All observation and firing was carried out with the aid of periscopes. The 75mm guns were loaded far below ground, laid on their targets, raised, fired and disappeared with the recoil. Hundreds of machine guns were worked by gunners sitting some 50ft below them and traversed according to the terrain of the ground in the firing sector covered by each gun. Each fort was self-contained for air and all were provisioned with fuel, food, water and ammunition for 6 months. They could be pressurised to prevent the ingress of gas and to prevent any of the doors from being opened. Unusually, for French troops, the Maginot forts were kept in a spotless condition.*[20]

Associated with these defences were a series of 'lines'. The Front Line or 'Ligne de Contact' was essentially a line of outposts. The Second Line or 'Ligne de Soutien' was supposedly a support line but, in some places, did not actually exist. Then came the Retreat Line or 'Ligne de Recueil' which was on the line of the Maginot forts. Finally came the Stop Line or 'Ligne d'Arret' but again, this was often only a theoretical line.

In the Saar the 'Ligne de Contact' was up to 7 miles in front of the 'Ligne de Recueil'. When the 51st occupied the line it was certainly not in any fit state to be considered an effective line of defence. The French troops, who had previously occupied this sector, had done little to strengthen defences. Bradford was of the opinion that the French were relying too much on the Maginot Line holding firm. However once the front-line was breached, with the honourable exception of the French Artillery [75s] who were attached to the Highland Division and the French Cavalry who fought fiercely with the Division just before St-Valery, the French did not appear to have the stomach for a war.

In this part of the line the French, who had held the position before-hand, had established a compact of sorts between themselves and the German forces opposing them. Patrols of fewer than six men were allowed to go unmolested and artillery ceased fire for meal times. Even provision trucks were left alone providing they kept to specific hours. At night the French were very loathe to do anything which might annoy the Germans. Stephen reported, of one forward post where men from the 1st Black Watch were stationed alongside their allies, 'the French troops, repleat (sic) with good liquor used to go to sleep at nine o'clock at night and take no further interest in the proceedings'.[21]

Major James Murray Grant of the 2nd Seaforth Highlanders was taken by members of a French battle patrol on a recce (reconnaissance) of the forward area prior to 152 Brigade taking it over. He described an uproarious luncheon with drunken Frenchmen involving endless toasts to the Allies and much backslapping. Of the French commandant Grant recorded:

> He was a nervy wreck. Obviously no proper patrolling had been done by them and the Germans had the upper hand and complete freedom of movement in that area. When I tried to get permission to take out my officers during the next few nights i.e. until 152 Bde took over from the French, he nearly fainted. Shouted to me that there must be no movement at night and no contact with the enemy until they, the French, got out of the Ligne de Contact. Pointed out that the object of our coming up in advance of our units was to gain experience from his unit, to no avail.[22]

On the French Division which was relieved by the 51st Highland Division in the last days of April, Lt-Col C.G. Stephen commented:

> the impression one got from the French was of complete inertia. They were fed up with being in the line, very jumpy, and glad to get away. Their whole idea appeared to be that directly the Germans attacked they would withdraw behind the fortress area; but it was never laid down what constituted an attack and how much resistance they would show. On the other hand the British troops were determined to teach the enemy a lesson and make any advance as costly as possible.

It was not until the beginning of May that action proper started and by then the Division had been several weeks on the Maginot Line, with battalions taking it in turn to man the front. Apart from a few skirmishes the phoney war continued. The 'action' was sufficient, however, to justify sending home a signal that things had begun to hot up. In fact the 1st Bn had beaten off a small but fierce attack on posts in the Ligne de Contact near Hartbuch Wood.

30 April 1940

I have been so busy that I haven't had a moment to write anything except that P.C. At any rate I'm not allowed to say much.

We have been having a most interesting and exciting time. There is a lot of activity and we have had quite a bit of fighting and shelling. It seemed funny to be back in my old bedroom [*he was billeted in the same house as previously*] after such a long time.

There are masses of cowslips here – more than I've ever seen at home. Also masses of other spring flowers too. I saw several French soldiers with bunches of Lilies of the Valley which they must have got in the woods.

The references to flowers are a recurring theme in Bradford's letters home. This determination to write of everyday peacetime subjects was, of course, to allay his parents' concerns and, indeed, in the circumstances of censorship, to give him something to write about. Wild flowers were, and remained, a genuine interest throughout his life.

2 May 1940

I met an officer showing War Correspondents round yesterday, and entertained them for a time. He lives in Limerick and breeds horses, and says he'll give me a hunt or two after the war!

I have invested some money in Vogelstmisbult Gold Shares, which Cox's recommended. I hope they don't go bust.

I went and had a bath and a good dinner in ------ near here two nights ago. We had dinner in a very nice restaurant, all gilt and pink brocade which looked just like a scene from the Merry Widow – with no music.

The CO of the 1st Black Watch, Lt-Col C.G. Stephen had been hospitalised with stomach problems for some time and Bradford wrote of his concern:

2 May 1940
The Colonel is still in hospital and I'm very much afraid he may be sent home, as he doesn't seem to be at all well. I don't know who we shall get instead if he does go. I don't particularly want Honeyman, as he can never make up his mind, and is awfully fussy.

154 Brigade had been in position since 21 April. On 2 May they were joined by, on the right, 152 Brigade and, on the left, by 153 Brigade. As with 154 Brigade the new arrivals first placed their one regular battalion on the front line – the Ligne de Contact of the Maginot Line.

Meanwhile, back in Britain, Neville Chamberlain resigned and was replaced as Prime Minister by Winston Churchill who took office on 10 May 1940.

The German offensive against France and the Low Countries started in earnest on 10 May with the main thrust being through Belgium and Holland, far to the north-west of the Saar. In response to this the north-western flank of the French Army and the BEF commenced a swing to the north into Belgium. The idea was to bring Belgium's twenty-two divisions within reach of the allies and to keep the enemy away from the important mining and industrial region of northern France. The plan also had the effect of shortening the line of defence by 35 miles. The advance was in contravention of Belgian wishes. They had declared their neutrality and forbade the BEF from entering the country. This new line ran from Antwerp, along the river Dyle and thence via Namur to Sedan on the river Meuse. From this point eastwards the front remained as it was, along the French border. By evening on the 12th there was no reason to believe that this plan had not gone well. The forces were established in their new positions.

It turned out that the execution of the Dyle Plan played into German hands. The main thrust of their offensive was not through Western Belgium but through the Ardennes where the front was more lightly defended as an attack in this area of difficult ground was thought to be unlikely.

It was not until the afternoon of the 11th that the Highland Division first made contact with the enemy on anything more than the usual skirmishing scale which had become the norm over the past week. By the 13th the Division was heavily engaged. After a heavy barrage the Germans attacked all along the line and the 1st and 4th Bns Black Watch bore the brunt of the fighting.

This attack was the first major assault and the Germans advanced on a front that covered two whole brigades of the 51st as well as on the flanking French troops to their left.

It was about one small element of this attack that Bradford wrote the following account which predates the remainder of his diary by two weeks. As Adjutant he certainly shouldn't have been doing what he reported.

2

One Day in the Saar: May 1940

About 13 May 1940,[23] when we had been some time in the Saar, and had had various German attacks or large-scale raids and considerable shelling, our two left company positions (C & D) were attacked strongly about 06.00hrs. This attack had been preceded by really heavy shelling throughout the night, which by 06.30hrs had lifted to our reserve positions & Coy HQ etc. The gunners estimated that there were ten German batteries on our battalion front, including some 8in Howitzers – the shelling was really heavy and far more than we had had further north. We only had one battery of 25 pounders and one troop of French 75s.

Bradford was not complimentary about the fighting capability of most of the French units but he made an exception about the French gunners with their 75mm field guns. 'We were thankful for them' he said, 'they were quicker into action than ours (Royal Artillery) and they were very good'.[24]

We were very well dug in, being in the old British sector, and suffered few casualties, but the 4th Black Watch, on our

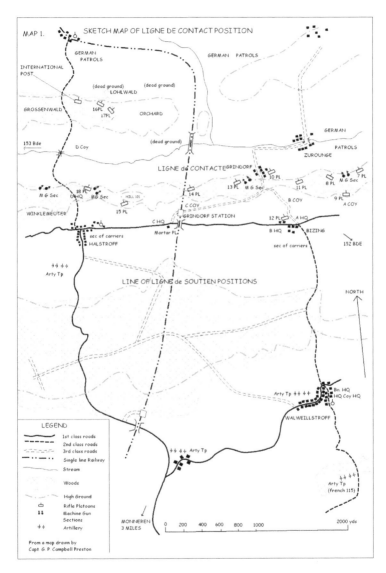

MAP 1. SKETCH MAP OF LIGNE DE CONTACT POSITION

Maginot Line.

left, in a sector recently French [*and therefore less well dug-in*]
suffered quite severely. Fairly soon, communications to forward patrols of D Company were cut, and reports came that
they were being heavily attacked, and that German infantry were right up to them in the wood, while the Company
Commander [*Patrick Campbell-Preston*] could see that they
were behind his forward positions to the right.

By 09.30hrs, the situation did not sound very good, and
reports were not explicit, so I persuaded the CO to let me
go up, find out what was happening, and if necessary collect
a troop of light tanks to try and mop up a mortar, also some
machine guns, which D Coy reported were worrying them.

Telephone communications were too bad by then to refer
things back to the CO as most lines were cut. I went off on
an M/C [*motor-cycle*], collected the troop of 1st Lothians and
Border Horse from near C Coy, and went to D Coy. Patrick
was still uncertain about his forward patrols – companies
were spread out over an absurd area and his HQ was about a
mile back from forward positions – but knew they must want
more ammunition. [*On seeing Bradford arrive Pat Campbell-
Preston recorded, '"You would come up" I thought, but I was pleased
to see him'.*]

We decided to go up together, standing on the back of a
tank, with some SAA [*small arms ammunition*]. One tank got
ditched moving around a road block, so only two came up,
and halted behind the Grosenwald. I told them to stay there
until I came back to tell them where to go, and Patrick and
I set off, revolvers in hand, carrying several bandoliers and a
box [*of ammunition*] between us.

There was a lot of firing in front, and we rather wished we
had got an escort. After some 600 yards, we got within sight
of the most forward section posts, having passed the other to
the right. Someone shouted to us to 'look out' and then they

opened rapid fire away from us. We doubled through the wire entanglement, and into the trench, to find the Germans were only 30 yards in front, in some thick bushes.

One could see movements in the bushes, but it was difficult to get a shot. The Jocks just couldn't reach them with a grenade so Patrick and I got some, and landed them right among the bushes, causing shouts and forcing them to move to where we could get shots at them.

[*Of this incident Campbell-Preston recorded: 'We threw some hand grenades at a German sniper who was reported lying close to the wire – Bill's black moustache bristling with excitement.'*]

Soon we had cleared up that lot and, rather miserably, I decided I had better go back to tell the tanks about the mortar and machine gun to our right flank. Patrick wanted to come too, or go instead of me.

They arranged to fire like hell, while I got out. Of course I couldn't find the exit through the wire, but did at last. I felt very silly looking for it while people were shooting at me. When I got back near to where I had left the tanks, I saw some men there, but as I got near them they fired at me, and I saw that they were Germans – a small patrol I suppose. I dropped down, fired back and crawled away.

[*Again, Campbell-Preston's comment is worth recording: 'It was clear to Bill that all was well with 17 pl. so he returned to Bn HQ. On the way back he had a long shot with his revolver at a German sniper – so he said afterwards. I always thought that sniper must have been a rotten shot or else Bill very lucky.'*]

I got round and found that the tanks had gone out in the open and had been knocked out. I set off for Coy HQ, when an automatic opened up on me from my left rear, so I had to crawl again. Then they began shelling the road, exactly where I was. An Observation Post must have been able to see me, and was amusing itself, as each salvo was exactly on my line. I covered about 100 yards between each salvo, but the last lot landed all round me – the nearest was in my ditch and 6ft from my head.

Just as I was getting into cover, someone shot at me with a pistol – and I found the driver of one of our tanks – very shaken poor chap. They were shelling Coy HQ fairly well, and just as I was going to leave, there was a terrific explosion, which shifted tree tops, sandbag emplacements and men. (The 6ft-thick sandbag walls moved sideways complete.) I was 20 yards or so away from Coy HQ and thought everyone must be dead, but went over and found them all right. The anti-tank minefield in front had been hit and about an acre had gone up all at once.

After a decent interval I set off, on my M/C, and telephoned from one of the other Coys, saw all Coys, and then set off for Bn HQ. As I was going along the road, at about 40mph, there was a spurt of flame 10ft to my left front, and I was hurled sideways and off. A shell had landed on the left of the road and made a good crater. Rather battered, I collected my M/C and went on. Going round a corner under the railway bridge at Halstroff, I ran straight into two craters across the road and fell off again.

By the time I got back, the M/C was rather battered, and I got a raspberry from Sgt Matthewson for the state of his bike. Both he and RSM McNaughton were very angry with me for having gone up myself and angrier still when Patrick C-P told them what we had been up to.

This particular attack near the village of Betting was repulsed. The Germans suffered heavy casualties with 2nd-Lt John Moon's platoon alone claiming at least forty Germans killed. 1st Black Watch losses were a mere 5 dead and eight wounded. The Germans had attacked with hugely superior numbers and supported by eight artillery batteries compared to three supporting the 1st Black Watch.

To the left of the 1st Battalion the 4th Black Watch however faced an even sterner task. 153 Brigade had had some two weeks less in which to strengthen the defences that their French predecessors had largely ignored. Nevertheless the German assault was repulsed.

The Battle of Rémeling on 13 May was but a small part of a major onslaught by Germany which had no few than 126 divisions plus ten armoured divisions given to the front line between Switzerland and the North Sea. Stationed against this force was a very similar number of Allied Divisions. By rights the German advance could have been repulsed but more than half the French Army stood on the southern and eastern sectors of the French border which left fifty-one French and British Divisions of the First Army Group to face seventy German Divisions on the French – Belgian border between the North Sea and Longwy.

On 13 May, the BEF became aware that the main thrust of German force was against the French 9th Army which was holding the west bank of the Meuse between Namur and Mezieres and by night-fall German troops were established on the west bank of the Meuse at Dinant and Sedan. The French troops, where attacked by German Panzer [Armoured] Divisions and carpet bombing, were in total disarray and the enemy was able to advance at great speed.

The BEF to the north was still in position, but on its left flank the Belgians were retreating to the Antwerp defences and on the coast itself the French 7th Army was retreating at high speed.

The assault on the ground held by the 51st, though repulsed on 13 May with heavy German losses, continued. On the 14 May in the sector held by the 5th Gordons, to the left of the 1st Black Watch, the German artillery fired 3,600 shells into a company front [normally around 250–300 yards] in 90 minutes – a rate of a shell every one-and-a-half seconds. An infantry attack followed this barrage but the Gordons held their ground and the Germans were, once again, sent back with bloodied noses.

On 15 May Holland surrendered. The Dutch had attempted a conventional defence by blowing bridges and flooding large areas of land.

They had fought a retreat across the country and at the moment when they were parleying with the Germans for the surrender of Rotterdam the Germans attacked with a large-scale air raid on that city rendering some 78,000 homeless. The Dutch General Winkelman surrendered the forces under his command. The Dutch government continued to fight in exile however and gave the Allies the use of their colonies and resources, their navy and merchant navy.

On the morning of 15 May the Germans attacked yet again and this time the 5th Gordons, heavily outnumbered, were forced to withdraw from their forward posts. This loss of ground was actually of little import since the French forces, on either side of the 51st Highland Division had given ground and the Division was in danger of being outflanked. Withdrawal of the 51st from what was becoming a dangerous salient was necessary and this took place only a few hours after the Gordons gave up their ground.

It was at 07.30hrs on the 15th when Churchill gathered that French morale was already broken at this early stage in the campaign. In a telephone conversation with the French Premier he recorded: '"We have been defeated" said M. Reynaud. As I did not immediately respond he said again, "We are beaten; we have lost the battle."' [25] This astonishing sign of defeatism after just a few days of conflict was an extraordinary admission for an army of 10 million men (including volunteers) and which was described with great confidence in the Daily Mail Year Book of 1940 as the world's most formidable fighting machine.[26]

In fact, a breach of some 50 miles wide had been established through the French 9th Army and, by the evening of the 15th, German armoured vehicles were reported to have advanced 60 miles. This caused some problems for the BEF as it now had to defend its south flank, where the 9th Army had been.

On 16 May, facing mounting pressure on their front, the BEF was ordered to withdraw to the river Scheldt. Churchill flew to Paris to meet the French and records 'At no time did we sit down around a table. Utter dejection was written on every face.' He was flabbergasted *when he asked 'Ou est la masse de manoeuvre?' (Where is the strategic reserve?) to receive a reply from General Gamelin who, with a shake of his head and a shrug, said but one word, 'Aucune'; (There is) none.*[27]

To have retained no strategic reserve goes against all military logic.

Saul David writes: 'From here on, as the military situation worsened, Churchill was forced into an intricate game of political chess, with the 51st Division as a pawn, as he tried desperately to persuade the French to continue to fight.'[28]

Back with the 51st Highland Division, although forced to withdraw from the Ligne de Contact to the fortresses of the Maginot Line, they still held firm on 17 May. However, the French Division immediately to the south of them was suddenly withdrawn to face the northern German advance, and 154 Brigade extended to the right to cover part of this ground.

18 May 1940

I'm afraid I haven't written for some time as I have been very busy. We have had quite a bit of fighting, but I am very well though tired.

I hope the fighting in Belgium goes better. It doesn't sound too good at present.

20 May 1940

I listened to Winston Churchill talking last night, but I didn't think he was very encouraging. I suppose it isn't possible to be. I suppose it is a good thing putting Marshall Weygand in Supreme Command, but it must be an awkward time to make any changes.

I managed to get a sort of bath the other day which was a blessing. They are not too easy to come by.

The French premier Reynaud replaced 68-year-old General Maurice Gamelin with General Maxime Weygand on 19 May.

On 20 May, the 51st Highland Division was removed from the command of the French 3rd Army and ordered to move on the 22nd about 25 miles west of Metz to a concentration area at Etain. Here they were put into reserve under the control of the French High Command.

By this time it was apparent that the main thrust of the German advance had turned towards the sea. On 20 May General Kleist's Panzer had reached Abbeville and thereby closing off any escape route for the French and the BEF. The following day German units reached the coast in the vicinity of St-Valery-sur-Somme. The encirclement was complete and these German forces on the southern flank now headed northwards to close the trap. With the French 9th Army in total disarray and the reluctance of the French 1st Army, on the immediate south of the BEF, to move to face this attack in the Somme it became clear that a withdrawal and evacuation at Dunkirk was for the BEF the only alternative to surrender.

At this stage Bradford's account takes up the story.

3

From the Maginot Line to St-Valery-en-Caux: May – 12 June 1940

Towards the end of May, 1940, after having held several positions about the Maginot Line, we moved suddenly on 23 May to Etain, a small village some 40km west of Metz on the Paris road.

As the village had been bombed we were not allowed to billet there and Maj. Dundas had therefore arranged for us to go into a nearby wood, with the MT [*Motor Transport*] parked round its perimeter. It was around dawn when we arrived and cooking was difficult as fires were not allowed and very little water was available, and, expecting air attacks at any time, we did everything possible to keep concealed.

I motored back to Metz to see Col Stephen in hospital about some matter on which Col Honeyman wanted his opinion. [*Contrary to Bradford's hopes Honeyman had taken over command following Stephen's illness.*] I had an excellent dinner in the Moitrier, with some 1893 Montrachet, before returning to the wood. The Moitrier was a really good restaurant in Metz which we had known from our previous tour in the Saar in December 1939. [*In anticipation of the invasion, the best wines were being eagerly consumed.*]

The plan was, ultimately, for the 51st to rejoin the main body of the BEF. Having concentrated the Division near Etain the plan was then for a move by road and rail to Pacy-sur-Eure, north-west of Paris. However, no sooner had the Division completed its concentration than orders were received for a rapid move through Verdun to the Varennes area. The 51st had been sent by French High Command to join its 2nd Army as reserve behind the French forces holding the southern flank of the German salient.

The battalion rested throughout the day and night, and needed it, as no one had had much sleep for some time. It began raining about 02.00hrs and we all got pretty wet, and the trucks bogged down. At about 06.00hrs we began to try and get them out. With a length of rope it took fifty men to get each truck out of the wood and onto the road. Having concealed them in the village and other places, we opened the battalion out into orchards.

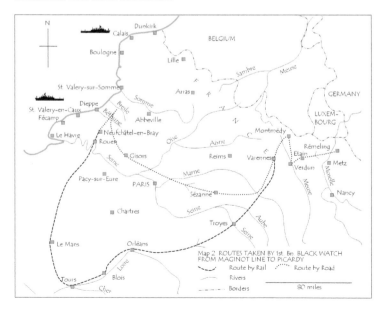

Map 2 ROUTES TAKEN BY 1st Bn BLACK WATCH FROM MAGINOT LINE TO PICARDY

In the evening we moved down to the village and billeted there. At 22.00hrs on 25 May we were ordered to send a liaison officer to Brigade at once, and an hour later orders came to be ready to move at 00.15hrs by MT. Maj. Dundas went on as advance party and, eventually, some inadequate transport arrived about 03.00hrs and we crowded on board and set off. I was feeling rotten with 'flu.

25 May 1940
We got some news on the wireless for a few days when we were on the electricity, but now we can't get it again. The Germans seem to get through far too easily don't they.

We moved through Verdun to Montmédy where we billeted at about 07.00hrs. We rested a good deal, but thought we were only there temporarily to fill a gap between French troops and stop a breakthrough. There was considerable confusion in orders. After 24 hours there we were told we should stay for some time as part of the French 9th Army, and so began reorganising.

Most of the Division had arrived at Varennes, but six battalions which had left Etain by train had not been heard from. Later that day Divisional HQ gathered from the French that these battalions had been re-directed by French command to Rouen, while the remainder of the Division should move to Pacy as originally intended.

Battalion HQ was in a lovely old farm which was full of animals almost dying from hunger. We let them all out including many caged hares and rabbits which, while they loved rushing about in the grass, must have been subsequently killed by dogs, but at least they didn't starve.

The Division was instructed to move to Pacy via a route to the south of Paris via Fontainebleau and as preparations were made by the Division (advance parties etc.) the orders were changed yet again, both in route and destination. Now they were to travel by road to the north of Paris to Gisors some 40 miles north-west of Paris. Meantime the rail parties would follow the six missing battalions moving to Neufchâtel-en-Bray via a loop to the south of Paris.

At about noon on the second day we were ordered to send an Advance Party by MT at 13.00hrs to 'West of Paris'. Maj. Dundas and one officer from each company set off to recce. The battalion was told that it was unlikely to move until the next day.

The plan had changed yet again as, with the speed of the German advance, it was now not possible for the 51st to rejoin the BEF. Instead the plan was now for the Allied armies to hold the line of the Rivers Somme and Aisne. A large proportion of the Allied armies, in Belgium and north-western France, were now cut off by the rapid advance of German armour towards the coast. The size of the Allied force remaining to resist the invasion was by now only sixty-five divisions – barely half the total that had been available a mere three weeks earlier.

On 26 May, at 18.00hrs we received orders to entrain at a station some 15 miles away at 23.00hrs. This meant leaving at pretty short notice and was complicated first, by the 4th Seaforth thinking that they were going on the same train; secondly by trying not to move in daylight; and finally by French artillery completely blocking the roads. No one knew the route, and I set off just before dark to mark it with Despatch Riders.

It was all I could do to get through the artillery. Just before the train was due to start, I found one rider missing and went back to find that he had broken down, so I towed him in.

A muddled move! The 4th Seaforth were not even in our brigade but were the only battalion nearby.

Somehow we reached the station in time and entrained. As it happened the train then started 4 hours late. After about 20.00hrs we were told we were going to Rouen, but on arrival there, were sent on to Neufchâtel, where we arrived at about 03.00hrs on 28 May [*after 2 days on the train*]. 2nd-Lts Moon and Campbell met us, owing to Capt. Sandford having gone to sleep in the station, and no one being able to find him.

We were supposed to be met by transport, but as it hadn't arrived and, as both station and town had been bombed several times, the battalion marched to woods some 5km out and got under cover. The CO and I went on to meet the 2IC [*second-in-command*] at Guerville near the River Bresle. On arrival there, I set off to Divisional HQ to try and locate transport for the battalion which eventually arrived (Paris buses).

It should be noted that the Division was entirely under the direction of the increasingly disillusioned French. Reynaud, the French premier, having appointed the 73-year-old General Weygand as his Commander-in-Chief, had recalled, on 17 May, another veteran from the Great War, this time 85 years of age. Marshal Philippe Petain he appointed as deputy Premier to try and strengthen the war effort. Little did he know that even at this early stage in the campaign Weygand and Petain were already considering capitulation. Reynaud later wrote: 'I knew on 24 May that Weygand, and with him Petain, were to form a coalition in order to demand an armistice, if, as unfortunately there was some reason to believe, the battle which was to be waged on the Somme were lost.' It was a cruel betrayal for a man who had, just a week previously, placed his confidence in them.[29]

In blissful ignorance of this mood within the French command the 51st Division took up position on the river Bresle, with 154 Brigade on the left and 152 Brigade on the right

with 153 Brigade as reserve. Since the move to the Somme the
Division had been joined by a composite armoured force consist-
ing of serviceable units from the British 1st Armoured Division,
which had received considerable damage during an attack on 27 May.

Meantime the German Army Group A which had reached
St-Valery-sur-Somme by 21 May had continued to reinforce their
position to the north of the Somme Canal. They had not ventured
across the Somme and were actually advancing up the coast in a north-
erly direction to tighten the noose around the BEF which was encircled
and retreating to Dunkirk.

We took up position in woods overlooking the Bresle river,
from Gamaches on right to about Incheville on left, with
three Coys forward and one in reserve. By then it was raining
fairly hard.

One of the causes of confusion lay in the totally inadequate
supply, and often complete absence, of maps. At this point the
entire Battalion was working from only five Michelin maps.

29 May. At about 12.00hrs orders were received to move
forward immediately to a position North of the Bresle from
Buingy-lès-Gamaches to Dargnies. While this move was in
progress, further orders were received to move instead to a
position in front of Valines, which was about 8km further
ahead. The CO was told to get in touch with a French cavalry
Commander under whose orders the battalion was placed.

On arrival there it was learned that our orders had once
again been changed. By this time, although Maj. Dundas had
received the new orders, our Coys were moving in every
direction and, without any means of wireless communication, it was extremely difficult to co-ordinate each new order.

Eventually, at night (29/30 May), the battalion took over
from the French in a position from Toeuffles on the right
to Miannay, with Bn HQ at Acheux-en-Vimeu. There was

considerable firing during the evening from Moyenneville, but later it was learned that the French troops had been firing at each other.

29 May 1940.

We haven't had any mail or news for ages now. I haven't had much time to write, as we never stay still. We are in nice country with quite a lot of woods. I have found six different kinds of orchids – the ordinary dark pinky/mauve one, the lighter spotted mauve one, a very pretty one which had half the flower dark mauve & the other half light, the bee orchid, a much smaller flowered green orchid in a wood, and a big white flowered one in fields with a lovely scent. I daresay there are many more as I wasn't really looking for them. There are masses of wild flowers all over the place.

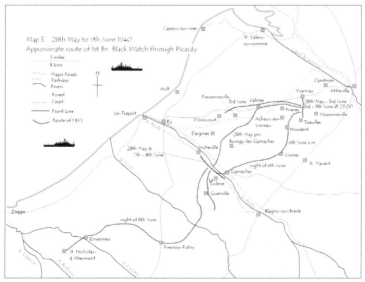

Retreat from the Somme 40-05-28.

Considering the activity on this day it is astonishing that time was
found to write a letter, let alone look for orchids.

During the week other units of the brigade and the division
arrived and relieved the French. The 1st Bn Black Watch
was moved [*temporarily it was intended*], to 153 Bde [*replacing*
4th Black Watch who were put into Divisional Reserve]. We were
told that the enemy only had bridgeheads over the Somme
at St-Valery-sur-Somme and Abbeville and that we were
going to attack and push him back. Precious days were lost
and nothing was done, while we could see that the enemy was
gradually digging in and extending his position.

Under orders from the French, B Coy was ordered (about
31 May) to attack and capture Grand Bois on our left. This
was supposed to be in conjunction with a French attack on
Cambron. B Coy attacked and captured the wood with slight
casualties, however the French attack never came off and
this left B Coy right out in the open and they were forced
by enemy attacks to withdraw. As a result of this attack,
our front was extended from about 7,000 to 8,000 yards An
M.G. [*machine gun*] platoon of Northumberlands, supposed
to support us in this attack, motored straight through our
field positions and into the hands of the Boche. Later Nogi
Dundas did a very good patrol right up to their trucks, which
their own officer had come back from but found that the
Boche had collected everyone.

2nd-Lt Freddy Burnaby-Atkins commanded one platoon in
B Company. Having advanced successfully they held the forward edge
of the Grand Bois de Cambron being fired at intermittently from a
small wood some 400 yards away. After the French attack failed to
come off he received a message by runner to withdraw and rejoin the
battalion at Miannay. There he was met by a carrier platoon which

was preparing to come to his rescue should they have got into difficulty in withdrawing.[30]

This attack took place on French orders without consultation with Divisional HQ. This was in direct contravention of the agreement between the French and British. The order to attack was issued only 2 hours before the planned start. The CO of 1st Black Watch, Lt-Col Honeyman, remonstrated with the French that there was insufficient time to carry out reconnaissance. Consequently the attack was put back by fifteen minutes. Following this development, coupled with the failure of the French to carry out their promised supporting attack, General Fortune subsequently had considerably less faith in the reliability of his French allies.

The Northumberland's Machine Gun platoon which motored into enemy hands was, it was later claimed, directed by someone in British uniform. One theory is that this person might have been a fifth-columnist as rumours abounded that there were many of them about. Bradford later recorded, 'we quite believed half these rumours, but we couldn't tell – there were lots of refugees and endless nuns! We had our doubts about some of them.'[31]

1 June 1940. I have suddenly had a mass of letters from you dated 19 and 22 May – so they must have been held up somewhere. I wonder if you have had any of my letters? I can't of course tell you where I am. It is a pity as you would be much interested having fought over all the bit where the fighting is going on now. [*The marked letters S, O & M in this sentence indicated the Somme.*]

We get very little news about what is happening elsewhere as we never see a paper or hear a wireless. All batteries seem to be run down and we can't buy new ones.
Some battery has just begun ranging on this village with ranging shells bursting in the air. I hope they don't start shelling us, as so far the village is fairly intact.

A few days later we were relieved by 5 Gordons, 153 Brigade and marched into reserve with 154 Brigade at Woincourt, Fressenville etc. arriving about 04.00hrs. We were supposed to continue that morning towards the sea, but at 11.00hrs orders were received to march back and take over our original position, coming under command of 152 Brigade. The battalion therefore got even less rest and more marching than if it had not been relieved at all.

I had found a big farm wagon (a Somme wagon) and two horses abandoned on the road and appropriated it, together with quantities of butter, cheese and wine. Sgt Matthewson drove it down full of supplies. Unfortunately it arrived at Battalion HQ just when the CO was there – he didn't really approve.

Lt-Col Honeyman was, by all accounts, keen to do things 'by the book'. According to Bradford the CO, overcame his disapproval and drank some of the wine for lunch.[32]

On 3 June our original position was taken up but with Battalion HQ at Frieres. The next day, 4 June, 5th Gordons attacked Grand Bois on our left and suffered heavy casualties before taking it. Their attack was supposed to go much further forward, while the 4th Seaforth attacked on the right towards Cambron. If the attack had been successful, the plan was for the battalion to move forward and push down to the Somme Canal. The attack was completely held up and failed.

Bradford and Pat Campbell-Preston, both Old Etonians, joked beforehand that this attack was doomed to failure from the start as it was to take place on the Fourth of June which was an Eton holiday and therefore a 'Non dies' – a day off! As he observed, precious days had been lost while the enemy bridgeheads across the Somme were being strengthened. The objective of this attack was to destroy these bridgeheads.

The 51st were, at this time, holding a front some 16 miles wide – approximately four times the usual front allocated for divisional defence.

This counter attack was, despite the brevity of the diary entry, a very major attack involving the 51st and a French Infantry and Armoured division. It went badly wrong. The French heavy tanks (24 Chars B tanks of Groupement Cuirasse) were late to start, lost the rolling barrage's protection and suffered in consequence. Likewise the French armoured escort (Chasseurs Portées) for the 4th Seaforth was also late – most, in fact, failed to turn up at all. Twenty-three hours after the start the 4th Seaforth's losses were 11 officers and 223 other ranks. The 4th Camerons also suffered heavily and overall 152 Brigade lost 20 officers and 543 other ranks on that dreadful day to no avail.

On 152 Brigade's left the French 31st Infantry Division made their attack and it was reported that the French troops 'shambled their way into attack, with rifles slung on shoulders and smoking cigarettes.'[33] Less than an hour later they returned and it is thought that they mistook retreating French tank crews as an enemy counter-attack and retreated.

The 1st Gordons, supported by 1st Black Watch, did, in fact, achieve their objective but, with all the other elements of the attack a failure, had to give up their position that night, as they would have been left dangerously exposed.

While this attack was going on the final debacle at Dunkirk ended. The evacuation had saved some 338,000 men from captivity. The Isle of Man steamer, the Mona's Queen, which had brought Bradford to Cherbourg on the stormy crossing the previous autumn, had played her part. She brought 2,000 British troops from Boulogne on 22 May and on the 27th rescued 1,200 from Dunkirk. Returning to Dunkirk on *the 29th she hit a mine and broke in two and sank, taking 24 of her crew with her.*

Germany now turned her full attention to the French armies (with the 51st) holding the southern flank. This operation had the code name 'Fall Rot' (Case Red). Over the next week the Germans, having already isolated the BEF at Dunkirk, were to advance through the Somme in a south-westerly direction, driving before them the French forces and with them the only British forces, the 51st Highland Division and the remnants of the 1st British Armoured Division. In total, between Reims and the sea the French 10th, 7th and 6th Armies, totalling 32 divisions were to face 50 German Divisions. Ominously the 7th Panzer Division under Generalleutnant Erwin Rommel headed across the Somme in the vicinity of Amiens and proceeded south-west at high speed.

On 5 June the enemy attacked and walked through the 7th Bn Argyll and Sutherland Highlanders on the left of the 5th Gordons, getting behind and on the flank of the Gordons, who had to withdraw.

Owing to the way the withdrawal was carried out, our left flank was left completely exposed. As soon as I saw what was happening I went and told Brigadier Burney, as I knew he hadn't meant this to happen. He came back himself but was too late to alter it [*the exposure of the left flank*]. We could see all from Bn HQ and the enemy came through our flank to within a short distance. Our carriers counter-attacked. The line had always had an awkward bend in it. The 7th Argylls were spread over miles of country in an impossible position.

I went to see Brig. Burney to ask him to stop the 5th Gordons withdrawing from our left flank and leaving it completely exposed. I wanted him to tell them to leave one Coy forward on our left and to swing their battalion back pivoting on this Coy.

Bradford later reported that one of the problems about visiting Brigade HQ was the sheer difficulty of finding it. He said: 'It was very diffi-cult keeping track as to where Brigade Headquarters had got to — they were so well concealed and very cagey about putting out signs that very often one couldn't find them.[34]

Eventually, in the late afternoon, C and D Companies (on the left), and Battalion HQ were withdrawn to Houdent. The battalion was thus very strung out and communication with A and B Companies was difficult, as all approaches were under M.G. fire. CQMS Crawley was unable to get up and wounded, I think. About 21.00hrs orders were received for the battalion to move at 23.00hrs to a new position near Vismes. Orders were only got to the two forward companies with difficulty, and our new positions were only taken up at about dawn.

Meanwhile the transport of two companies was missing, as B Echelon and Transport had got scattered.

I went up with orders on a motorcycle to A Company and got fired at in the dark by one of our own sentries at about 2 yards range.★ I couldn't find Maj. Noble for ages and then couldn't get him to understand anything, and had instead to pass the orders to CSM Wardlaw and the Platoon Commanders. (Maj. Noble was just like a man walking in his sleep.)

★ I had tried already to send another officer with these orders but he had been too windy to go. I gave the sentry a raspberry — a) for firing at me in the first place and b) for missing!

Bradford frequently used motorcycles for communication as they were fast and manoeuvrable. He later recorded, 'we had the most unsuita-ble transport for commanding and staff officers, we were desperate for a jeep, all we had was enormous great trucks, 8cwt & 15cwt. Before the war we had two-seater Austin Seven cars which would have been invaluable as they were so narrow'.[35] *This was clearly a comment made with the benefit of hindsight as Jeeps, in 1940, were unknown and unheard of in the British Army.*[36] *A few days later Bradford commandeered a small saloon car to overcome this problem.*

6 June. We occupied our new position at about 05.00hrs. The enemy was soon up to us but were held off although only very inadequate artillery support was available.

The whole Bn was now very tired, as no one had been able to get much sleep or rest for some weeks.

In the afternoon, orders were received to withdraw at 21.00hrs to a position on the River Bresle. Although at the time all Coys were closely engaged with the enemy, and a village, through which B and A Coys had to withdraw, was being heavily shelled, the withdrawal was carried out successfully. At one time the situation looked very serious, as the enemy attacked strongly, and our artillery had withdrawn some 4 hours previously.

After crossing the River Bresle, the bridges were blown. Enemy aircraft came over and dropped flares and a few bombs, and they also machine-gunned the main road, along which the battalion was marching, but we suffered no casualties.

7 June. By dawn the Bn had taken up position on the River Bresle which was approximately the same position as held previously [*on 28 May*], but did not extend so far to the left. It was held with D Coy on the right, A in the centre and C on the left with B in reserve. Maj. Noble had gone sick on the march back and Capt. Walker, who had arrived about 4 June, was put in command of A Coy. Battalion HQ was in the village of La Tuileries, but in the evening moved to a wood nearby, owing to the danger of air attacks. During the afternoon an enemy

pilot was captured close to Bn HQ and by this time the enemy were once again up to our new positions.

For the night we moved the Coys down to forward positions on the bank of the river to prevent any enemy crossing, returning them at dawn to a position at the forward edge of the wood. In the evening a report was received that the enemy had crossed some ten miles to our left and had broken through the mixed brigade of Royal Scots Fusiliers, Royal Engineers, etc. B Coy therefore took up a position on the left flank. The enemy was engaged by long-range M.G. fire on our front.

By this time the rapid advance of the German 7th Panzer Division to the east of the 51st had cut the defensive line and this north-western flank of the French line was now clearly in danger of being encircled with their backs to the sea. Gen. Fortune wished to fall back in the direction of Rouen, thus permitting escape from encirclement should the need arise but this was forbidden by the French Command which, by then, was disintegrating.

8 June. In the morning D Coy and M.G. positions were shelled and eventually one anti-tank gun had to be abandoned until dusk and one M.G. Section moved. The enemy had definitely broken through to our left and our left flank was threatened. At about 18.00hrs information was received that the battalion would withdraw that evening and the CO was sent for to Bde HQ.

While he was away, Bn HQ in the wood was shelled twice with great accuracy, so that we suspected that spies, dressed as civilians, may have reported our position. There were a number of civilians about and it was difficult to check up on them. There were a lot of nuns about and it was often thought that at least some of these were fifth columnists however to the best of my knowledge no steps were taken to stop or search them.

The Col's batman was killed and the RSM, Cpl Sharp, and a number of others wounded. Stewart Matthewson, Provost Sergeant, took over RSM temporarily to avoid interfering with the Coys. When I told him to do this, his remark was characteristic – 'Right you are Sir. Now there will be a spot of discipline.'

Orders were given for the river to be held until 23.00hrs but to begin thinning out one hour before. Maj. Dundas was sent off with the Motor Transport as we had not been able to regain contact with B Echelon for some 36 hours. The battalion was to go to Envermeu, where orders would be given them.

It was later learned that B Echelon had been heavily bombed by aircraft, the Padre and others killed, and had had to move to new position just before the battalion moved so that they could not report their move to us, and we could not find them.

Ever since our first withdrawal, communications had been rendered extremely difficult by a total lack of field telephone cable, which was also unobtainable from Division. Shortage of maps was also acute. When the Division moved from Northern France to the Saar all maps of North France had been handed to Corps HQ and could never be obtained again.

The battalion withdrew successfully, although parachute flares and lights seemed to be quite close on three sides, and aeroplanes were overhead. After the companies had rendezvous-ed, they marched some 8km to buses near ----- -. However HQ and B Coys had to march the whole way to Envermeu [*a distance of approximately 30km*] as there was not enough transport.

At the embussing point there was absolutely no organisation and no one at the brigade staff made any attempt to allot buses or do anything except sit in their car. Buses were parked in the open, head-to-tail, along a narrow road, which was packed with French troops and transport. To add to the confusion, a French mule column had halted in the same place, and it was almost impossible for a single man on foot to fight his way through.

Somehow Coys were embussed and despatched individually. Embussing was done at dawn, and the remainder of the move took place in daylight. Although enemy bombers came over, they fortunately did not attack. They dived low several times, but, I think, had pity on us. We were very vulnerable and completely exposed as the whole brigade was embussing at one time and on the same road.

David Campbell insisted to me that this move, in vehicles, on very crowded roads was madness and while I agreed with him, there was, by then, no option but to continue.

9 June. The road was crowded the whole way down. There were no guides at Envermeu, where traffic resembled the Brighton road at Whitsun, as the whole of our Division and several French columns had met together. The Bn was wrongly directed to Wanchy some 10km on the wrong road, whence it had to be collected and turned round.

We found the CO at a wood near St-Nicholas-d'Aliermont (he had gone on from RV the previous night to meet Maj. Dundas and recce) and three companies were put in position in a wood overlooking River Eauline with HQ and B Coys in orchards at St-Nicholas. These positions were occupied by 08.00hrs. It was not a defensive position as the river was only to be watched. However, we dug in against air attack, meaning to rest in the afternoon.

However, at 13.00hrs orders were received to move about 3km left to positions in Foret d'Arques. This move involved all companies except one, and it was extremely annoying as it again prevented anyone from getting any rest and wasted all our previous digging.

I collected a modern Citroen saloon, which I used from then on as my car. It was much quicker for getting about in.

By 9 June Rouen was occupied and it had been rumoured that the line of retreat of the whole corps had been cut. That evening at Arques-la-Bataille, which incidentally was the birth-place of William the Conqueror, General Fortune held a divisional conference. The only escape route, he explained, was towards Le Havre. However, he anticipated that the Germans would arrive there before the planned date of evacuation from Le Havre on 13 June. He was sending a strong force immediately to join up with French troops on the Fécamp-Blobec line, some 20 miles east of Le Havre. The new force would also prepare for an inner line of defence around Le Havre to cover the actual embarkation.

Brigadier Stanley-Clarke, commanding 154 Brigade (the 1st Black Watch's original brigade from which it been moved), would lead Ark Force which would be comprised of 154 Bde, 6th Royal Scots Fusiliers, 1st Kensingtons (less two companies), 17th and 75th Field Regiments RA, 204 Battery of 51st Anti-tank Regiment, RA, the 236th, 237th and 239th Field Companies, RE and relevant back-up troops. While this was, on paper, roughly half of the entire division, Ark Force was comprised of units that were in a weaker state of equipment, personnel or training than the remainder. It should be noted that all the regular battalions, armoured regiment and nearly all the anti-tank guns were to remain behind, a sure indication that it was expected that the rear-guard would face the sterner trial in the days ahead.[37]

After this conference the commanders returned to their brigades and the orders filtered downwards.

At 20.30hrs, during dinner which was well served in a forester's house, orders were received for the CO and me to be at Brigade HQ [*three miles away*] at 19.00hrs for orders; and the battalion had to withdraw at 22.00hrs to a position on River Varenne with our left flank at Martigny. By the time I had returned with these orders, there was very little time left for the move. No warning had been received, and Maj. Dundas could only set off with the Recce Party at the same time as the Battalion.

To add to the muddle, we had managed to get in touch with B. Echelon, and were ordered by Bde to move them forward to Foret d'Arques. B. Echelon arrived at 22.00hrs, just as we began to withdraw, so that we met, head-on, in a narrow lane at night.

During the march back, men were so tired that they could not keep awake, and if they halted, had to be shaken hard to get them on their feet again.

10 June. [*Italy declared war on France and Great Britain.*] Battalion withdrew to a position on River Varenne, which was taken up about 03.30hrs. Some companies' transport was still missing, and D Coy's disappeared that day with their CQMS and our Liaison Agent Vaquier.

(I met Pierre Vaquier in Marseilles in October. He had got to Le Havre by truck and embarked, being subsequently sent back to France. He said he had never been told where to go,

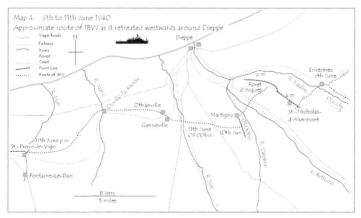

Retreat from the Somme 40-06-09.

but for some days past he had been maintaining that all was lost and the only thing to do was to make for Paris at once.)

Some of the bridges over the Varenne were blown – not very adequately but for some reason no attempt was made to blow those bridges on the rear branch of the river, which was the line we were ordered to hold. The bridges which had been blown were able to be bridged and crossed by our truck driver, who arrived late, in no more than 15 minutes.

There were crowds of refugees mingled with the army, and blocking every road with their carts. After the bridges had been blown, refugees on foot continued to cross, and mingled with them came German infantry, who suddenly opened fire about 400 yards from B Coy's HQ. The enemy soon had their mortars up and in action.

By the afternoon, the whole position, including Battalion HQ was being shelled by artillery and forward companies were closely engaged.

Communications with forward Coys were difficult, as roads were being shelled and machine-gunned and there was

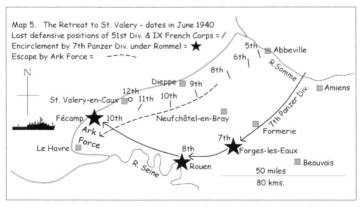

Encirclement.

no cable for telephones. All our cable had been left in the Saar weeks before, and since then we had only been able to get what we could salvage. The Gunners were very helpful with assistance this evening, as they had got communication to their Observation Post and passed messages on. They were getting short of ammunition however.

Despite the fact that their own telephone cable had all been lost some time before they still had salvaged cable by the time they reached St-Valery-en-Caux. 'We wound up all the Gunner's stuff which they left behind them' said Bradford later, 'we still had cable at St-Valery-en-Caux but things were in such a muddle by then that you couldn't direct anyone to where they could lay a telephone wire'.[38]

At about 17.00hrs enemy were reported to have broken through 4th Camerons on our left and numbers of Camerons came back through our position. By this time we were heavily engaged. Soon afterwards orders were received to deny the river until 21.00hrs. The Artillery were unable to give much support and withdrew early. At about 20.30hrs this was altered to 22.00hrs and at 21.45hrs, after forward companies had thinned out, we were told to deny river until 23.00hrs. It was almost impossible to communicate with companies but somehow we held our line until the required hour. Capt. G.P. Campbell-Preston was slightly wounded in the head and sent back for dressing. The battalion was to withdraw and embus near Genneville – then move to Ouville-la-Rivière (on main coast road to St-Valery-en-Caux) where orders would be given.

Prior to this, orders had been received to throw away everything except fighting material, in order to make room in transport for personnel. All kit was therefore dumped in ponds and wells, and we had the fun of breaking up our wireless sets, and throwing our trews etc. into middens. [*By now food, water and ammunition were in short supply.*[39]]

Ark Force had got out of the trap with minutes to spare before the Germans closed off the line of retreat for the rearguard towards Le Havre. The fact that the 51st, with the French 9th Corps, were now encircled was described by Churchill as 'a case of gross mismanagement [by the French Commanders], for this very danger was visible a full 3 days before.'

11 June. The Bn eventually withdrew, embussed after a fairly long march, and moved off in a long column, under the CO at about 03.00hrs. Major Dundas had been sent off with Recce Party, but to a different position than that for which we were making. As no one knew till the last moment where we were making for, the column soon got split up and half was lost.

We took a wrong turning early on as the map was poor, and lead the column to Offranville, near Dieppe. We thought the enemy might be holding this town, but after scouting ahead on motor-cycles, we decided it was safe and proceeded.

At Ouville, we received orders to take up position on the railway at St-Pierre-le-Viger, near Fontaine-le-Dun, with

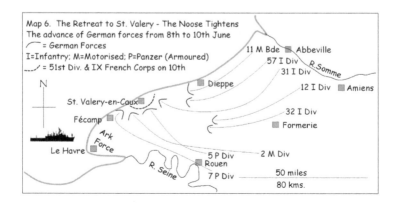

Map 6. The Retreat to St. Valery - The Noose Tightens
The advance of German forces from 8th to 10th June
⌒ = German Forces
I=Infantry; M=Motorised; P=Panzer (Armoured)
_ _ _ ⁄ = 51st Div. & IX French Corps on 10th

5th Gordons on our left and possibly the French on our right. The orders were most vague, and we were told 'to extend as far as we could to the right'.

From Ouville onwards, the road was packed with double lines of transport, and we were often stationary for a long time. It was a perfect air target, and looked more like Derby Day traffic than anything else.

When we could turn off, the CO went ahead with the RIO [*Regimental Intelligence Officer – Roger Sandford*] and me, leaving orders for the battalion to follow.

After a brief recce companies were got into position on the ground. It was a really bad bit of country – the forward slope of a hill with practically no cover. To make it worse, the line turned at this point and we were holding a salient, with no one at all to the right of us. B Coy was on our right, A centre and D left, with C reserve. Battalion HQ was in a small cottage and orchard. It was difficult to find anywhere for the transport and as most of B Echelon had got lost, there were no rations. However, 2nd-Lt J. Moon found some hard biscuits (from the site of a NAAFI dump), which were distributed and later a cow was killed and eaten.

The French army was streaming over the crest in front and up the main road through our position. They were in complete disorder. The Germans came through on their tails, and got their mortars into a position only 1,000 yards away, without difficulty, as everyone assumed that they were French Chasseurs who were alleged to be out in front.

At about 13.00hrs, orders were received to send recce party forthwith to line from Guetteville-les-Grès to Cailleville, some 12 miles in rear near St-Valery. We were told that Bn would probably withdraw there about 17.00hrs, and that we could begin thinning out now. We were also told to be ready to embark that night or the next.

D and C Coys, and all HQ, except one Section of Carriers, were sent back to a wood at Houdetot, leaving A and B Coys and a skeleton Bn HQ in forward position.

During all this time, enemy could be seen occasionally in front, but there was practically no firing. Enemy aircraft flew over several times very low. PSM Royle was killed by Sgt ------, who went quite mad.

About 16.30hrs CO left for Brigade HQ, and soon afterwards tanks were seen in front, and the enemy began to engage us with mortar and machine gun fire. The Signal Officer was sent off to the rear HQ to order up the Anti-Tank Platoon.

B Coy was not dug in at all, as their tools were missing with their transport, and, in any case, it was thought that the position was only going to be held until 17.00hrs. Bn HQ and A Coy were dug in slightly. (Our best trench was used for burying PSM Royle in and later we regretted it very much.)

Some French Cavalry had arrived about 15.00hrs and taken up a position round Bn HQ mixed up with our men.

By about 18.00hrs, we were being heavily engaged and shelled and B Coy withdrew without orders to the line of the sunken road only 150 yards from Bn HQ. Their position had been exposed completely to continuous M.G. fire from a flank, and they had had fairly heavy casualties, but by withdrawing, they let the enemy advance very close to our position.

The Signals Officer had not returned with the Anti-Tank Platoon, and at about 19.00hrs 2nd-Lt Moon was sent on motorcycle to try and get into touch with the CO at Bde HQ or to get some sort of orders, as the situation was getting difficult. Maj. Dundas had left with Recce Party at 13.00hrs and only the Adjutant [*Bradford*] was left at Bn HQ.

Freddy Burnaby-Atkins wrote: 'I ought to say that during the battle leading to the surrender at St-Valery, Bill Bradford, for long periods, was virtually commanding the battalion and communicating mostly on a commandeered bicycle!' [40]

The position we were holding was roughly as shewn. [*Map 7*] B Coy had the left forward position. At about this time firing began on our left flank and rear, which was also completely exposed. The enemy were also getting round our right flank.

Soon after 20.00hrs, I saw the French Commander, and told him that we were suffering heavy casualties and might not be able to hang on much longer. He said we must hang on until dark, and that his orders were to stay until dark and then to withdraw before us. The shelling, mortar fire and machine-gun fire was almost continuous, but the shelling, though accurate, was not really heavy. The French troops were excellent, and continued to fire and keep their heads up in spite of the shelling. Their commander was badly hit and had to be helped round his positions.

At about 20.15hrs the enemy got into position on our right flank, and one Section of Carriers were put into dismounted position out on right flank to stop them working round further. At 21.00hrs we decided to withdraw at 21.45hrs in conjunction with the French – rendezvous at a road junction in the rear and then make for Guetteville – Cailleville line. The enemy were very close up by this time and movement round Bn HQ was difficult. Several runners had tried to get into touch with remainder of Bn since 19.00hrs, but we had had no news back. I wanted them to extend their line to join up on track with B Coy.

As many wounded as possible were piled into the office truck, which L/Cpl Farquharson drove across the fields to the road to try and get to hospital.

Map 7. Position held by part of 1st Black Watch on evening of 11th June 1940. From sketch by B C Bradford.

Woods

5 Gordons

German Advance

Transport and remainder of Bn. about 1 km.

Bn HQ & French

sunken road

B Coy's new position

A Coy

St. Pierre-le-Viger

Open Right Flank

B Coy

Railway

Road

German Advance

N

German Advance

500 yards

To Fontaine-le-Dun

St-Pierre-le-Viger 40-06-11.

(I saw him later, just after we had been made prisoners, with arms badly wounded and having lost a lot of blood. He told me he got to the hospital all right and had then tried to get back to B Echelon, which he did. In the morning B Echelon were ambushed when on the move trying to rejoin me at Cailleville. The Boche tried to make him walk but after arguing with an officer I at last managed to get him put with the RAMC. I learnt later that he died.)

Just before 21.45hrs, one platoon of A Coy, with its commander, withdrew and caused confusion in the remainder of A Coy. Everyone got the idea that the enemy were right on top of us, and it was difficult to keep men at Bn HQ in their positions.

The Carrier Section was withdrawn from the right and got into position round a cottage at Bn HQ. They were ordered to act as rear-guard, and to remain behind 5 minutes after the remainder had left. B Coy, I learned later, did not withdraw for some time, as the Coy Commander was trying to make arrangements for the wounded. As we had no stretchers and only one 8cwt truck without driver, this was impossible. Wounded were put on Carriers, but I'm afraid many were left. It was awful.

I withdrew with Bn HQ slightly after rear of A Coy. On getting some way, I found that my servant, Gardiner, whom I had posted as a flank, had not come, and had to go back and fetch him. I had told him not to move unless I told him to. On reaching the road in 5th Gordons' position, I found a number of men from A Coy who had got lost from their Coy Commander. I tried to find Capt. Walker, but couldn't. I also collected a number of men from B Coy, and the Carriers joined us there.

The Gordons told us to avoid the road (their front line), as the enemy were close on the other side, so, with a party of some 100-120 men, we pushed on in the ditches on either side. There was a good deal of firing. We turned left at a cross-roads some miles on, and then had a bit of a skirmish with some French troops, who were 'withdrawing' in the opposite direction.

12 June. We reached Guetteville at about 01.30hrs I found some anti-tank gunners, but no one knew anything of our brigade. The Anti-tank gunners were about to march off and told us that no one else was in the village. The men were incapable of moving further, so I decided to halt for 2 hours. I was

literally asleep, and had to make Sgt Matthewson walk beside me and keep me awake and on my feet. We lay down on the stone floor of a schoolhouse, with a guard on the crossroads, in case any of the Bn appeared.

Burnaby-Atkins commented on the struggle to keep awake. 'The difficulty from the point of view of a junior leader was that, when we had a ten-minute halt during these night-marching withdrawals, one had to keep awake oneself in order to be sufficiently alert to wake one's soldiers at the end of the break. It was agony.'[41]

St-Valery-en-Caux is a small port lying in the only break in the chalk cliffs that line this section of the coast. The cliffs are around 300ft high. The men of the 51st were still expecting evacuation by sea from St-Valery but fog in the Channel on the night of 11/12 June prevented this. By the following morning German troops had reached the cliffs to the south and the beach was under fire from their guns.

At 03.45hrs, we continued the march. It had been, and still was, raining. For some reason, two of the Carriers had turned off and tried to find the Hospital, leaving only one with us. We lost the way a little and halted at about 05.00hrs near the road to St-Valery, where the column of deserted transport began. I collected a bicycle, and went to Cailleville to find the battalion but it was deserted except for a few French cavalry and was obviously not being held by us.

I collected two good mackintoshes, and a tin of chocolate biscuits out of some dumped staff cars, which I put out of order, but while I was doing so, someone pinched my bicycle. However, I managed to get another off a French sentry and returned to the troops.

I then set off for St-Valery alone, to try and find someone from the Bde but before I got there I met Maj. Dundas, who had some food looted from trucks, and about 40 men. On the

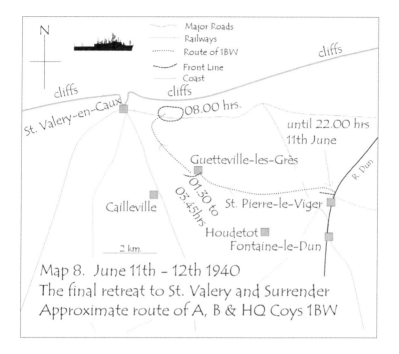

N

	Major Roads
	Railways
	Route of 1BW
	Front Line
	Coast

cliffs

cliffs   cliffs

St. Valery-en-Caux

08.00 hrs.

until 22.00 hrs
11th June

Guetteville-les-Grès

R. Dun

01.30 to 05.45hrs

Caileville   St. Pierre-le-Viger

Houdetot

Fontaine-le-Dun

2 km.

Map 8. June 11th - 12th 1940
The final retreat to St. Valery and Surrender
Approximate route of A, B & HQ Coys 1BW

road leading to St-Valery there were hundreds and hundreds of dumped trucks, cars, guns and equipment for some miles. The roads were completely blocked, and even on foot one had to climb over mudguards etc. much of this equipment was undamaged and in good condition.

We collected both parties together, and issued some bully beef and biscuits. At about 07.45hrs we found the Bde Major, who ordered us to take up a position on the high ground above a cemetery about 1.5 miles NE of St-Valery. Maj. Dundas went off to recce while I organised the men into Platoons under Sergeants, and then sent them off to collect Bren guns, anti-tank rifles and arms and tools from deserted trucks.

Each platoon was soon well equipped and armed. A mortar section was organised with mule transport, a large reserve of rations was collected, Signal Section and 2 Despatch Riders with M/C's arranged and the position taken up. Major Dundas and I even had a Lewis gun as our own weapon. Men only had rifles on arrival, as we were a motley collection and not organised in Platoons.

At about 09.00hrs, various other parties arrived, including Maj. Milne, Lt Elphinstone, and Capt. Walker. At about 09.30hrs, we saw a number of French officers with white cloths on their backs, to our right flank, but we imagined they were doing some flanking movement and wanted us to distinguish them. The position was being shelled by mortars from front and rear, but we had no casualties. A tank attack was put in on our left flank.

At about 10.00hrs Major Rennie, GSO2, arrived and told us that orders had been received to capitulate and that we were to cease fighting and surrender. I could not believe this at first, but knowing Maj. Rennie well, we obeyed the order. Various men were absolutely in tears on getting this order. The mortar detachment did not get the order at once, and continued firing at an enemy tank for some time. We destroyed what equipment we could, and the British troops were collected on a hill.

I got a bit behind, as I was burning some papers, and a tank came along and ordered me, Sgt Rogers and Cpl Anderson, who had stayed with me, to go the wrong way with the French. I expostulated, and the officer immediately swung his tank into me and knocked me over. I was then put on the tank and taken to join the others.

I believe St-Valery might have been defended if any organised attempt had been made. There were guns, anti-tank guns and anti-aircraft guns, each with a certain amount of ammunition all over the place. The breech blocks had been thrown away and no effort had been made to get these guns into any position at all. We were certainly attacked on all sides, but hundreds of troops were sitting about doing nothing useful, and there seemed no organisation at all. In fact I think we and a Seaforth Bn were the only troops who took up a position for all-round defence. The French were largely responsible for this [*lack of activity*] as there were thousands of them, and their Army Commander and Staff were there. They appeared to have given up any idea of resistance at all, and had actually surrendered the night before.

A letter written to Bradford on 26 October 1941 by Lt Roger Sandford gives a different perspective on the events during the night of 11/12 June 1940:

As far as I can see the French were holding the perimeter to the West of St-Valery, and as evening came on they surrendered to the Germans and allowed the German light tanks and AFVs [Armoured Fighting Vehicles] to cut our defences in half. Then Brigadier Burney and staff according to PSM Clarke left for St-Valery about 10.00pm. How we never got the message to retire before 12.20[am] will someday be told maybe. I have had many hours thought on whether I did the right thing when I arrived at Bde HQ at Moneville which was certainly not more than 1¼ miles from our HQ. I knew the Gordon officer was certain to get back to inform A Coy BW + the Gordons to move. The information I gleaned from C & D Coy men was that we seemed to be the last to commence retiring to the Beaches. PSM Clarke had lost all the transport 1½ hours previously in the first ambush and had rallied his men twice after that. So rightly or wrongly I stayed with this party of approx 100 men who had no officer. Piper Tait, A Coy runner & Pte McGowan the assistant mess cook & also Pte McCreadie, John

*Hopwood's batman, escaped from the first ambush and got down to
the sea and got on the same boat as myself.*

*When I got to the crest the whole cliff top was alive with
Frenchmen trying to get down the cliff. There was not a single break
from St-Valery to Veules-Les-Roses about 7 miles [to the north-
east] the average height was approx 300ft or a little more. When I
eventually got down on car tow-ropes tied together there were again
about ninety French men to every ten English on the beach. There
was a summer mist on the sea and no life-boats had come in as they
could not tell what was happening. The mist soon lifted and after
signals they towed life-boats in with naval pinnaces. As the life-
boats touched the beach, all the French panicked and made a dive
for the boats in front of the wounded. They broke up 3 and made
them unseaworthy. A 2nd-Lt in the Duke's Regt. who had quite
a lot of men with him fixed bayonets and drove the French up the
beach killing a Colonel and about fifty others. Major De Chimery
from 1st Kensingtons of all people suddenly turned up. He was the
MG Coy Comdr and we got grenades to hold the French off until
all the wounded were shipped off, then the men and finally we both
swam and were hauled in the pinnace. We begged the Navy to hang
on but about 6.15 to 6.30 they started shelling with A/T guns,
three went slap through one boat and bounced across the water for
about a mile before sinking. We then to our sorrow had to weigh
anchor and get out while the going was still good. There is a hell of
a lot I cannot write about, but I have told the whole story in detail
to Col Stephen.*

In total over 10,000 soldiers of the 51st Highland Division were taken
prisoner at St-Valery. Approximately another 1,000 were taken in
the Saar and on the Somme. Fatalities among the Divison's infantry exceeded 1,000 with more than four times this number wounded.
The units comprising Ark Force, which was sent to defend Le Havre,
comprised many of the 5,300 who were rescued from Le Havre and

Veules-les-Roses. It seems almost certain that if Ark Force had not been sent then its soldiers too would have had to surrender at St-Valery.

The loss of so many of the regular battalions was a particularly bitter blow. The Divisional Commanders were trying to use the regulars and particularly 1st Black Watch as the rearguard and moving them to any potentially dangerous spot. They were regarded as being more capable than the Territorials. Accordingly the regulars had comprised a large proportion of the rearguard. However, in placing such dependence upon 1st Black Watch the commanders inflicted a heavy price. As Bradford said 'In the last 2 days we were still capable of functioning, but in the last few nights before St-Valery we were moved repeatedly from one brigade to the other – often we marched away as instructed, only on arrival to be told to go back, thus getting no rest – we were tired out.' [42]

Salmond in his book '51st Highland Division' wrote of the tendency to think that the Division had 'lost its soul' at St-Valery and that it only found it again at Alamein. 'While it existed as a fighting formation, the Division never lost its soul. At no time in all its history did the 51st show more courage, more determination, than during those long and weary hours when it fought from the Bresle line to the streets of St-Valery. Nothing in all its history exceeds in gallantry the show it put up in those last days.'

4

A Prisoner of War:
12 June–19 June 1940

Since 5 June the vast German attack which had encircled the 51st Highland Division at St-Valery also advanced rapidly to the south. On 9 June the French held a line from Montmédy at the northern end of the Maginot Line to Le Havre directly westwards. A week later the front line had reached as far south as Autun, south-west of Dijon, an advance of some 200 miles. Churchill had tried hard to persuade the French of the effectiveness of carrying out a house-to-house defence through Paris which, though it would have ended in defeat by Germany, would have tied them up for a considerable time. This was refused by the French and they sought an armistice on the 17 June. In five short weeks the huge French army had been brought to its knees.

Meantime the defeated soldiers of the 51st Highland Division were being marched north-eastwards towards a railhead for transport into captivity.

12 June 1940. Our arms and equipment were taken off us and most of the men lost their haversacks and everything else, as the Germans ordered them to throw them down as well. We were marched off to the East at about 11.30hrs. I broke

my automatic, compass and binoculars so that the Boche shouldn't use them. I had no kit at all, as it had all been in the CO's car the evening before when he went off. The remains of the battalion marched off last past Brigadier G. Burney.

It was extremely hot and we went for some miles across country. We saw German mortar detachments carrying their weapons – a heavy load on harness – a long way; also anti-tank guns on caterpillar chassis, guns and section positions, and several knocked out tanks.

Gradually the troops in front began to throw away their tin hats, gas masks, blankets and even their haversacks, if they had them, so that those of us who had nothing were able to pick up some kit. I only picked up a blanket, as I was very tired, and didn't want to carry much. We made our own men hang on to all their kit as far as possible.

There was no organised halt, but we got so tired that we broke into various houses and managed to get some cider at one, and some water. Finally I managed to get some red wine which I mixed with rain water.

After we had passed the position held by half the battalion the night before, we halted at last at Fontaine-le-Dun where we were herded into a farmyard and the officers into an attic in the farm. There we slept for an hour and a half, and moved off again at about 16.30hrs. We met many of the battalion at this farm, including the CO. He had been unable to get back to us, owing to fire on the road, and had rejoined the other half of the battalion.

They had been attacked on the evening of the 11th with tanks, and again very heavily on the morning of the 12th, when they had finally been captured. Capt. N Grant-Duff had been killed, among many others; also L/Cpl Gardiner, Officers' Mess cook, 2nd-Lt A. Telfer-Smollet was also thought to have been killed, while Major Odo Russell and Lt S. Russell were both wounded.

From the Colonel, I learnt that the orders about withdrawing to the Guetteville – Cailleville line had been cancelled, but of course we hadn't heard that.

When we marched off about 16.30hrs, we were told we had only 5km to go. I was feeling rotten and was sick – probably the red wine on an empty stomach. In addition, my feet were pretty sore, as we had marched most of the night and early morning. David Campbell kindly helped me with my blanket which I almost wished I hadn't picked up. We straggled on and on. By about 20.30hrs, I was some distance behind with a Gunner Captain, who had been FOO [*Forward Observation Officer*] with us several times. We could only go on very slowly, and lay down hoping not to be noticed, but were moved on again with a bayonet.

We eventually got into a small farmyard, where we lay down as we were about 22.00hrs. There was no food at all, but we got a small bottle of schnapps out of a German staff car.

That evening the following officers were present. Lt-Col G.B. Honeyman, Majors Dundas, Milne and Russell; Captains Walker, Campbell-Preston, Adjutant [*Bradford*]; Lieutenants Elphinstone, Jardine-Paterson and Howie; 2/Lieuts. E.F.D. Campbell, Burnaby-Atkins.

It was drizzling. Noel [*Jardine-Paterson*] and I got into a loft, but were turned out soon afterwards by a Boche. We then got under a cart and shared our blanket and coat. The farmyard was filthy and slushy.

All that night I kept waking Noel up, and imagining that we were still fighting, and telling him to do something. Then we would realise that we were prisoners and go back to sleep again for half an hour, when the same thing would happen again.

2nd-Lt Leslie Hunt, in his book The Prisoners' Progress *recorded his first camp as a prisoner being located at Buchy, to the north-east of Rouen a distance of some 25 miles from St-Valery-en-Caux. However, he was there on 11 June, while Bradford and his half of the 1st Black Watch were still fighting. In light of the distance and timing it would not have been possible for the column to have reached Buchy on the first day of marching and it seems probable, therefore, that Bradford and his group spent the night of 12 June somewhere between Yerville and Cléres, north-west of Rouen. They caught up with, and merged with the larger group of captives at St-Léger-lès-Domart some days later.*[43]

13 June. We got up fairly early – about 05.00hrs and left soon afterwards in lorries – fairly crowded. Very few British troops got on the lorries; I suppose they wanted to separate us from our own men. We arrived in a prison camp at Formerie. The

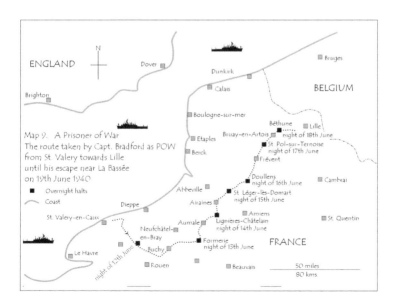

Map 9. A Prisoner of War
The route taken by Capt. Bradford as POW from St. Valery towards Lille until his escape near La Bassée on 19th June 1940
■ Overnight halts
Coast

camp was only a large open field; the ground was already fouled and dirty from previous camping. We managed to get a little drinking water after some hours, and at about 16.00hrs got about a port-glass of hot soya-bean soup, which tasted delicious, but was hardly sufficient. It was the only food most of us had had for many hours. We were told that we might get some more food, but never did. [*Noel Jardine-Paterson recorded that this was the first meal that they had had for 3½ days.*[44]]

The guards at this camp were particularly brutal and unpleasant. When I took some drinking water over to some of our men, who had been marched in about 14.00hrs, and were tired and hot, one of the guards knocked me over with his rifle, and poured away the water in front of the men.

Hunt records of the camp at Formerie: 'Slept in a field. No cover. Desperately cold and miserable. Took coats of men killed in action a few days ago.' He also noted 'the German N.C.O.s controlled columns and camps; their officers rarely seen' which may explain Bradford's comment about the guards.[45]

French troops abandoned Paris on 13 June. It had been declared an 'open city' 2 days previously.

14 June. Everyone got up early, as we were told we should be off at about 07.00hrs. The column actually moved off at 12.30hrs, having had no food. The Colonel got me a place in a lorry as my feet were in a bad way. We went off about 14.00hrs – 35 in a small lorry that normally wouldn't have held 20. We arrived at a better organised camp and were issued on arrival with a piece of bread, some meat and soup. There were a few wooden shelters about and I got a shave with some borrowed things – the first I had managed for over a week. [*This camp was at Lignières-Châtelain. Hunt describes the 'wooden shelter' in which he slept as a pigsty.*[46]]

By now German troops had entered Paris.

15 June. We marched fairly early, and about 13.00hrs after some 30km arrived at another camp near a stream, in which some of us managed to get a complete bath before that was stopped. [*It turned out that they were bathing in a lovely clear stream but upstream of the point where they drew the water for cooking.*[47]] The ground here was as dirty as ever and the place very smelly. After some hours, we were formed up again to move on by lorry, but only a few people went. As a result of this we managed to pinch some corrugated iron sheets and make a shelter of sorts for us seven – two Davids, Patrick, Noel, John E, Freddie BA and self.

We eventually got a little soup about 15.00hrs – all the food for that day. We had been told we should reach rail-head next day. Lt-Cols. were allowed to chose a batman here – I got the Col to have Sgt Matthewson (Provost Sgt).

About half the officers got into some lorries about 15.00hrs, but there wasn't enough transport for all of us. It began to rain, and they let us go into two small houses. We found some flour and fat, lit a fire and made some chupatties, which gradually improved.

Then we found thirty-two eggs in water-glass, which had escaped everyone's notice. These we hard boiled and distributed among the regiment. After that, other officers, who had been rather scornful of our cooking efforts, began to get more interested. We also fried some potatoes, and put a stew of turnips etc. on to cook. We found several pounds of dried peas and beans, and a large copper saucepan all of which we took along with us. [*This halt was at a camp at Airaines.*]

About 17.00hrs there was some more transport, and twenty or so officers got left behind. We had to leave our stew, which was a pity, and crowded onto a lorry. It was a most dangerous journey, as there were far too many of us on the lorry. I really thought we must overturn several times. We caught up the others at this next camp – only an open field, very crowded. We formed up for food several times, but never got issued with any although all the French were given a good meal and a quarter loaf of bread. Naturally there was considerable ill feeling over this.

It must seem as if we thought of nothing but food, but we were most frightfully hungry and tired, and our cooking efforts hadn't filled us much. It looked as if it would rain, and all Field Officers were taken off to a barn. Luckily it just kept fine. [*This camp was at St-Léger-lès-Domart.*]

16 June. We were issued with some biscuits and cheese about 07.00hrs and then marched straight off. I had left my kit and had to go back for it, and so got issued with two breakfasts which was marvellous. I kept half for later on. We were told we should definitely get to rail head at Doullens. We had a long march of some 9km and the pace was frightfully slow as the Colonels were marching in front.

We camped at the Citadel at Doullens, where there were many other Highland Division officers, also the Quartermaster. We got a bell tent with some straw between 12 of us, which was luxury. We were issued with a fairly reasonable meal about 16.00hrs, and in addition had a stew of peas, beans and a mangle, which someone had picked up – also an Oxo cube, which David had bought for two cigarettes. The French were all very excited about reports of an armistice having been asked for.

Reynaud's cabinet, which had relocated to Bordeaux, was ousted by Pétain.

17 June. We marched fairly early again, for St-Pol-sur-Ternoise, about 30km. Some of us managed to get most of our

kit onto lorries carrying Colonels, sick, etc. We had no halt for the first 3½ hours, but before that we got a bit out of hand, and managed to get into shops etc. in Frévent, and bought eggs, butter and bread. There were not enough guards to keep us in column. I knocked four loaves out of a French officer's hands and we collected them. In addition, civilians were giving away slices of bread, milk and wine. We bought quite a lot, and had some lovely bread and butter, when we did halt.

We arrived at St-Pol, and were made to give up all our knives, forks and cigarette lighters. I had mine down my trousers and kept them. We were then given some stew and biscuits, and the officers marched to another camp near the football ground. Here we had sort of tents.

Someone had discovered a dump of Army biscuits, which they issued out – as much as we wanted. The Germans never discovered that we had helped ourselves to these. We also made a row about them taking our knives, etc. and these were ordered to be returned. Of course very few people got their own pocket knives back.

There were crowds of civilians round the wire near the entrance to the camp, and we could, with considerable patience, get them to buy eggs, butter and wine. The latter took Nogi and me absolute hours. The whole business was like Port Said, and unless you spotted your buyer returning, someone else would grab the things out of her hands, and claim them. We had a good meal with plenty of bread and butter.

Pétain made a broadcast to the French people urging them to lay down their arms. He also requested terms for an armistice from the Germans.

18 June. We again marched fairly early for Béthune, about 30km. I had got some food in my pockets, and was determined

to try and get away with David, at a suitable place. It may seem curious that we hadn't tried before, naturally escape was always in our thoughts, but we had been so tired that we couldn't do anything. One needs to have been like that to appreciate how we felt. Besides we were going in roughly the right direction, and into a more and more friendly part of the country.

We had been told by our own senior officers, who motored, that we must be more disciplined and not forage on the line of march. We tried to be so, and succeeded until after our first halt at Bruay-en-Artois some 20km without a halt. There we were in a wire enclosure, and the civilians crowded round and gave us all sorts of food and drink, which was most kind of them. Of course this was a part where British troops were well known, and we were most popular with the civilians. Some of the French prisoners tried to persuade them not to give things to the British, but the people were most indignant, and said we were all soldiers, and all their friends.

We continued after about an hour. Bruay stretches a long way, and is a mining town. It was packed, and people were handing out food and drink. There were pails of beer, wine, lemonade and milk, but we couldn't break ranks much for the drinks. The lemonade looked particularly inviting. We collected quite a bit of food, and also some sweets and sugar, for which we were longing. I managed to get a boy to go and buy me a toothbrush and paste, which I wanted more than anything.

We arrived at Béthune and were marched into the football stadium. This was packed, and the ground was more fouled than ever, as it had been successively dug up for latrines and then filled in. The officers were in the grandstand – packed and filthy. There were about 1,000 British and 7,000 French, all ranks, our usual column strength.

Some British Aertex pants were issued out, as the Germans gave us a lorry full. A man was taking orders for things in the town, and people bought quite a lot. I didn't get anything as I had been looking for a chance of getting away all day, as I was in a country I knew. I had tried once to get away in a village but was spotted and came back by myself. Also I had very little money and wanted to save what I had.

We got quite a reasonable meal soon after arrival. David Campbell and I had long talks with several Frenchmen about our chances of escape. All the British officers seemed to think it was pretty hopeless, and Col Roney-Dougal gave out officially that we were not to think it was our duty to try and escape at present as it was too dangerous. In the evening, many officers went to sleep in the rifle range, also many British troops. I stayed in the grandstand as it was at least airy.

19 June. About 07.00hrs, without any warning, we saw that some queues had got breakfast. The few of us who slept in the grandstand dashed off and tried to make a queue. We were dispersed by the guards as being too late, but four of us got in with the Belgian wounded queue, and got some filthy 'coffee' (soya beans again) and bread. There was a lot of good French bread, but the Frenchman issuing it would not give me a bit, and said it was being kept for French officers.

There was no transport for baggage, and we walked on for about 2km, when we halted in the town. I gave my blanket and pack to a wounded L/Cpl, who managed to get on a truck, as I couldn't carry it all the way. Nogi was carrying an enormous load.

The others, who had slept in the rifle range, caught us up here having had no breakfast. While trying to get breakfast I saw a German hit an elderly officer in the face with his rifle, because he wasn't quick enough in moving – absolutely unnecessary and unprovoked.

All Colonels were on foot this day, and British were in front. We got well fed on the route by the population. I looked about for a place to get away, but couldn't see a chance. I very nearly stayed in a piece of scrub I got into, but too many men came in there, and a sentry waited. David Campbell was all ready too. We went along the main road towards La Bassée, and turned off right short of the town for Billy-Berclau and Seclin. Halted past Billy-Berclau at about 10.30 a.m. lots of civilians came and watched us. Many of us had just bought berets from civilians on the road, to replace our tin hats.

We were halted beside a wood on an old slag heap on our left; there was another wood a few hundred yards back on the right. I thought the one on the right looked bigger. (It wasn't!), and tried to make someone come with me. [*Noel Jardine-Paterson recorded, 'I sat down to rest and eat a bit and while I was there Bill came up and said he was leaving. "It's no use asking you to come with me?" I shook my head so he went off alone.'*] David wouldn't come, and everyone said it was stupid to go without out a definite plan, so I went off alone. I knew that Thomas Rennie and Col Mackintosh-Walker had gone about the same time, and later I tried to find them. Thomas had actually asked me to come with him the previous day, but I was fixed up with David.

Bradford admitted afterwards that he had turned down the opportunity of going with Rennie and Mackintosh-Walker because, as he told them, he thought they were too old to get anywhere! As it happened they got away far quicker than he did. They bicycled to Marseilles where the American Consul got them moved to Spain. From there they went to Portugal and flew home all within about six weeks.

Bradford had no plan. David Campbell, who had won an MC in the Saar some weeks beforehand, refused to go at this time. 'He didn't think it was safe to go; he didn't want to get out of uniform and be shot as a spy;' said Bradford 'I quite expected to get a bullet in my back when I first went away.'[48]

I got off the road without being noticed, and into the wood, which was very swampy. I lay down with my mackintosh over my head to keep off the clouds of mosquitoes. The wood was much smaller than it looked, and had tracks through it which were used. Some children came and played about quite close to me and I was afraid they would scream and give me away.

I didn't hear the column go off, but after about one and a half hours, I crept back on to the road, and found it clear. I went up the road, where some civilians asked what I was doing, and said I had missed the column – a bit obvious. I said I had got a pain, and couldn't walk, and went across into the other wood, which was much bigger than I had thought.

After a bit I crept back near the road, threw a stone near some people, and then beckoned one of them up. He came up a round about way, and was a Polish miner. He promised to come back with some clothes to a certain place in an hour, and was obviously pretty scared. I looked around for Thomas Rennie, and called out but couldn't find him. Then I hid myself and destroyed any papers which might give me away.

Soon after 13.00hrs the Pole returned with two suits on, and gave me one. I didn't take the pants and vest which he offered me, as mine were cleaner. I changed into a white shirt without collar, black striped trousers – old and rather short – blue waistcoat, and a smooth and fairly good black coat. With my moustache cut a bit, a beret, a black American-cloth bag, which every Frenchman seems to carry for his bread and wine, and my stick, I thought I looked quite like a Belgian Refugee schoolmaster.

I buried my uniform, and left my new Cording mackintosh, which looked too military. Then I slid down the slag-heap, and walked off down the road. I couldn't pay the Pole, as I only had about 60 Frs, so I gave him my fountain pen.

In dressing in civilian clothes Bradford thought he was running the risk, if caught, of being shot as a spy. This seemed to be a common concern at this time. Flt Lt Bob Hodges who was shot down in northern France in 1940 and headed towards Spain recorded that he and his Sergeant Gunner with whom he travelled wore civilian clothes but carried their uniform tunic in sacks over their shoulders so that they could prove they were British servicemen. The paths of Bradford and Hodges crossed that autumn.

Later in the war officers were taught that there was a category under military law of 'escapers and evaders' who were not liable to be shot if out of uniform, unless of course they were operating against the enemy or actually spying. They must not be armed, however – even a penknife was questionable.[49] From some of his later activities it is clear that, if found out, there was no question that Bradford would have been treated as a spy.

I wasn't sure of the road out of the village, and went straight on till I met the canal, which I followed to La Bassée station. As I came out of the side road by the station, to cross the main road, a German staff car came by very fast, then pulled up with a jerk, and an officer lent out and shouted something. My heart was in my mouth as I continued to walk towards him.

5

On the Home Front (1)

As Roger Sandford recorded in his letter to Bradford, units had got off in boats from the beaches below the cliffs north of St-Valery-en-Caux. Larger numbers, in Ark Force, sent to form a reserve line around Le Havre and which had by minutes escaped encirclement by Rommel's 7th Panzer Division, were also safely evacuated. The return of several thousand troops brought home the news of the disastrous loss of most of the 51st Highland Division.

Frantic efforts were made to find out what had happened to those who didn't return. Bradford's parents and friends were probably no more active in this respect than others and the news, or lack of it, can be gleaned from fragments of correspondence that remains.

In this chapter, and later on, I have tried to give an idea of the anxiety and efforts made by Bradford's parents to gather news and, later on, to help their son. This correspondence has not been inserted into the main account as it was difficult to know whether to use the date the letters were written, or received. Sometimes those two events were months apart. Bradford's father, Lt-Col Edward Austen Bradford, kept copies or at least drafts of some of the letters he wrote and so we are fortunate to have both sides of part of the correspondence.

Telephone calls were limited to three minutes and no doubt the news spread fast. It is quite evident that Bradford's parents knew of the disaster long before they received official notification as to the whereabouts of their son. From the record of correspondence it seems most likely that the first news came from the regimental family, The Black Watch. This will have triggered off an immediate effort to glean news from those who had been evacuated.

Thursday, 20 June, 1940

My Dear Mrs Bradford,

I was not able to answer your letter yesterday, because information was not available. Tonight we fear that only eleven private soldiers of the 1st Bn have reached home, of that splendid Bn. How many, and who, are prisoners, nobody yet knows, and it will be a long time before we do know.

As far as I can trace, Bill was with the Bn at St-Valery. It would be wrong of me to lead you to hope that he may have escaped.

That he may do subsequently is another matter. Yesterday a few of the Rifle Brigade from Calais got home after being taken prisoner a month ago. So there is always hope.

I grieve to write and give you these bare facts. As one who has served over 25 years in the Regiment, you will I think know, how sad the knowledge that that fine body of men should have had to give in together with Seaforths, Gordons and Camerons.

I read today that the 1st Bn changed places with the 4th Bn in the 154 Brigade and that the 4th Bn got out almost complete, with two other Territorial Argyll Bns. They are in Dumfries now. Brigadier Stanley Clarke Commanding this Brigade may know more than I do as to the whereabouts of Bill just before the time of surrounding when his Brigade was told to take up a position covering Havre. Then the Enemy Armoured Division broke in and closed the line of retreat. More I do not know.

As one who knew Bill well may I offer you my sympathy and express the hope that he may be well and unwounded. Should I hear any more I will let you know at once.[50]

In light of our current knowledge the letters give little information. At the time, however, it would seem likely that these snippets of news were, at least, helpful in filling in the almost complete void of knowledge that Col & Mrs Bradford would have had about the last few weeks of the activities of the 51st Division. Brigadier Stanley Clarke wrote a few days later:

H Q 154 Infantry Brigade
Dumfries
Scotland
25 June 1940
Dear Colonel Bradford
I was away home on 48 hours leave and found your letter on my return this morning. I am glad that you wrote but I fear I can give you no really definite information about your son in the 42nd. On Friday Sandford came here having been sent back to the beaches at St-Valery by the CO Honeyman and he had eventually got away. He and a few men were not off the beach but at the foot of the cliffs. Up to the time that he left there had been few casualties and your son was alright as far as he knew.

But the difficulties of getting anyone away from that coast were very great and we are now forced to the sad conclusion that most of the division was surrounded and cut off.

Sheer chance brought it about that General Fortune had sent my brigade with some gunners and sappers back to form a rear line for them to fall back upon covering Havre. [Ark Force.]

But the 42nd were no longer with me. After earlier fighting on the Somme I was ordered to send them as a reserve to another brigade. Later on I had the 4th Black Watch sent as my third battalion. During the next 3 days no chance of changing over again occurred. I feel terribly sad at not having them still with me. They were a grand fighting battalion and had greatly distinguished themselves on the Saar and your boy had done remarkably well as Adjutant.

He was to have come for a short time to Brigade HQ to understudy the Brigade Major with the prospect of sending him on the War Staff Course at home on our leaving the Saar but operations of course intervened. I am not indulging in any flattery or exaggeration when I say that he was an exceptionally fine adjutant and a first class officer of marked ability. We were all very fond of him at this HQ.

Your nephew Edward was in my old regiment and in the summer of 1906 or 1907 I played some cricket with his father Sir Evelyn Bradford. I am more sorry than I can say at your anxiety and only wish I could give you something more certain by way of comfort. If I do hear you can rely upon me to let you know and I am keeping your address. I am proud to have had the honour of having the 42nd under my command and your son among them. With much sympathy believe me

Yours sincerely

A.C. Stanley Clarke

Sir Evelyn Bradford had played cricket for Hampshire. His First Class career ran from 1895-1905. In 1896, playing against Essex, he got 6 wickets for 28 runs in the first innings and 5 for 40 in the second. In 1899 against Leicester he scored 102 when the next highest score in the innings was 39. In military cricket he was a prolific run-scorer. In May 1913 he had an innings of 251 runs playing for Shorncliffe Garrison against Folkestone.

Finally on 27 June Col and Mrs Bradford received official notification:

POST OFFICE
TELEGRAM

27 Ju 40
MRS E A BRADFORD, EMPSHOTT LODGE, LISS,
HANTS
REGRET TO INFORM YOU THAT LT. B.C. BRAD-
FORD BLACK WATCH IS REPORTED BY HIS UNIT
AS BELIEVED MISSING. FURTHER PARTICULARS
WILL BE FORWARDED AS SOON AS RECEIVED.
Under Secretary of State
For War

One correspondent, to a cousin Kitty Wood, did little to raise hopes:

3 August 1940
Many thanks for your letter of 29th which I should have answered
sooner, but I have again been on the move & have eventually now
fetched up here, where I am likely to remain for 2 or 3 months at
least, as we are now reforming the 1st Battalion.

I am afraid I can give you no news of Bill Bradford, whom I
knew well, except to say that he is missing as is the whole Battalion,
officers, NCOs & men: they must either all be killed or captured.

2 out of the 3 Brigades of 51st Highland Division were cut off at
Saint Valery, and no one has heard of them since, that is why we
are now reforming 1st Bn & most if not all other Highland Regts
are similarly situated some having lost more than one Battalion.

The best that one can hope is that any individual is a prisoner,
but it may be months [if ever, before end of war] before one hears
any authentic news. Actually only 12 men of our 1st Battalion got
away but they can throw no light on the fate of the remainder. I am
sorry to be so unsatisfactory.[51]

The War Office can't have helped allay fears for Bradford's safety
when they wrote on 12 July:

Madam,

In confirmation of War Office telegram dated 26 June, 1940, I regret to inform you that a report has been received from his unit that Lieutenant B.C. Bradford, The Black Watch, is ~~killed~~ missing.

No further information is available at present, but you will be immediately informed as soon as any definite news is received. In the meantime, should you receive any further news regarding your son from any source, it would be appreciated if you would communicate with this Department.

The fact that the word 'killed' had been typed in and then crossed out in ink, but remaining legible, can have done nothing to lessen their anxiety. A few days later a more encouraging letter was received:

17 July 1940

I know your son because the 42nd were with our brigade during the last days before St-Valery.

I saw him on the 10 June in company with Colonel Honeyman when he was fit and well. I am afraid I cannot give you any later news than this, but as there were some five thousand prisoners taken, there seems to be every hope that your son may be one of them.

There were also many French, Belgian and others taken prisoner and it may be some time, therefore, before accurate records will be received from Germany. I do not think, therefore, that you should be unduly anxious.[52]

Five weeks after St-Valery the best that Bradford's parents could hope for was that their son was a prisoner.

In looking at the domestic situation we have now moved considerably ahead of events back in France where Bradford, having just escaped, walked apprehensively towards the German officer who had summoned him from his staff car.

6

Alone:
19 June–25 June 1940

It seemed to take ages to approach the German officer and as he started to speak I feared the worst but he only wanted to know the road to Béthune. I told him and he drove on.

Greatly relieved I went on down the main road for quite a long way, hoping to get a lift to Béthune. [*Bradford's initial intention was to get back to the coast as fast as possible and find a boat across the Channel.*]

However, I had no luck, and went back to the canal before Cuinchy station. The canal was in an awful mess, as all the barges had been sunk or set on fire. People were trying to salvage things out of the water – coal, beetroot, and wood. It was interesting to see the defensive posts, which we had spent so much time in building last winter.

I went on past Béthune, where I heard two rifle shots from the camp, where I had spent the previous night. I thought I was being followed by a man, who would keep about 400 yards behind, and I didn't like to stop at a farm, but at last he disappeared, and I went on to a farm at Hinges, and asked if I could spend the night. The people were friendly, but said

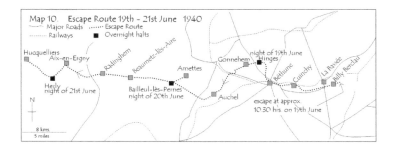

Map 10. Escape Route 19th – 21st June 1940

it was too near the road, and Germans often came in. They gave me some food, and suggested I had better go on to a big farm, where the people were kind. The man got out a horse, and pretended to be harrowing a field until he could shew me the way.

I went to this farm, and found the J------s, who were charming and said I could certainly stay there. They made me lie down in a clean stable, with a coverlet until supper, then I had a wash and shave with a borrowed razor, and afterwards fed with them in the kitchen. They told me that the Germans had accused the villagers of shooting at them during their advance, and had collected the first ten they saw, including two old women, and had shot them, thrown grenades on the bodies and told the rest to bury them.

I went to sleep again fairly early in the stable. They wanted me to sleep in the house, but I thought it was too much of a risk for them.

20 June. I breakfasted with them – bread and coffee – and left about 08.00hrs. They gave me a baddish map from the Post Office Calendar, but explained the whole way to me – by small roads and along a railway. I found the way fairly easily, and was not much on any large road. I didn't rest much

till I had passed the mining area, and was back near Amettes, where I stopped and ate my sandwiches. I then went back to the house of the ------ at Bailleul-lès-Pernes, but it was locked, so I hid nearby till 13.30hrs when I tried again.

They came out and knew me at once, although I had cut off half my moustache and was dressed like a tramp. They were really pleased to see me, although I had only been billeted there for about a week, and couldn't stop looking at me. They were two dear old women, who farmed by themselves. They gave me an excellent lunch – eggs, potatoes, beer, bread, butter and cheese. I wanted to rest somewhere for two nights and they thought I would be safer with the niece, a few kilometres off, as it wasn't on a road.

After lunch, Madame and I set off. Going through the village, I was unfortunately recognised by the Garde Champetre and others, who said, 'Mon Dieu, c'est Monsieur le Capitaine', in a loud voice. On getting to the niece's farm, we found that the Germans had given warning that they might be coming that night. The niece was frightened at any rate, so after a glass of beer, and the gift of a blue shirt, we had to go back, entering the village across the fields, so as not to be seen by too many people in the street.

I had a wash in what had been my bedroom. They had taken all the nice things out of it and had hidden them, and the farm hand now slept there to keep the Germans out. They wanted to put me there for the night, but I didn't want the whole village to know I was there, for their own safety, and I insisted on sleeping in the little attic room, where Gardiner used to sleep. Even then they tried to make me have sheets, but I wouldn't.

It was amusing to hear how the owner of the house we had used as a mess had been treated. He was a nuisance when we were there, and complained of everything, although the house was not lived in. When the Boche arrived, he started complaining at once and said he didn't want an Officers' Mess there. The Boche said 'All right' and put a company of men there instead. I also heard that some RASC were caught in bed by the first Germans to arrive. They took away their trousers and boots, and left them to be picked up later. After supper and a long talk, I went to bed and slept very well.

21 June. For breakfast, I had some milk and bread, and then black coffee with the yolk of an egg, which was just like coffee and cream and was excellent. They gave all the whites to the calves, with the skim milk. I left about 08.30hrs and went by Beaumetz-lès-Aire, Radinghem to Aix-en-Ergny, where I tried to find a farm for the night. There were a lot of Germans about all the last part of the road, and the farmers were frightened of having me, as they thought more were coming for billets that night.

After trying many farms, I went south to *Herly*, which was off the main roads, and where I thought there would not be any Boches. I picked out a lonely farm, but as I went in at the gate, two German soldiers came out of the house. There was nothing for it but to say 'Bon Jour' and go in.

I went up to the farm and asked if I could stay the night. The old woman said I would have to wait for the Patron, and that she was only a servant, so we sat and waited. She looked and was a talkative old lady, and I didn't dare tell her who I was. Several more Germans came to buy eggs and butter, and two came and bought bowls of cream, which they ate in the kitchen, as noisily as pigs. I was left talking to several Germans by myself at one time, and had to find butter for them, as I couldn't find the old woman. I was thankful when they left, as one of them spoke French too well for my liking.

At last a man arrived, and I found that he was the servant and the old woman the Patronne. They agreed that I could stay the night, and gave me some milk and hard-boiled eggs. I helped them with feeding the beasts for a bit, and later went to sleep in the barn, which was full of rats. I could feel them squirming under me during the night and several ran over me.

22 June. I started early and went fast to a place near Boulogne, called Ecault. From there I went on to Boulogne and tried hard all round the harbour and town to find some old fishermen, who would row or sail me across the Channel. I asked several, but they all said that the boats had gone and that it was all hopeless. None of them suggested anything or was at all hopeful. I got there about 15.00hrs, and left about 19.00hrs, having accomplished nothing. I had counted so much on Boulogne, that I returned very disappointed to Ecault, where I slept the night in a barn.

France surrendered formally to Germany on 22 June 1940, signing the declaration at Compiégne in the very same railway carriage that was used in 1918 for the surrender of Germany. It was subsequently destroyed by the Germans to avoid further use. Reynaud, the Prime Minister, was forced to resign owing to his refusal to surrender and he was replaced by Maréchal Philippe Pétain. France was divided into two parts, an Occupied Zone and an Unoccupied Zone governed by the collaborationists under Pétain based in Vichy. Charles de Gaulle, who was in London at the time of surrender and refused to acknowledge the Pétain government, subsequently started organising the Free French forces.

23 June. I left early, and went by Lefaux to Etaples. It was much the same as the day before, and, although there were a few boats lying about, I couldn't get anyone even

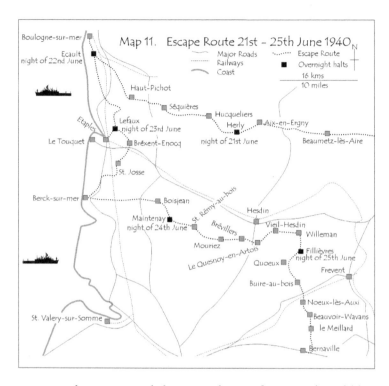

Map 11. Escape Route 21st – 25th June 1940

interested. I even tried the Curé, but unfortunately told his sister, who opened the door, that I was a Belgian, and so he wouldn't let me explain who I was, and said 'Go to the Belgian Committee.'

Both Boulogne and Etaples were full of Germans. To make it more difficult, an order had been issued that all refugees would be 20km clear of the coast by 23 June, so that I was rather a conspicuous figure that day, and had been stopped and questioned by the Germans several times. On one occasion the patrol was not satisfied with my answers, and took me along to HQ. There I saw an officer, who pretended not to believe me, but when I stuck to my story that I was a

Belgian, who had lost all his papers and his family in the quick evacuation, he finally let me go. I didn't speak French very well, and so I spoke as fast as I could to try and muddle him, but I was a bit shaken when I got out.

I returned late in the evening to Lefaux, where I had seen a good farm. It turned out to be the Maire's and he let me stay although he was frightened. He hid me away in a barn, and brought me some soup, meat and cider, which was an excellent meal. I was still quite extraordinarily hungry, and was always longing for food. The Maire had been falsely accused by the Germans of hiding a prisoner some days before. They had held a revolver to his head and had badly shaken him. I slept very well as I was tired.

24 June. The Maire made me leave about 06.00hrs, and I went by Bréxent-Enocq to St-Josse, where I met a very nice Curé. I asked him what on earth I could do, and although he couldn't help me, he talked so kindly and gave me his blessing, that I left him feeling much happier.

I tried near Berck-Plage again for a boat but with no result. Today the Germans asked everyone who looked like a refugee for papers, so I set off inland. I went by Boisjean, and then tried to find a lodging in a big farm, but without success, though they gave me some cider.

I then rather lost my way across country making for St-Rémy-au-Bois, and came into a village [*Maintenay*] where I saw some Germans. I asked a woman at a cottage, where I might find a lodging, and she said, 'Try at the first big house up the road, where they are always very kind.' I went up to a lovely Château, coming in through the farm, and a lady looked out of a window, and asked me what I wanted.

I said who I was and found she spoke English. She took me into the house, where I met her sister. They gave me some coffee, bread, butter, meat and boiled eggs on the lawn outside — also some strawberries and sugar. I never seemed to have enough to eat and my thoughts were often on food. Then they let me have a hip bath in a summer house or bureau in the garden, and the Polish gardener lent me his razor etc. After that, they shewed me a little cottage across the road, where I could sleep the night, as I refused to sleep in the house.

The cottage was empty, and had been used by a lot of evac-uees. There was some straw, an old Belgian greatcoat and a lot of rats in it. I picked a tin of red and white currants out of the cottage garden, and then went to sleep. I didn't sleep very well, as I had to open a window, and kept feeling that some-one was looking in at me. The de France's were awfully kind and made me promise to come back and see them after the war. [*He did, on his honeymoon. Today the château is readily found a short distance outside Maintenay. The roadside gates and wrought iron fence open onto a large farm yard, now used as a builder's yard, with the pretty château beyond. The cottage, just across the road, is now derelict.*]

25 June. I left the cottage at Maintenay about 06.40hrs, and walked for about 45 mins, when I breakfasted off my cur-rants. I had decided to go to a little village called Willeman, where we had lunched several times, when we were doing field firing in March, and where I knew I could get a bed for the night. It had been decreed that all refugees would be inland of the road from Hesdin, by the 25th, and this village was well inside that line. I didn't hurry much all day, and halted whenever I wanted, as I didn't want to arrive too early at this café.

There was a great deal of troop movement, both march-ing and in lorries, all round Hesdin, and I found it difficult to find a quiet place where I could eat my lunch, as the country was so open. I very nearly gave myself away, by asking some German workmen the way. They were engaged in building a shed, and a soldier came out just as I was going up to them.

I arrived at Willeman about 16.00hrs, and went to the café, and asked for a glass of wine. They recognised me at once, but didn't say anything until the café had emptied. Then they told me that there were some more British soldiers in the village, and sent out for the man who had helped them. He was a refugee schoolmaster from Ronbaisc, and said that they had gone on a few hours before, but that he thought there were some more in a hut in a wood. We went off to try and find these, but couldn't – they probably hid from us.

We went back to the café, and I had a quick meal in the kitchen of soup and rabbit stew. They gave me some bread and butter to take with me, and also lent me a ladies bicycle. The schoolmaster, his friend and I bicycled off over the field firing range, and caught up the others at the entrance to Filièvres – four of them dressed as workmen. Our friend went off with the bicycles, and we five went into a café, where the people were very friendly, and gave us bread and pâté.

They were four young soldiers of the 4th Camerons, and had escaped from Frévent 2 days before – since when they had fed well, and covered only some 15km. They were McKay, Bernardi, Hardy and Mackintosh. McKay and Bernardi looked very French, the other two not at all. We decided to go on together towards the South and then Spain – an ambitious programme.

I went out as a German lorry had stopped outside and the driver was coming in, and found a farm next door where we could sleep the night in a barn – right on the main road. The others stayed on talking for half an hour in spite of several German lorries in the street.

Two of them then went off to forage and came back some time later with bread, butter, jam, eggs, biscuits, champagne and rum – also two shirts, some soap and a towel – much better than I could ever have done. I got a pail of milk from the farm, and also a very old coat, which I exchanged for my black one, so as to look more like a workman, and fit in with the others.

We washed and then had a meal. They had no idea of saving any food for the morrow, and would have liked to have stuffed themselves, till they couldn't eat any more. There was plenty of straw and some sacks, and we soon made ourselves comfortable, and after talking for some time, went to sleep. It was really wonderful not to be alone again and to have someone to talk to.

7

Travelling in Company: 25 June–2 July 1940

26 June. We had plenty of milk left over, and breakfasted off that, bread and butter and hard-boiled eggs. We didn't set off until 08.00hrs as they were very slow in getting up. We decided to march with me in front, and the others in pairs at about 400-yard intervals. McKay had a pitchfork, another a hoe, and another a sack, as if they were going to work in the fields.

We had to make a detour to avoid a German aerodrome at Quoeux, and eventually came to one of their Remount Depots at Beauvoir-Wavans, where there were far too many Boches about. I had borrowed from the café at Willeman a map – a *marketing* gift of Suze or some *other* aperitif – which showed about half France, but was not quite detailed enough for us. However it was much better than the Post Office one I had had before.

At about 14.30hrs, after we had lunched behind a hedge, we came to a main road where our map showed our road going straight across. There was no road straight across and, as a German staff car pulled up beside me just then, I had to hope

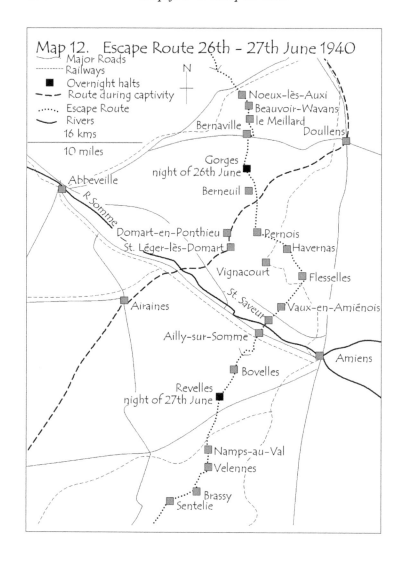

Map 12.   Escape Route 26th - 27th June 1940

for the best and turn right and then first left. Unfortunately this took us into the fairly large village of Bernaville.

I went on slowly through it, and saw McKay and Bernardi go into a boulangerie behind me, so I waited at the next cross-roads. After about 20 minutes I went back, and heard a man in a cart call to a friend that there were two Scottish soldiers in a farm there. I went into the farm, and found they had gone in for some butter, and stayed for some coffee and a cigarette. They had done nothing about seeing if the next two took the right turning or about telling me. I sent Bernardi off to try and find the others, and fixed up where to meet him. Then a woman dashed in to say that there were some Germans coming, so we hurried out a back way.

On arrival at the fork road, where I told Bernardi to meet us, we found a group of Germans, who looked very excited and were gesticulating. We went on a short way, and then McKay went back to look for Bernardi. At last we found him, but he had seen no sign of the others. I said I would wait at the Calvary where I was, while they set off again to look for the others. While I was waiting, an old woman came up and asked what mischief we were up to. When I explained who we were she became a little less unpleasant.

After about 2½ hours, we had to give them up as lost, and went on to a small village, Gorges, where an old woman told us we could sleep in an old building across the road. She gave us some milk at her farm, and cooked us an omelette about 20.00hrs. She also boiled us some eggs, which we had, for the next day. A labourer told us we must avoid Berneuil and Vignacourt – German aerodromes, where they might ask for papers.

We had a wash and climbed into a loft over a threshing machine. We slept on straw which had not been threshed and was all going to waste through shortage of labour. We had not made a great deal of progress and had already lost half our party. The other two had got all the provisions, two shirts, towel and our valuable bit of soap.

McKay and Bernardi both came from Inverness, where McKay was a bus driver, and Bernardi a ladies' hairdresser. His parents were of Italian origin. They were both about 22 years old, and were dressed in blue canvas suits and berets.

27 June. We didn't wake till about 07.20hrs. We had some skim milk from the evening before, hard-boiled eggs, and bread, and then we set off. It was rather a complicated route to avoid the aerodromes, but we were lucky to hit off a track to Pernois, and another from there across the fields to Havernas – neither of which were marked on our somewhat indifferent map.

From Havernas we had to go for about 6km along the main road, past enormous dumps of burnt British petrol tins. Acres of lovely beech had been destroyed in burning these dumps. No wonder we hadn't been able to get petrol when we were on the Somme.

The country was largely evacuated and bread unobtainable. There was nothing else to buy at all, except eggs, butter and cheese from the farms, and they usually gave those to us, when we said who we were.

Just after Fleselles, which was full of Germans, we had to cross a level-crossing, where a German column was halted. However, no one took any notice of us, though some of the soldiers shouted 'Bonjour'.

At Vaux-en-Amiénois I asked an old man in the fields which was the way. He asked if I was English, and when I answered, asked us all to come to his farm for lunch. We went with him to a small farm, where his wife received us kindly. We had to wait about 2 hours till 14.00hrs, during which we slept in the barn. Then they gave us a lunch with meat, purée of potatoes, cider, bread and cheese. His daughter had returned from buying bread at Ailly-sur-Somme by then, and told us we could cross without difficulty, and that there were no sentries.

Vaux had been an Artillery School in the last war, and there had been a British aerodrome nearby this time, so the population were well used to British soldiers and very friendly.

We crossed the Somme from St-Saveur to Ailly by a temporary wooden bridge built by the Germans. Both villages had been badly knocked about in the fighting. Ailly church was partially destroyed, and many buildings were still smoking. Looking at the river and swamp, it seemed ridiculous that we hadn't been able to stop the Germans crossing. There were a number of Germans in Ailly.

From the river up to the top of the valley, going south, you could see all the different positions held by the Germans as they advanced, where they had used their mortars, the little scrapes they had dug in the ground, the use they had made of ditches on either side of the road, and how they used every bit of dead ground, which hid them from the French. The French positions had not been heavily shelled judging by the number of craters near them. There were many groups of graves of German soldiers, marked with a cross, with the man's tin hat on it. In a large wood a few miles south of Ailly we saw stacks of French anti-tank mines, which had never been used.

We stopped for the night at Revelles, which was mainly evacuated. During the last few miles we passed a number of refugees returning north in their huge Somme carts with four or six horses. It took us some time to find a farm, which was occupied, and would let us sleep in it. Even then they could only give us a little milk, and let us go in a barn across the road. However, I tried several other farms, and at last got some more milk, some of which we kept for the morning, and some hard-boiled eggs.

The others at last began to realise that we must keep a reserve of some sort, as we had not been able to buy any bread all day. They both liked to eat six eggs, half a loaf of bread with half a pound of butter each at every meal, and to rely on the civilians to supply them. I had rationed them strictly that day and continued to do so, as we had practically no money, and it was unfair to eat more than the civilians were getting themselves. Bread was only obtainable for local residents and was strictly rationed. It was brownish and had been quite unobtainable for several days before this, as the bakers had departed.

I didn't get to bed till late as I didn't want the others to go foraging and give away to all the refugees who we were. We had quite a lot of straw but no sacks. We had made about 30km in a direct line and must have walked much further. We were all very tired, but glad to have crossed the Somme.

28 June. I didn't wake up till about 07.15hrs, as I was very tired. The others never seemed to wake by themselves, and used to start about 10.00hrs, before we met together. Today I told Bernardi to be responsible for waking us at 06.30hrs in future, and he did it effectively every day from then on; usually waking me up at 05.00hrs, to see the time as he had no watch.

After a quick snack, we set off. We missed the way slightly at Namps-au-Val. At the entrance to the village, we waited for Bernardi, as McKay and I had been together in front for a change. We had talked to him some 5 minutes before, but he couldn't be seen. McKay went back to the cross-roads to look for him, while I sauntered on through the village, although there were several Germans about. I had told McKay the names of the next two villages, and explained the way.

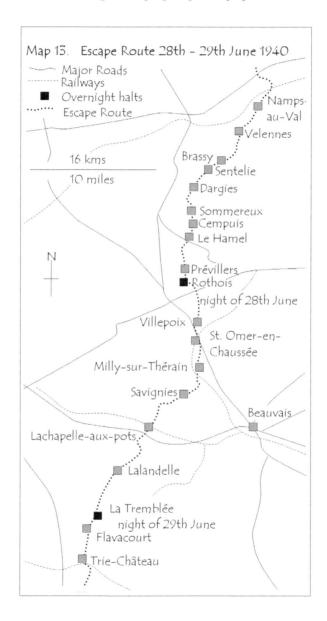

Map 15. Escape Route 28th - 29th June 1940

After I had passed a long column of marching troops and horsed transport Bernardi caught me up – without McKay. We decided to continue to the next village, Velennes, where we waited some time and looked about for him. Then we went on to Brassy, which was the last village I had told McKay. We went down one street to find a German column coming up it so we turned back and tried another, but the village was full of Germans.

We went into a farm in the main street and asked for a drink, and then arranged that I should keep a lookout for McKay in the village, while Bernardi went back along the road. While I was waiting and eating a piece of bread and butter, a German came in to buy butter. He hadn't got enough money and said he would come back. After about ten minutes, McKay and Bernardi came back together, so we left at once, as the Boches might be suspicious of three young men together.

When we could talk together, it turned out that Bernardi had missed the first cross-roads in Namps-au-Val, but had taken another street and so missed McKay. McKay, after looking about for a time, had come on, but when he met the German column on the road, had cut across the fields to another road, as he didn't like going past them. I was very glad we had found each other again, as I was afraid we were split up for good.

There were a lot of troops halted in the next village, Sentelie, so that I couldn't ask the way, and didn't take the road I meant to. It wasn't much further round though, and I decided to go on by Dargies and Cempuis.

When I was in the main street of Dargies, a German lorry, coming the other way, pulled up suddenly and soldiers got out. One of them shouted 'Venez Ici' to me. Fearing the worst, I went over. They got out a big container and said, 'Manger'. I found they were offering me soup, and wanted everyone to come, so I shouted to some civilians, and beck-oned the other two, who had stopped 400 yards away. They of course thought that I had been rounded up.

I had nothing to eat out of, so I borrowed a very small cup from an old woman in a house, and ate out of that. The others were luckier as they got a saucepan and a big bowl from the same house. The civilian population came with saucepans and big dishes and took away food for their families.

The old woman of the house near us was most garrulous, and I was frightened that she should give us away, as she kept on shouting out, about me, 'Monsieur peut parler le Francais assez bien [*sic*].' I kept trying to shut her up, and luckily the Boches only knew a few words, and suspected nothing; even when McKay said, 'Cigarettes comerade' in broad Scots, and got a packet out of them.

We refilled our bowls, but I rather lost on the deal, as they got three bowlfuls to my three miserable cupfuls. I was only keen to get a move on, as the soldier would keep talking to us, and I was afraid we would get caught out. I tried to stop McKay having a third bowlful, as I was full of apprehension.

We went on about 2km off the main road, and then rested in a wood, and took our boots off. Bernardi was getting very sore feet – largely his own fault as he would not wash them every evening.

We went on to Prévillers, which was mainly evacuated. We tried to find a farm, but had to go on to Rothois, which was off our road. After some time we found a barn, with no straw, and as the farmer was most unhelpful, we looked for another. The woman at the other farm was rather frightened, but gave us some raw eggs and milk. Bernardi went off to buy bread, and I to get more eggs and milk, which I at last managed to get – also some butter from a very kind woman at a big farm.

The baker wouldn't sell any bread to Bernardi, so I went down, and induced him to let me have half a loaf.

We had a wash, and ate the raw eggs in milk, and then slept rather badly, as the shed was stuffy, and had hens in it, which made it stink. We had done about 29km direct.

29 June. One of the farm hands woke us up about a quarter to six, and asked us to leave, so we went off down the street till we found a deserted barn, where we sat down and ate our meagre breakfast. We didn't want to start walking much before 06.45hrs as the farmers didn't keep summer time and there was never anyone about till then, so that one was conspicuous.

As we went through the village after breakfast, the baker offered us another half loaf of bread, which we gladly took, and we were able to buy another half loaf in the next village, so that we were fairly well off.

Later on, near a little village, Villepoix, four French soldiers, in uniform with white bands round their arms, came and asked McKay and Bernardi where they could buy butter. Naturally McKay couldn't understand or answer. We supposed that they were prisoners who had been released, as the rumour was that all French prisoners were being sent home.

A few kilometres further on we had to go through Milly-sur-Thérain, which turned out to be a German HQ of some sort, and was full of German troops, sentries and officers. We were not stopped, but owing to the number of officers about, I couldn't remain long enough at the road junction in the town for the others to see me. They turned the wrong way, but when they came to the end of the town, and couldn't see me, turned back, and luckily we all met again.

We continued via Savignies to Lalandelle, where we got a drink of cider, and then to La Tremblée,[53] where we found a big farm up a lane off the road. I found the Patron, and he kindly said we could stay in his barn, so I called the others in. They usually hung about some way off until I had made arrangements for the night, so as not to put anyone off with the sight of the three of us.

We found that the Patron was the Maire, so we kept fairly concealed for his sake. His wife and daughter were charming, but said they couldn't give us much to eat, so the others went off, and collected about a dozen hard-boiled eggs – which proved to be not so hard in our pockets the next day. I don't know what Madame thought we expected to eat, as she gave us the best meal we had ever had. She gave us some cider and cherries at once, and, at about 19.15hrs, an omelette and potato purée, a bowl of milk each, and a bowl of cream cheese which hadn't really set and which she was going to throw away, but was excellent.

I washed my socks and shirt, and hoped the latter would be dry enough to wear in the morning. Madame was horrified at the idea of my wearing it the next day. As it was Saturday we tried to borrow a razor for a shave, as most of the farmers shave for Sunday, and it was less conspicuous to do the same, but we couldn't get one. We listened to part of the news at 21.00hrs, which was very nice, and then went to sleep in an enormous barn, with plenty of sacks which Monsieur kindly collected for us. It had been a boiling hot day again and we had done about 30km directly south.

30 June. They gave us some more milk in the morning, and we started off a bit later, as it was Sunday. After Flavacourt, when we were on a small track, we came to a branch which wasn't shown on the map, and took the track with the telephone poles. After about 1.5km this ended in a large and lovely farm, so I went in to ask if there was any road through to Villers-sur-Trie.

The owner – a very pleasant man – told us the way straight through the farm, and when he found we were British, called down his son, who spoke English and was still in pyjamas. I asked them if they could give us a map, and they gave us a good but old large-scale map.

As they were so kind, I asked if we could shave and wash. They lent us an old cut-throat – very blunt – which Bernardi tried painfully on me. The shaving brush shed all its hairs on our faces. Then they found an old safety razor, and as I had some Gillette blades in my pocket, we got a decent shave. They had only returned from the South a few days before, and the Germans had ransacked the place, so that they couldn't find what they wanted.

After shaving in hot water, they gave us tea and toast, which was excellent. We were thankful that we had taken the wrong road. We took a small track from the map through woods to Trie Château, and then on to Lattainville. After that we had 3.5km along a Route Nationale, which we did very fast in spite of the intense heat.

When we had got off this, we went into the first big farm, and asked for a drink and something to eat. They gave us some really good bottled cider, which we mixed with water, and some eggs and bread. We went on a short distance into an orchard and ate our lunch. We had to move several times owing to the number of ants.

During our travels we drank a lot of cider. I used to think that French cider was too bitter, but most of it is really excellent, when you are really hot and tired. The farmers drink a lot of it in the fields and at meals. The home-made bottled cider is delicious – sparkling and quite as good as any made in England. I was surprised to find that cider was made over such a large area of France – right down to the Loire in fact.

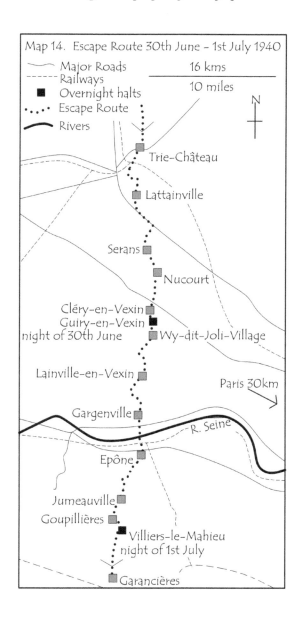

Map 14. Escape Route 30th June - 1st July 1940

Major Roads
Railways
Overnight halts
Escape Route
Rivers

16 kms
10 miles
N

Trie-Château

Lattainville

Serans

Nucourt

Cléry-en-Vexin
Guiry-en-Vexin
night of 30th June

Wy-dit-Joli-Village

Lainville-en-Vexin

Paris 30km

Gargenville

R. Seine

Epône

Jumeauville

Goupillières

Villiers-le-Mahieu
night of 1st July

Garancières

During the last few days we had heard strong rumours that the British had landed at Calais and Dunkirk, and even retaken Lille. I very much doubt if any of them are true.

Just before Clery I had a glass of cider with an old lodge-keeper at a Château. I had to wait about a quarter of an hour for the others, who had got very tired and footsore, so we stopped to eat a piece of bread and butter in a wood. In Cléry-en-Vexin we all had a glass of cider at a house, and then went on through a nice rough piece of wood with some fir trees, which was full of rabbits, down to Guiry-en-Vexin – a small village. There weren't many people in the village and we went straight into a big farm where they immediately said we could stay the night. The owners had only just returned and were busy unpacking their carts. Their house had been turned upside down. In spite of this they were very hospitable and told us we could take as much milk out of a big can as we wanted. It was lovely creamy milk, as it had been standing since the morning.

We had a good wash in the stable, and I darned my socks, which I had had to do the last two evenings as they were nearly finished. Our good hostess cooked us some meat and roast potatoes, which were excellent. We couldn't obtain bread or anything else in the village. M. Huppé took the trouble to give me an introduction to his friend at Gargenville, who, he said, would help us to cross the Seine. I then had a long talk to him about religion, and it was most interesting to listen to his arguments. We listened to part of the news, which was somewhat interfered with, and then went to bed in a nice open-sided loft with plenty of sacks and straw – wheat straw, very stiff and crackly. Poor McKay and Bernardi had got very sore feet and had to get bandages and powder from Madame. They also got an old pair of socks, but they were very thin and worse than their own.

I was afraid they wouldn't be able to march much further without a long rest.

We had done about 26km direct, which was surprising in view of the time we had stopped to shave. We hadn't hurried too much as it was Sunday.

1 July. Monsieur took the trouble to milk specially early to give us milk before we started. We set off fairly early as we were all keen to get over the Seine. We managed to get a little butter at Wy-dit-Joli-Villages and a glass of water later on. It was a very pretty road through a forest after Lainville, and it was quite hilly, so that we got very hot, as it was a grilling day without a breath of wind. We got to Gargenville and found the friend we had been directed to, but he was most unfriendly and wouldn't help us at all.

So we went on down the road to Rangiport, where I knew the road had been blown. There had evidently been a number of low-flying air attacks along the road, as the houses were riddled with MG bullet holes. We found a boat without difficulty. The boy, who rowed us over, told us that the Germans had a post at the railway crossing, so we got him to drop us well upstream. Both bridges had been thoroughly blown and will take some rebuilding. We only paid 6 Frs, and then cut across the fields for Epône church.

We were rather conspicuous in the open fields and crossing the railway, as we had some 2km to go, and there was no one about. In Epône there were a number of troops about, and we pushed on hard for some miles till we got to a small village. There we got some cider from a farm, and soon afterwards stopped under a fruit tree in a vineyard and rested.

It was very hot indeed, and we were really tired, as we had gone some 20km in a direct line fairly quickly. We had actually walked at least 25km and the last 10 had been under rather anxious conditions. By '20km direct' I mean the actual distance as the crow flies from point to point.

An aeroplane flew very low over us, as we were crossing the Seine and again when we were in the open fields. During the rest of the day there were a number of aeroplanes about and we felt that they were looking for us, which was of course absurd – but the hunted feeling we had. It had been much easier to cross the Seine than we had expected, and it was another milestone on our road. We now felt that there was only the Loire to cross.

We went on, after resting nearly 2 hours, to Goupillières. On the far side I stopped at the entrance to a Château, and had a glass of good strong cider with the lodge keeper, who said there were some German officers at the Château. I had several glasses with him, as the others were so far behind. They were very tired when they came up, though their feet were holding out well, so we stopped in a wood by the main road and had something to eat.

We then went on a few miles to Villiers-le-Màhieu, where, after looking about for some time, we found a biggish farm, which turned out again to be the Maire's, but he let us stay, and refreshed us with some milk. As our only decent map, (from the café) had finished some miles back, I decided to go off to the Château to try and get another. I tried to borrow a bicycle for this, as my legs and feet were weary, but the men wouldn't trust me with theirs, as the refugees and Germans had taken so many. The Maire hadn't got one himself, but his sister-in-law finally produced one.

There was no one, except servants, at the Château, which was very old and lovely. It formed a square with its farm buildings, and had a tower at each corner, and there was a moat around the whole group. When I got back, I had a wash all over, and McKay sluiced me down with a bucket of water. Then I talked to the Maire for a long time. His wife kindly cooked us some potatoes in their skins, and gave us some butter, pâté and cider. We heard the news clearly, as they let us eat in the house.

We then went to bed in a big Dutch barn, with some sacks, and slept well. We had made 28km direct, and had had to follow a very roundabout route.

2 July. There was no one up when we left and we couldn't get any milk or say goodbye. After a few hours, we saw a big farm by itself, and asked the woman for some milk. They couldn't give us much, as they only had one cow, but they gave us a litre. Her husband then came up, and they were so nice that I asked them for a map. He gave us an excellent Michelin map, which took us as far south as Chateâudun. It had been left by the Germans. They also gave us a large bit of cream cheese in a wet cloth, and some bread.

About 10.00hrs, as we were going through Grosrouve, I saw a boot repairer's sign, and as my boots were almost in pieces, I went in and asked the old man to re-stitch them for me, and put a patch on, while I waited. At first he said he couldn't, but when I told him who I was he said he would do it. Then his wife gave me a good meal in the kitchen. I had told the others to go on and wait somewhere till I came. I didn't like to fetch them to come and eat, as the house was so small, but luckily Bernardi came in to have his boots seen to, and the good woman went off to friends and collected some jam, eggs and bread for them. They also gave us some lettuce, which was good, as we never got any vegetables. The old man wouldn't let me pay for my boot, and when he had finished, I went off, and found the others lying at the only road junction in the village, so that once again the whole village knew that three soldiers had been there. After that they followed about 50 yards behind me, which was annoying.

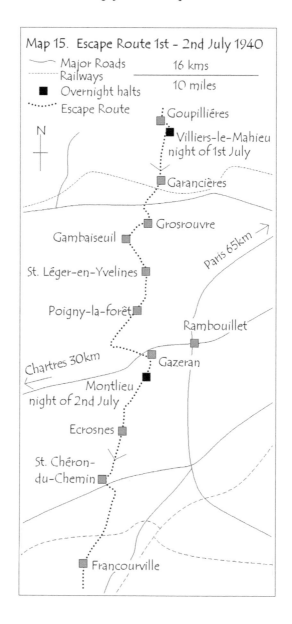

We pushed on fast, as we had spent a good deal of time. We went on for some time through a big forest, which was mainly fir trees, and was very hot. Just short of St-Léger-en-Yvelines, we halted to look at the map, and I told them to follow the main Rambouillet road for 3½km out of town, and then fork right for Poigny-la-Forêt, where I would wait. There were Germans in the town, as we expected. The road went straight through, and I went fast along the main road although it was terribly hot. At the road junction, I sat down and waited under a small copse.

After half an hour I began to eat my lunch. I waited over 2 hours till 15.00hrs, but could see no sign of them along the road, so I went on alone. I think they must have taken a wrong turn, as there was a 'No Entry' sign on the main street in St-Léger. I didn't have much of a lunch as they had got all the bread – luckily we had divided our eggs, but they had the soap, and everything except the cheese and jam.

I bought some rather poor bread in Poigny, and then went on several miles through a lovely oak forest. At about 18.00hrs, I saw a small village about a mile away on the left, so I went and asked the only farmer there if I could sleep the night. He asked for my papers, and, when I told him who I was, told me to get out.

I went on a few kilometres to a Château – unoccupied except for refugees in the stables. I found the old caretaker, who said I could sleep in his Dutch barn on a cart of fresh hay. This was near his cottage.

My feet were very sore, and I had got a cut right across the top of my foot, which was bleeding. Also my ankles and legs were all sore from sweating in thick socks. I think it had been an even hotter day, if possible, and I was really tired. The old man gave me some soap, and I had a good wash in a not too clean pond. I even washed my head, and then sat with my legs in the water.

They gave me some talcum powder and bandages for my feet, and also some sardines, cheese and wine for supper and a plate to eat it on. They also gave me two old army blankets for the night. There were piles of French equipment, rifles etc. lying about near the Château, and I collected the top of a mess tin to put my cheese in. I went to bed early and slept very well. I had done over 30km in spite of many delays. I was really sorry to have lost the others, but I couldn't see any way of finding them.

8

Alone Once More in Occupied France: 2 July–10 July 1940

3 July. I slept soundly till 7.15 a.m. when my host brought me a can of milk. As I got out of the cart, two German officers came in at the gate. They took no notice of me and only wanted billets for the night. My feet were much better with bandages, but I decided not to do more than about 20km, and to try and get a map from Chateâudun to the Loire, as my map would only do about 2½ more days. I tried at every big farm I could see. One was run by black Senegali labourers, who looked most out of place.

I couldn't find a quiet place to stop and eat till about 13.15hrs as the country was very open. I then sat in a hollow hedge-row, which had evidently been used by several escaping French soldiers, as it was full of straw and bits of uniform and equipment. I rested for about 2 hours with my boots off, and then went on several miles to a big farm by itself – near Prunay-le-Gillion. I got there about 17.00hrs and found a lady, who said I must wait for the Patron.

I waited until 18.30hrs, and was just going to move on, as the lady had not been very helpful or optimistic about the

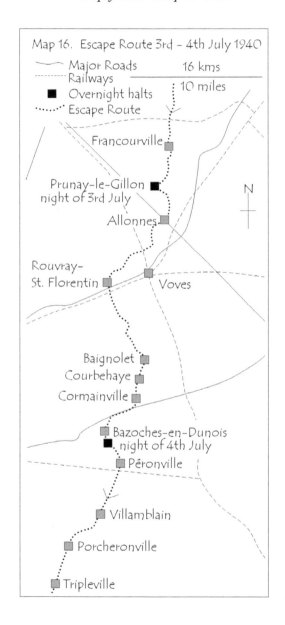

Map 16. Escape Route 3rd - 4th July 1940

Patron letting me stay, when he returned in a gig. He was a charming old man – somebody's factor – and took me into the house at once and invited me to eat with them. I declined to do this, as they had servants, who might talk and get them into trouble. I asked for a map, and he kindly gave me a fairly good one. Actually this map got me into a certain amount of trouble later on, as it was apt to mark as tracks what turned out to be good macadam roads.

While I was talking to them, a motor-cycle arrived, and we all thought it was a German soldier. The Patron went out and everyone got very alarmed and dashed about, till the motor-cyclist left. The Patron said it was a spy, who was known to be working for the Germans, and they were alarmed. They told me to pretend to go off and then work round to a big barn at the back. So I went off and shouted 'Au revoir', and got round to a big Dutch barn, where I found a tarpaulin, and some sacks in the straw. As I got there, I thought I heard the motor-cycle start up again and go off, so he might have been watching.

I was a bit worried as in the last village, where I was trying to get a map, when I approached a farm, a man on a cart asked me what I wanted. When I told him 'a map', he asked a lot of questions loudly, and wouldn't believe I was British. He shouted out 'Je connais bien les Anglais, et vous n'êtes pas Anglais du tout. Jamais des moustaches comme vous. [*sic*]' Several people must have heard him, and I was afraid this spy might have too.

After 20.00hrs, the Patron brought me some very fat bacon, bread, wine and showed me the track across the fields to the next village, in case anything happened. He also told me to avoid Voves, the next day, as it was a Kommandantur. This meant a long detour, but I was grateful for the information.

I was also much cheered up by finding that I had not got half as far to go as I thought, as I was making for friends near Blois, but I thought they were between Blois and Tours, and that I had about 140km to go before I crossed the Loire. Now that I had got a map, although their village was not marked, I could see that it must be north-east of Blois, and that I only had some 85km to go to cross the Loire. I decided from the map to make for Mer and try and cross there.

Before I went to sleep, I listened to the noise of hundreds of rats, and mice eating the grain in the sacks. There was a steady noise of eating all round me. I'd done 30km direct again, without pushing too hard, and my feet were less sore than on the previous day. This farmer had driven to Blois the day before and would have given me a lift, had I been there.

4 July. The Patron woke me up about 06.15hrs and tried to give me some bread and a bottle of wine, which I refused as I had some left over. He was anxious for me to be off and I left at once, though it was earlier than I liked. It had rained hard during the night, and looked as if it might again. After going through Allonnes, I found a little copse, and ate my breakfast. I also got a drink of milk at Allonnes.

In spite of having to make a long detour, I had done 22km direct by the time I stopped for lunch in a little copse near Courbehaye. I rested there quite a long time with my boots off, and then went on to Cormainville, which was full of Germans, along an old Roman road, which was all grassed over, to Bazoches-en-Dunois – also full of Boches. I said 'Bonjour' to several, who saluted back politely.

At about 18.00hrs, I found a farm, by itself, and the woman said I could stay in the barn, which had a little straw in it. There were some chickens at one end and it was rather smelly.

I had a wash, and waited until about 20.30hrs, when they brought me over some potatoes in gravy and some milk. The potatoes were excellent. The farmer had returned by then and was not very pleased at my being there. He also said, rather

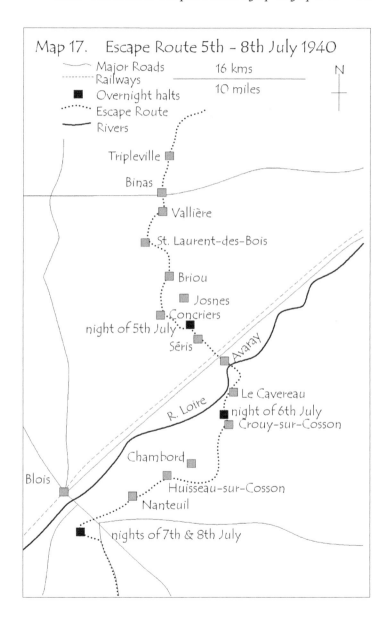

Map 17.   Escape Route 5th - 8th July 1940

Major Roads
Railways
Overnight halts
Escape Route
Rivers

16 kms
10 miles

N

Tripleville
Binas
Vallière
St. Laurent-des-Bois
Briou
Josnes
Concriers
night of 5th July
Séris
Avaray
Le Cavereau
night of 6th July
Crouy-sur-Cosson
R. Loire
Chambord
Blois
Huisseau-sur-Cosson
Nanteuil
nights of 7th & 8th July

pointedly, that I wouldn't find many people kind enough to give me something to eat without working, and that it was a waste doing so. I couldn't tell him how much more pleasant and kind my other hosts had been. I made a good 32km direct, and must have walked well over 40. I slept indifferently, as the place was smelly and none too clean.

5 July. I got some more milk in the morning and left soon after seven. I had to go through Péronville, where there were a lot of Germans in the streets. After Péronville, I bought four hard-boiled eggs in a big farm, and they gave me a slice of bread and butter, and some water. I then tried a track across country to miss out the next village. It looked all right on the map, but after a bit it fizzled out, and I got a bit lost. However I got to Binas at last, and had rather a nasty time going through, as there were too many German officers about for me to be able to ask the way.

I was just going to eat my lunch, when it began to rain, so I went to Vallière, a small hamlet, and asked if I could eat in a barn. Afterwards the farmer offered me a glass of calvados – a liqueur made from cider. As he was so pleasant, I told him who I was and asked his advice. He told me I could safely go through St-Laurent-des-Bois, as the Germans had left the day before, but to miss out Josnes somehow, as it was a Kommandantur, and the Germans were apt to ask for papers.

Soon after St-Laurent, I passed a man in the woods, who said 'Evade aussi?' I didn't tell him till I was satisfied that he was an escaped prisoner, and then I talked to him for a bit. He had escaped three times south of the Loire, but had been caught again very quickly. This was bad news, as I had thought that the Loire was the Demarcation Line – between occupied and unoccupied France – everyone said so further north. Last night he had swum the Loire near Amboise, and was making his way to Paris. He was a swimming instructor, and the Loire was very dangerous unless you were an expert swimmer, he said. He also warned me to use the little tracks in the woods and wouldn't believe I was using the ordinary road. He tried to persuade me to come back to Paris with him, and live in his house, but when I wouldn't, we shook hands, wished each other 'Bon Voyage' and set off again. I really had thought my difficulties were nearly at an end, and that I should be in Free France once I had crossed the Loire, so I wasn't exactly cheered by this meeting.

About 17.00hrs, as I was getting near Concriers, I stopped to ask the way of rather a smart lady coming out of the fields. She said at once 'Vous êtes Anglais'. This quick recognition was shattering, but she quickly told me that they had had three French soldiers at the farm the night before. When she told me that both Concriers and Séris, where I had meant to stay the night, were full of Germans; I asked her if I could stay at the farm, and she said 'Certainly'.

She was a Parisienne, staying with her brother-in-law. The farm was a lovely old one, and had been part of a Priory. The old dovecote was still there, and there were enormous cellars under the house. The whole family was extremely kind to me, when I got to the house. Monsieur and his brother from Paris were out in the fields and didn't come in till late. We all had an excellent dinner at about 21.00hrs, when work was finished, and I heard a bit of the news. After we had talked for a bit, I went to bed in a lovely old barn with a blanket. Distance – about 32km.

Both Monsieur and his brother hated the Germans like poison and made no secret of it. One had been a prisoner in the last war, and had been sent to work in the salt mines. The brother was really a Corn and Seed Merchant from Paris, and not at all used to heavy farm work, but he was working like anything just to occupy himself. He had always been extremely interested in gardening, vines and any cultivation, and he had shown vegetables for years at shows in Paris, so he was not really out of his element.

They confirmed that the Germans were south of the Loire, but didn't know how far they occupied. They were very gloomy about my prospects of getting anywhere near Blois, as they knew it was a big HQ and that Chambord park was full of soldiers. They agreed that Avaray was a good place to try and cross the Loire, and explained the road across the fields, which avoided Concriers. They also told me that any Germans, who had come to the farm, had said they would kill British prisoners found escaping, which was encouraging. 'Francais bon, Anglais kaput.'

In 2002 we arrived at the farm, called Les Heaumes, and met the current occupant who had farmed there since 1955. I explained briefly what we were doing and asked if the farm had enormous cellars underneath it as my father's diary had described. 'Peut être', he replied somewhat warily but then went on to talk about a 'vieux pigeonier'. This was a relief as I had no idea what the French was for a 'doocot'. We then knew we were in the right place and I gave the farmer the full details and he opened up and took us to see the doocot. He told us that the farmer at the time of Bradford's visit was a M. Va La Don and that the farm was an old one which had once been part of the estate belonging to the Château de Fontenoy.

6 July. I was not in any hurry to leave, as I thought I was unlikely to be able to cross the Loire before dusk. I was told that I shouldn't be able to find any boats, as they had been taken or smashed by the Germans, to prevent people crossing except at the proper bridges, which had been mended by pontoons, or at the ferries.

I was determined not to swim unless I was forced to, as one would be such a conspicuous figure in wet clothes, or even in dry ones which had been wet. I had an excellent breakfast of café-au-lait, bread and butter. The coffee was made with milk only, without using any water at all and was quite excellent. Afterwards I shaved with an old cut-throat, which Monsieur lent me, and looked years younger as a result, so that I was quite sorry that I had.

They gave me food for the day, wished me 'Good Luck', and I set off through the fields to Séris. After Séris, I had to cross the railway, and was a little nervous as the gates were shut, but no one took any notice. Then I crossed the main road, where there was a lot of traffic, and a number of soldiers on bicycles. I went on down a track through the fields, and looked about for someone to ask where I might find a boat.

As luck would have it, I picked a man who was stone deaf, and after bawling at him, I had to go on to a woman, who told me that the Germans were in the main part of the village, and that I might get a boat at the top part of the village, where my track happened to lead.

At practically the first house I came to there was a man loading up a cart and just setting off to spray his vines. I asked him to help me, and, though he didn't seem too enthusiastic to begin with, he took me into his barn, and sent his son off to see about a boat.

He produced some good scale maps, which we looked at, but they didn't go as far as Nanteuil, for which I was making. However, he showed me where I must make for after crossing the river. The son came back to say that the owner of the boat was away in it, and wouldn't be back until 19.00hrs, so I was taken to a small shed behind another barn, where he said I could stay till evening. He then brought me an excellent goats-milk cheese and a bottle of wine, and said he wouldn't be back from the fields till after I had gone.

On saying goodbye, he gave me 1,000 Frs, and insisted that I should take it, although I tried not to. I ate my lunch and lay down in some straw to sleep.

At about 15.30hrs, the man's wife dashed in to say that the Germans were coming at any moment to put 10 horses into the barn, just beside my shed, and that I must leave at once. She got a young fellow, who said he would take me to the riverbank near where M. Gilbert tied up his boat, hide me there, and then somehow find M. Gilbert when he returned. We went down to the river, just as German troops came into the lane, and I hid on a small island in a clump of willows.

It soon began to rain, and I had nothing to cover myself with. At about 18.15hrs I saw a boat passing, well out in the river, and it came in and tied up about 100 yards below me. I was certain that it was Gilbert, but I found that I couldn't get off the island, as the boat I had walked across on had drifted back.

However, the boat came nearer to tie up, when it had been unloaded, and I shouted to the boy in it. He said he would take me over. I nearly fell in getting aboard, and we pushed off. The current was very strong, and we got stuck on a sand-bank which we couldn't avoid. By this time the youth who had hidden me returned with Gilbert, and shouted to us. As we couldn't control the boat at all, we put back and picked them up. We crossed easily after this, and I paid him 10 Frs and set off into the fields.

[*When we visited in October 2002 the Loire at this point was some 200 yards across. In early July the flow would normally be twice the October level.*]

It was still raining and I couldn't find a track, so that I was soon soaked, as I had to go through very long, wet grass and thick bushes. I found a track after about half an hour, and arrived at Port Pichard looking somewhat bedraggled. I then found I had got to go 1½km along a main road through a village, up which German troops were marching, and where there were a good many officers and men standing about. I didn't like this at all, as people had said that they were collecting all the French soldiers who had been liberated.

At last I turned off this road, and after about 2½km came to a big farm, where an old farmer was unloading some hay in the rain. He wasn't very pleased at all at seeing me, but said I could stay in the barn. About 20.00hrs they called me into the house and gave me some bread and milk.

There were several women and more children, and the house was indescribably filthy with chickens and cats all over the place, and old bones, pieces of bread, a bit of fish and inches of dirt lying on the floor. They didn't even wash out the bowls they were eating from. The children were all dirty, and one leg of the old man's trousers was torn off at the knee. I was given some sacks and climbed up on top of the hay in a huge barn, which was pitch dark, as it was so full of hay. I was still very wet and had nothing at all to change into, so I didn't sleep very well.

7 July. They gave me some milk and bread for breakfast, and I set off about 07.00hrs along a very small track with long wet grass to Crouy-sur-Cosson, where there were several Germans and a considerable number of lorries and despatch riders moving about.

Owing to the amount of troop movements on the road to Chambord, I turned up a track, which I hoped would lead me direct to the Forest of Boulogne, which encircles Chambord Park. However there were more Boches up the track and in farms off it. I was particularly anxious to avoid any troops that day, as everyone was saying that French soldiers were being collected into a camp at Beaugency, and I eventually had to wander in the woods, avoiding parties of Germans, till I came to a cottage.

There a very nice peasant, an oldish man, gave me some bread and bacon cooked in dripping, and some wine. He offered to lead me to the beginning of the road in the Forest of Boulogne. He took me about 2kms, and I went on through the forest to Huisseau-sur-Cosson, without meeting anyone. I couldn't remember exactly where Nanteuil was, and it was't marked on my map. Had it been marked, I could have avoided Huisseau, which was full of troops, and also the 4km of main road towards Blois.

I had hoped that Nanteuil was too small to be occupied, but as I turned down the hill, I saw German troops on the bridge. I hadn't been there since about ten years ago, when I was learning French with a family. I saw an old woman come out of the back of the mill, and so, when I saw German flags at the Château gates and lorries parked in the drive, I turned into the mill, which joined it. There were more soldiers in the yard, but I knocked at one of three doors and then at another. When no one answered, I walked in as I didn't want to appear as too much of a stranger.

I found a woman and tried to explain who I was and what I wanted. She wouldn't play at all and got very excited and hysterical. Then her husband appeared, and I asked him to get in touch with Madame G-B [*Gardnor-Beard*] and ask her to meet me here. He said he would but that there were German officers in the house, and he wanted me to return in half an hour. I walked up to the top of the village and hung about.

Billy Gardnor-Beard and his wife Anne-Marie 'Souris' Denisane bought the Ch. de Nanteuil in 1921 and established a crammer-cum-language-school for the improvement of young British gentlemen anxious to advance their knowledge of the French language and literature, culture and social graces. She was born in the Ch. De Savonnieres near Blois which belonged to her grand-aunt the Marquise de Perrigny.

In 1930 Bradford spent a few months at Nanteuil attending one of these courses. The Gardnor-Beards had two daughters, Muriel (Moune) and Beatrice (Betty) and an English nanny, Nesta Cox, who had been in residence since 1925. Billy G-B died in 1938 and, unknown to Bradford at this stage, his widow had recently re-married to Conte Pierre de Bernard.

In common with many people in the area the de Bernard's and their household staff had fled southwards as the German armies swept towards the Loire. Progress, however, had been slower than anticipated and after 2 days the group set up camp in a field north of Châteauroux. De Bernard was very correct and formal even in these circumstances and the family continued to change for dinner and were waited on by their staff, who had eaten earlier and who also wore their service uniforms. After some days in the field the de Bernard's decided that camping wasn't for them and to chance their luck and return to Nanteuil. In the few days they had been absent they found that the property had been sacked and subsequently occupied by Germans.[54]

As I was returning, some soldiers, leading horses, asked me in execrable French, which was the way to ------, a place I had never heard of. I told them to go straight on, and they thanked me politely. The man had not found time to get in touch with Madame when I came back. He was terrified of being caught out and would continue talking to these German officers in his drawing room. He put me in the kitchen where I waited another hour.

Then he came and said I must go and return in another hour – at 17.30hrs, when he really would have Madame G-B there. He gave me a small piece of cheese and some bread.

By now it was raining and I went about half a mile off, and sat under some bushes to eat. On coming back an hour later, I was overjoyed to find Madame coming towards me with a man. I met them and was introduced to her husband, Conte de Bernard, whom she had married three weeks before. We went on to a house, where she thought there wouldn't be any Germans, but found there were. So they told me to go to the house of a Spaniard which was easy to find by following the old railway track till I got to the forest. We arranged to meet at a certain place in the forest, at 11.00hrs the following morning, by which time they thought the Germans should have left.

I went to the house, and M. Clement said I could certainly stay. His wife, a kind old Spaniard, let me sit in the kitchen and dry myself. They invited me to dinner – a very different meal from the previous day, with different plates for each course. We had soup, stew and finally haricot beans cooked in butter. I then went to bed in a little loft with plenty of new hay, and a nice clean blanket, having had a good wash.

8 July. I slept awfully well and didn't get up till 08.00hrs, when I had a good breakfast of bread and café-au-lait – really good coffee. I said goodbye to the Clements and went and hid in the forest till 11.00hrs, when I went to our rendezvous. [*This was a location in the forest where in 1930, when Bradford was at Nanteuil, Madame G-B had been thrown by her horse.*]

Madame and Monsieur soon came along, and gave me a lovely parcel of everything I could want – maps, a shirt, socks, food, a razor, toothbrush and money. They also said they had managed to get a bicycle, but it wouldn't be ready till the afternoon. This sounded almost too good to be true, as there was nothing I wanted so much. We arranged to meet again at 18.00hrs at the same place.

Madame said that the Germans would certainly have left by tomorrow, and wanted me to come to the Château for a few days, but I thought it was too risky for everyone concerned, as somebody in the village was certain to talk and then the de Bernards would get into trouble.

After they had gone, I went deeper into the forest, built myself a little hide and sat down to wait till 18.00hrs. I heard shots fairly near several times, but no one came too near me. I got lost for a time trying to get back to our meeting-place, but managed to find it again. The whole family, including Nannie, had come, and they had brought tea in a thermos for me, with bread and jam.

It was awful fun seeing them again and we had a most cheerful tea-party. Madame kept saying 'Pauvre Billy, I never thought to see you like this.' In the middle of our picnic, some Germans came past, but they paid no attention to us.

M de B had brought the bicycle which he gave me. It had one very dubious looking tyre, bound round with tape plaster, but it was grand to have it. Monsieur went over the map with me, advising me about the roads, and also gave me his brother's address near Clermont-Ferrand to make for. They again pressed me to come and stay for a few days.

When they had left, I went back, rather unwillingly. to the Clements, who again received me kindly, though I am certain they would have preferred my not being there. I changed into my new shirt and washed my old one. Monsieur de B had told me that the Germans were occupying the country as far as the River Indre, which would take me at least 2 more days even with a bicycle.

Bradford was the first of many escaping prisoners-of-war that received the de Bernards' assistance. His visit made them appreciate that there was something they could do to help the war effort despite France's

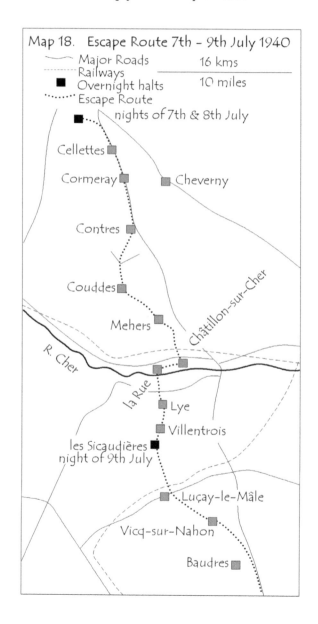

Map 18. Escape Route 7th - 9th July 1940

Major Roads
Railways
Overnight halts
Escape Route

16 kms
10 miles

nights of 7th & 8th July

Cellettes
Cormeray   Cheverny
Contres
Couddes
Mehers   Châtillon-sur-Cher
R. Cher
la Rue
Lye
Villentrois
les Sicaudières
night of 9th July
Luçay-le-Mâle
Vicq-sur-Nahon
Baudres

capitulation and in due course led to contact with Yvonne Rudellat [codename Jacqueline] who was the first female agent parachuted into France by S.O.E. A number of escapees were spirited into Free France as the 'corpse' in funeral processions. Nesta Cox, the old Gardnor-Beard nannie, stayed on during the war. The de Bernards and Nannie Cox helped many and became closely involved with SOE.

It was a fearfully dangerous time and there were numerous scares. On one occasion Madame de Bernard's teenaged daughters, Moune and Betty, took their canoe out into the mill dam to drop pieces of a radio into the deepest water under the eyes of the Germans. Eventually the de Bernards were both arrested and imprisoned in concentration camps during the latter part of the war – she in Ravensbruck, he in Belsen. Nannie Cox remained at Nanteuil and continued to look after the children and the château while clandestinely assisting the Sologne Resistance on behalf of her imprisoned employers. Nanny was sufficiently essential to the operation that on one occasion the RAF even parachuted in some tea when supplies ran short. She continued to live, and reign, at Nanteuil until her death, aged 93, in 1992. The de Bernards survived their incarceration to the end of the war but their health was adversely affected by the appalling treatment they received.

In 2002 we visited Nanteuil. I had made no arrangements to call and indeed had no idea if the family still survived. I had searched the internet but could find no reference and wasn't certain that the Château remained standing. I told my wife that we would do as one always would in France and find either the Maire or the Curé and ask. Coming down the hill we saw no German soldiers on the bridge, which we took to be a good sign. At the gate, in place of Nazi flags, there was a sign indicating that the Château was an hotel and restaurant with 'Même famille depuis 1929' – we were in luck. We were greeted by the Chef – a Frédéric Théry. The name meant nothing to us. Having established that they were open for business and after booking-in I then introduced myself. I had got as far as explaining in my poor French that my father had been a pupil and returned in 1940 as an escapee – 'Stop' he said quite forcefully and dashed off. He reappeared a few moments later turning the pages of a file and said 'I know exactly who you are' and then presented me with a copy of my father's obituary from The Times. *Frédéric turned out to be the grandson of Anne-Marie and Billy Gardnor Beard. Later that evening we met his mother – the same Betty – and, over a bottle of champagne, read out the details from my father's journal concerning his visit. She concurred with every word and remembered his visit in 1940 in perfect detail. 'He looked so English' she said 'I can't think how he had travelled so far without arrest'. Arriving at Nanteuil and meeting Mme Théry was a very moving experience.*[55]

9 July. I left the Clements about 07.40hrs and bicycled off. There was a German Horse Transport Column crossing the first crossroads, and I swung right along the main road with it. It was marvellous to sail along quite fast on a bicycle, after walking for so long. As I was getting near the head of the column, my front tyre blew up completely with a loud bang, and the German soldiers roared with laughter. [*The distance travelled on the bicycle was no more than 3km.*]

I then realised I was on the wrong road, but continued along the main road to Cellettes, and then through the other villages to Contres, trying in every shop and garage to get the tyre repaired or buy a new one. Unfortunately the wheel was an out-of-date size, and the tyre was irreparable. The flood of refugees and then soldiers had cleared out everything, and new wheel and tyre were unobtainable. The villages were full of Germans and there were numbers of Belgians returning north on bicycles.

I pushed this wretched bicycle the whole way to the Cher along small roads through Couddes and Méhers. In Méhers there was about a company of Germans doing physical training and I met another party marching along the road singing at the tops of their voices.

Just before Châtillon-sur-Cher, I asked an old man for a drink. He took me into his cellar across the road, to give me some wine and he was so friendly that I asked him about crossing the Cher. He said that for the last 2 days no one had been allowed to cross the Cher, not even the baker at Châtillon who normally got his flour from the other side.

At a level crossing, a sentry stopped me and asked me what I was doing. He called the guard-commander, and I explained that I was only going to try and get a new tyre at Châtillon, where I had heard there were some. I said I would be back in ¾ hour, and they let me go on. [*In 2002, while reading aloud this section of the diary as we drove along, we bumped across that same level-crossing literally two seconds after I had read the preceding paragraph.*]

I turned right at Châtillon to a tiny village called la Rue, 3km from Châtillon, where I had heard there were no Germans. However, on the way there I saw several piquets on the high ground, with field glasses, and there was a patrol at the ford, and others along the river bank.

I went down to the river behind an old woman and a girl, who were going to do some washing. They said there were more sentries on the far bank in the trees, and that it had been given out that anyone entering the water would be fired on.

Meanwhile the sentries had wandered up to the village. I arranged with the girl to go up and talk to them and to give them a drink – also to call out to her grandmother if they began coming back. I decided it was impossible to take my bicycle as the current looked too strong. I could see people moving in the woods on the far side and thought they were Boches. I set off, holding my coat and bag high up. [*The exact crossing place is easy to find from this description. Even in October, when the river is lower than in June, it was still a swiftly flowing and broad obstacle. We could find no sign of the bicycle.*]

The river was about 100 yards across and came up to my chest. The current was strong and I very nearly missed my footing several times. I was expecting a bullet in my back at any moment, but nothing happened and I scrambled into the wood on the other side. There were some men fishing in a small stream in the wood, and I hurried through, as I didn't want to be seen by German soldiers in my sopping wet clothes.

After going through some hay fields, I came across a farmer hay making. He told me that there were no Germans this side of the Cher, and that I was safe, which was almost too good to believe.

I pushed on to the village, where a farmer confirmed that there were no Germans, and gave me some bread and cheese, and wine to celebrate. My boots were full of sand and soaking, so I washed them out and changed my socks. A friend came in, and I went on in his cart to Lye, almost 2½km. I walked on to Villentrois, and then about 1½km further on to a small farm.

It was a lovely evening and it was a wonderful feeling not to have to worry about the Germans, and to be able to appreciate the country, and feel you were among friends. A very kind farmer and his wife gave me a good supper of soup, 2 eggs a la plat, and milk and then lent me some blankets. I went to sleep in an airy stable, absolutely dead tired but very happy. I had walked over 52km in the day. [*The farm is Les Sicaudières – in our 2005 visit we met the kind farmer's granddaughter-in-law.*]

10 July. I slept very well and was given café-au-lait before leaving. It was a very hot day again, and after about 12½km I stopped at a cottage and an old woman gave me a drink of wine. I then went on about 12½km along the main

Châteauroux road, when I waved at a car going my way and stopped it.

Unfortunately it turned out to be an army car, and Lieut Rogel, who was in it, soon realised that I was British. He wouldn't let me get out, and insisted on taking me to his General, who, he said, would help me on my way. I was not so sure of this.

I was well received by his staff officers and the General himself was most friendly and asked me to lunch in the Mess, but he would not let me continue on my journey.

There were some eighty officers at lunch, and I sat on the General's left, looking like the lowest kind of tramp. We had an excellent meal, and General Martin [*Lieutenant-General Henry Jules Jean Martin [1884–1894], GOC 87th African Division in 1940*] made a little speech, saying how glad he was to welcome one of our former allies of 1914–18, tactfully leaving out any reference to this war.

The General said I would be sent on to Marseilles as soon as possible, and thence home, but that I must not go at once. So I wandered round the town with Lieut Nicolas, who had been at Oxford.

In the evening I dined again with the General, and also talked to a General Barthélémy [*Brigadier-General Robert Jules Eugene Barthélémy (1881–1944)*], who had been at Calais with the BEF. He told me that he had been prevented from getting to a boat by British sentries with M.Gs. who had orders to fire on and hold up all French troops. This, and the fact that all French troops had been disarmed on arrival in England after Calais and Dunkirk, had made a bad impression on the French, but General Barthélémy was still fairly pro-British. [*It is interesting to note that this story is strikingly similar to Roger Sandford's description of events beneath the cliffs to the north of St-Valery-en-Caux.*]

After dinner I had a long talk with General Martin, but he could not let me go and has asked higher authority what to do with me. Lieut Mourot who is very pro-British, and speaks good English, looked after me and found me a bed in the Hospital, with a good many other officers.

I couldn't get to sleep for some hours, as it was very hot and they wouldn't open enough windows. Also one fat officer lay on his back and snored like a pig. I saw someone creep out of bed and dig him in the ribs, but it only stopped him for a few minutes and he was soon in his stride again.

At last I got up and opened another window, which made a slight draught, and I got to sleep.

9

From Châteauroux to Spain: 10 July–4 August 1940

I stayed at Châteauroux for 3 days and spent most of the time resting, as I was very tired. Lieut J. Mourot was very kind during this time and did what he could to make me comfortable. There was some anti-British feeling in the mess, and some of the conversation made me feel rather uncomfortable.

Captain de la Taille, a Royalist with old-fashioned views, who lived near Tours, tried to explain how they felt now. He was a most charming man, about 45 years old, and assured me that he had had every intention of going to England, and that most of the others had too, but that now we had shot up their fleet, and betrayed them, everything was different.

De la Taille was referring to the attack, by the Royal Navy, on the French Fleet at the expiry of Churchill's ultimatum either to surrender the fleet to the British or to sail the ships to the French West Indies and permit them to be demilitarised. At all events the aim was to prevent the fleet falling into the hands of the Germans or Italians. Operation Catapult took place on 3 July. All French

vessels at Portsmouth and Plymouth were taken over by force.
The French fleet in the Mediterranean port Mers-el-Kebir was
fired upon by the Royal Navy, with the loss of many French sail-
ors' lives, and much of the fleet incapacitated. Whether Operation
Catapult was a success or not is open to question as the French, true
to their promise to Churchill, scuttled the remainder of their ships
when the Germans entered the port of Toulon. What is certain is
that Anglo-French relations were greatly damaged. Bradford was
now on the receiving end of the ill-feeling in the immediate after-
math of this incident.

I also met General Hassler [*Major-General Joseph Louis Francois*
Hassler (1881–1966) GOC 22nd Division in 1939–40] – a fine
type of officer, under whose command we had been in the
Saar in December.

Every day I was told I was about to be sent home via
Marseilles, and so I made no effort to move on by myself, as
this sounded the normal thing for them to do.

13 July 1940. The third day I was sent for, and, after a lot of
waiting about, I was put into a car, and sent to Bélâbre under
Lieut Rogel. Before I left Lieut Mourot gave me all sorts of
useful things, including a map and some addresses and tried to
make me take much more.

On arrival at Bélâbre, I was taken to the headquarters of a
Senegalese battalion for internment. I was told I would only
be there temporarily before being sent home, and that it was
to avoid any unpleasantness in the Châteauroux Mess.

A lieutenant took charge of me and found me lodging
with an old couple, whose house was none too clean, but
gave me quite a reasonable bedroom. Then he took me
down to the Hotel, which overlooks the square, where I
had supper.

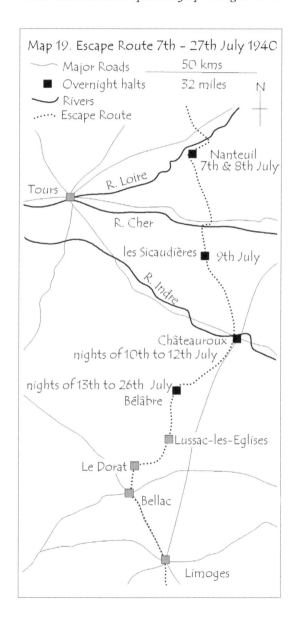

Map 19. Escape Route 7th – 27th July 1940
Major Roads
Overnight halts
Rivers
Escape Route
50 kms
32 miles
N

R. Loire
Tours
R. Cher
les Sicaudières
R. Indre
Nanteuil
7th & 8th July
9th July
Châteauroux
nights of 10th to 12th July
nights of 13th to 26th July
Bélâbre
Lussac-les-Eglises
Le Dorat
Bellac
Limoges

14 July 1940
chez M. Surreaux
Villa Bellevue
Bélâbre, Indre
My darling Mummie and Papa
I don't know whether this will ever reach you. I am sending it to the British Embassy in Spain and hoping he can forward it.

I was taken prisoner by the Germans on 12 June, but escaped on the 19th and after trying to find some means of crossing the Channel, I had to move on and eventually got down to this part of France, which is not occupied by the Germans. I walked the whole way till I got south of the Cher, when I stopped what I thought was a civilian car but was unfortunately a military one. Now I am a sort of prisoner in the category 'liberté surveillée.'

Can you try and get on to someone in authority about getting me exchanged with a French Naval Officer. I didn't realise they would keep me a prisoner, and the officer who gave me a lift thought his General, to whom he took me, would be able to help me on my way. I stayed for a few days in the barracks at Châteauroux & messed with the Officers. Yesterday I was sent here and am billeted in a small house, and feed in the village inn at the expense of the military.

There are a lot of refugees in the village which is packed. In the pub I have met an American, who works in Paris, & who is very kind. He has given me a flannel coat and trousers, as I only had a filthy & frightful pair of black striped trousers & an old purpley-grey coat which was almost falling apart. A Pole had given me my previous outfit when I escaped & threw away my uniform.

I was very weary of walking & this is a rest, but there is absolutely nothing to do & I would much rather still be walking slowly towards home.

How I am longing to get home and see you again. It was the only thing that kept me going on day after day. It is wonderful that God has brought me safely as far as this through all the Germans, and I thank Him continually.

This village is very nice – about the same size as Petworth – but too many refugees in it. I walked with the American this afternoon for a short way & then lay in a field & talked to him. They feed us well at the pub, but it takes a long time, as it is used to catering for perhaps 12 to 20 & has now to do about 100. No sugar is available & of course we get nothing between déjeuner at 12.15 p.m. and dinner at 7.15 p.m. which is a long wait. However, I am much better off than if I were in Germany, and also much better fed than when I was on the road.

I don't think you had better try and send me anything, except letters at present. Letters could either try through the British Embassy in Spain with above address or through the Red Cross. They don't know what to do with me at present and I am sure parcels wouldn't get anywhere.

I do hope you are all well. I wish I could see you again. Will you report where I am to the War Office. Col J.A. Barstow MC (AG2) might be able to do something for me.

Col James Anderson Barstow, MC (1893–1941) was commissioned into the Argyll & Sutherland Highlanders. He transferred to the Black Watch and had previously commanded 1st Bn Black Watch. It seems likely that at the time of writing he had already moved from the War Office to take command of the 69th Infantry Bde and in fact died shortly after leaving this post.

The Hotel, and in fact the whole town, was crowded with refugees but they say that many have left, and the others are supposed to be going soon. There were three Belgian youths at my table, who had bicycled all the way down in front of the armies. Their French was so bad I could hardly understand what they were saying.

After dinner I was surprised to hear a voice with a strong American accent, say 'I guess we can talk each other's language,' and turned round to find an American, Winthrop Whittaker, who was in business in Paris with Gillettes. He refugeed to Santes, and then started off back to Paris, when the Germans came, as they wouldn't let him go into the unoccupied zone. He got stopped at St-Aignan one night, and the next day found himself in unoccupied France, as the demarcation line had been changed. He had ended up here, as he couldn't get a permit to go into the other zone, and also had no petrol.

The next morning I went and saw the Commandant, to try and find out exactly what my position was, and when I should be sent home. He didn't give me a satisfactory answer, and I don't think anyone knows. Whittaker, the American, said he couldn't go on seeing me in my disreputable clothes, and very kindly gave me quite a decent flannel suit – though he was much shorter and stouter than I was. He and I watched a ceremony at the War Memorial, in the town square opposite the Hotel, when the few soldiers, who hadn't already got one, were given the Croix-de-Guerre; I suppose they had been in detention before.

After this some British soldiers arrived – Glasgow Highlanders, who had escaped from Argenta, when their transport had been ambushed. I had a long talk with them, and heard their stories.

Almost every day a few British were brought in, having been picked up somewhere, or having gone for help to the

French military on arrival in unoccupied France. We were determined not to stay long if nothing was going to be done for us, but we didn't want to miss our chances of being sent home.

I saw the Commandant most days, and also a Lieut Pic, from HQ, who was very friendly, and kept saying he would get us some money, and get a move on with our repatriation.

Two Sappers, Lieuts. Raikes and Hogg, and I tried to get bicycles to get away on when the time should come. They got theirs quickly, but I was unsuccessful, though I had a good map.

About the seventh day, when we had decided we must go, I was sent for and given 1,000 Frs – subscribed by the French officers – with which to pay for the food we had had at hotels, and to start Mess with! This was to be paid back to the Curé before we left as the Regiment is moving to Perpignan shortly.

Another officer, Ian Garrow, had turned up, and on the day before we finally decided we must go, as the French didn't seem to be doing anything for us, Freddie Fitch [*Capt. Freddie Fitch, Norfolk Regiment*] and Sellar [*Dr Sellar*] appeared – having escaped from a hospital in Tammai in Belgium.

They were not taken aback when we said we were all going tomorrow, merely wondered why we had stayed so long. Fitch and I planned to make roughly for Toulouse and then Spain, though he and Sellar were going to lorry hop, and I had, at the last moment, got a bicycle with the help of a Pole who gave me some money. He came from Auchel, and said that he had hidden several British up there till they were picked up by an aeroplane. I had been through there on 20 June. I suppose it's a possible story.

Raikes and Hogg were going to make for Perpignan, and so I gave them an address I had there, as I was unwilling to go there myself with the Senegalese Regt having moved there. They would think I had pinched their 1,000 Frs and they all knew me by sight. I went and saw the Curé and arranged to repay the money after the war, and he agreed to say nothing and wished me good luck.

27 July. We had to report daily to the office and after doing so next morning, we said goodbye to each other. M.M. [*probably Winthrop Whittaker*] promised to follow me with my bicycle and meet me about a mile outside the village.

It was grand to be on the move again but very soon my bicycle tyre went flat, and I had no pump, so I kept having to go to farms every mile or so and pump up my tyre. This was most annoying as I wanted to get a good way off before our absence was discovered which would probably be lunchtime or in the evening.

I got my tyre repaired at Lussac-les-Eglises, and also bought a pump and a 'Plâcque de Controle', which some-one had warned me to get. You buy these in a tobacconists, and in this one there was a Gendarme, who would not leave the shop, but when I finally went in, took no notice of me. By 12.45hrs, I had only done some 20km which was disappointing.

I took a wrong turn and got on to the main Le-Dorat to Bellac road, which I had meant to avoid. There was a military control just outside Bellac, which was stopping everyone, but I was coming very fast downhill and they let me through.

It was very hot, and my legs were getting very tired on this little ladies' bicycle, so that I had to dismount at the least hill. About 16.00hrs, I caught up a lorry, which was just starting up, and hung on behind. It was very slow, but a great relief.

After some miles, the driver saw me, and pulled into a café, where we had a drink. Then he put my bicycle on board, and took me slowly into Limoges, through the police post and all. It was an old US lorry from the last war and only averaged 10mph.

I bought a map of the Spanish frontier in Limoges – there had been quite a run on them and they weren't easy to get – but I couldn't get one of the country in between.

Going out of the town I just avoided a police post by going up a side turning (this one caught Ian Garrow 3 days later) and went on the St-Yrieix-la-Perche road. I was feeling so glad to have got past Limoges and to have covered about 100km that I went to a café at Glandon* and got quite a good meal.

*BCB's diary states Glandon but as this is south of St Yrieix-la-Perche [see below] it cannot be. It is far more likely that the correct location for this overnight stop is close to Solignac as the road south is uphill from there for many miles as described below.

There were a lot of refugees about, and the first place I tried wouldn't give me anything. At about 20.45hrs I found a nice farm a bit off the road, and went to sleep in their barn, in a blanket they lent me. [*Distance from Bélâbre to Solignac is approximately 106km.*]

28 July. Next morning I had a wash and then some milk and bread, and bought two hard-boiled eggs for later on. As it was Sunday, I left about 08.15hrs. It was all up hill for some miles, and I was making very slow progress when I managed to hang on to an old Renault, which crawled past me up a hill. It took

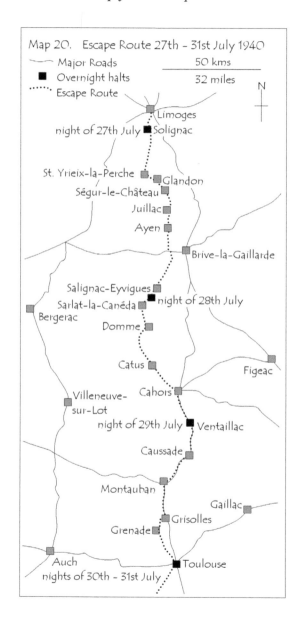

Map 20. Escape Route 27th - 31st July 1940

me about 8km fairly fast but as my tyre was getting flatter every moment, I had eventually to let go.

However, I wasn't too late in getting to St-Yrieix after all. I stopped for lunch soon after Ségur-le-Château, and when I was pumping up the front tyre afterwards, it burst, so I had to push the bicycle. I was lucky to find a man at a café by a crossroads some kilometres further on, who had a spare tyre and a tube. After some delay, he let me have them, and we put both on behind and changed the others to the front. [*Ségur-le-Château is an extraordinarily pretty village with an enormous ruined castle overlooking the houses.*]

At about 14.30hrs I got off again – rather behind schedule. It was hilly country, and my Esso map was far from accurate.

Some miles before Salignac-Eyvigues, I went to a farm and asked if I could sleep the night. The farmer asked for my papers, and when I told him who I was, called some soldiers, whom I hadn't seen, as I had chosen a farm which looked lonely.

They were very nice, and one of them spoke English well. The farmer then gave me some wine and jam, and pretended to be very friendly, saying 'I know you English like jam with your bread very much.' He then stepped away and his wife warned me that he was going to telephone the police at Salignac.

I went after him with the soldier who spoke English, and sure enough he was going off to phone. We argued with him, but couldn't make him change, so I hurried off.

(Curiously enough, some 8 months later, a man came up to me and asked me if I remembered this occasion. He turned out to be the same soldier, and was, by then, the manager of a big store.)

It was all up hill to Salignac, so I couldn't make any speed at all, and I was certain I should find the gendarmes waiting for me. However, no one took any notice of me going through the village, and I hurried on. [*Salignac has a very imposing castle on a bluff overlooking the northern approach to the village.*]

I hadn't had anything to eat since mid-day, and was tired. I tried several farms without success – one asked for my papers and wouldn't have me, another said he would look for the Patron, and came back with some soldiers who asked me to move on.

At last I got permission to go in a loft with some French troops, and was given a blanket. I told the soldiers I was a Belgian and had lived in Loire et Cher for years. As luck would have it they all came from that part, but I managed to keep the bluff up. I fell asleep at once and slept very soundly. [*Distance travelled approximately 110km.*]

29 July. The next day I got up early, and got a cup of black coffee from the troops. Then I bicycled to Sarlat-la-Canéda, and bought myself some café-au-lait at a smart restaurant, as I was so pleased to have got as far. When I went to wash, I found my face was perfectly filthy, so that I must have caused some surprises in this hotel.

I got on fairly well along the Catus road till lunch, but I made one long detour to Domme, as the map showed it on my route. It was a mediaeval walled town, standing on top of a hill, and in ordinary times well worth visiting, but I didn't appreciate it, as I was hurrying and had had to walk some five miles up steep hills, pushing my bicycle.

Domme is an attractive Bastide town standing on a hill about 400ft above the Dordogne. Bradford's route led up this hill and back down the other side. A perfectly good and very much shorter road leads past Domme on the river's flood plain.

Soon after lunch, my front tyre blew up. I got it off using a spoon and fork, and stuck a patch on it, but it didn't stay on for more than a few hundred yards. I repeated this exercise several more times but with no better success.

I pushed the bicycle till I found some soldiers in a village and got one of them to mend it – which lasted about 15 minutes. A column of transport was passing, and I got one of them to stop and got in the back with my bicycle till Catus, where I got a new tyre.

I bicycled on as fast as I could to Cahors. After a glass of beer, I was leaving the town, when I heard a shout. I went on hard, thinking it was the police, but then distinguished my name, and

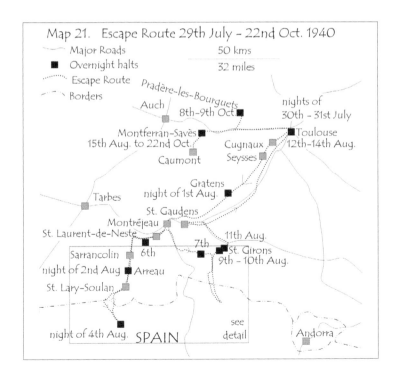

Map 21.   Escape Route 29th July - 22nd Oct. 1940

found Freddie Fitch and Sellar having a 'Bock' [*a variety of strong lager*] outside a café, so I joined them. We went on together, and ate our supper beside the road trying to get a lift.

Eventually we stopped a lorry, which took us some 10km to a lovely café and barn at a road junction – quite deserted. The barn was full of hay, and we got some water from the well, had a wash and shave and then slept. [*Distance covered approximately 90km.*]

30 July. We left together at about 06.15hrs, but I bicycled on, as they were still lorry hopping. We arranged to meet at an address I had in Toulouse. In Caussade I got some milk from a milk trailer, and the people at whose house it had stopped, gave me some coffee and a bowl to drink the milk from. It was a very hot day again.

There were many Belgians travelling north, who had been demobbed from Toulouse. I got a tow behind a car into Montauban, and coming out of the town overtook Freddie and Sellar again. Soon after this I got a lift on a wood-burning lorry to Toulouse.

The lorry had stopped to help a policeman with his tyre, and I made myself so generally useful that he gave me a lift. I arrived chez C--- about 12.15hrs, they were very nice, and gave me an excellent lunch. After a bath, I went to see some American Quakers, whose address C--- had got.

On getting out of the tram, I asked the way, and a lady, who was passing, asked if I was English. She was American, and helped me to find the Quakers, and then gave me tea in her house, almost next door.

The Quakers were very nice, but could only advise me not to go near Marseilles on any account, as all British soldiers were being put in prison there, and to tell me that Spain was not much better. I also got in touch with Martin*, D.L.I.

[*Durham Light Infantry*], who has been here some days and seems in no hurry to move on. [★*From Lt-Col E.A. Bradford's notes this is Martin Hogg.*]

31 Juillet 1940
Toulouse postmark
I wonder if any of my letters ever reach you. Don't write to the address I gave you before as I have now left there, and am travelling once more. I am very well at present but am longing to see you again. However that is no easy task. I have met some friends down here, which makes things better. We have been having a sort of heat wave the last few days. I hope it doesn't last too long, as I'm afraid it may aid Hitler's plans against England. We don't get much news over here, but it seems to me that I had better get back to the States when I can.

This reference to the States showed Bradford was thinking of all possible ways to get out.

I stayed about 3 days in Toulouse, expecting Freddie Fitch to turn up, and trying to get in touch with people who could get me into Spain. I had tea again with the American lady, who introduced me to her cousin, a banker, Conte de la Pleigniere. He very kindly gave me some money, including some dollar bills, but couldn't get me any pesetas. He also gave me a letter to a cousin of his near the frontier [*la Baronne Gauthier d'Annous at Moulis*].

I then got in touch with a very garrulous owner of a book-shop, who told me to go to a friend★ of his at a little village called Arreau, in the Pyrenees. [★*Dr Mounicq, of whom more below.*] I got some good maps with the help of C–, and asked Martin if he wanted to come. At first he said he couldn't start till the next day, but finally got himself ready after some delay, and we bicycled off with C--- to show us the road. C--- was a professor of philosophy, and quite unused to doing the many things I asked of him, but he did them admirably.

1 August. After we had said goodbye to C--- on the outskirts of Toulouse, we went on through Cugnaux and Seysses. It began to rain, and we sheltered for some time in barns, but finally pushed on to near Gratens, where we found a farmer who said we could shelter in his sheds. We had only done about 36km but were fairly wet.

When they had finished stacking the hay, the farmer was most friendly, and invited us into the kitchen to eat. His neighbours had been helping him and were there too, so we were about 14 round the table. We had an excellent meal, crowded in the kitchen, of soup, peas with pieces of mince mixed up in it, then grilled chicken with plenty of very strong wine. To end up we had some white wine – very

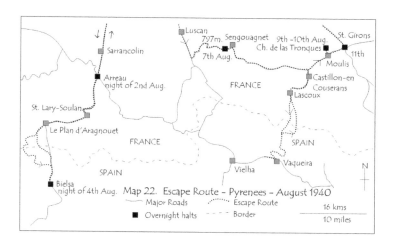

Map 22. Escape Route – Pyrenees – August 1940

good. They were all very friendly and we talked hard, till we noticed Martin was fast asleep, so we went off to our open-ended shed.

2 August. We set off about 06.00hrs the next day, after waiting a long time for Martin, who had a mass of kit and preparations to make. Perhaps I was impatient because I had nothing but an old mackintosh sheet that de Bernard had given me, and my black bag.

It was a nice day with a breeze, but the road was rather hilly and slow. We were both equally bad on the hills and had to walk up most. We went round St-Gaudens, and got into very pretty country where there were plenty of pears and plums – very good, as we seldom got any fruit and vegetables travelling like this, and one missed them.

We stopped for lunch in a field the far side of Montréjeau. Going through St-Laurent-de-Neste, a gendarme stopped us and asked where we were going. I said 'to Arreau'. He questioned us a bit more, but told us to go on when I said we were Belgians. We decided to miss out La Barthe-de-Neste after this.

The valley leading to Arreau was lovely and quite like parts of Scotland. The road wasn't as steep as we expected, and we made good going. At Sarrancolin, we were again stopped by a gendarme, but again he let us go on when he heard we were Belgians. This made us careful coming to Arreau. We went into a buvette, where Martin stayed, while I found Dr Mounicq's house.

He told me that there were two more British there, and of course they turned out to be Freddie and Sellar. I wasn't really surprised to find them as the librarian had told me that he had sent an Ecossais and an Anglais there, but Freddie was astonished to see me.

They had got to Toulouse a few hours after me, and were so tired that they couldn't be bothered to look for M.C-'s house, and went to a hotel. The next day they happened to go into M. Labradie's bookshop to buy a map of the frontier and he had told them of the doctor, so they had left at once. Freddie's wounded leg had broken out in boils and was hurting him a lot, so he had had to rest for 2 days.

The Doctor was charming, but a little shaken at this influx, as he had had nothing to do with getting people into Spain, but merely happened to know the mountains fairly well from shooting in them.

His wife was also very nice, and they insisted on us sleeping in the house – two to a double bed – while we went over to the hotel for dinner that night. We had an excellent meal at the hotel, but must have caused some comment, as the four of us talked English together. Afterwards we had coffee on a little terrace overlooking the river – very peaceful.

Bradford spoke no Spanish. His notebook contains a list of sixteen items of essential vocabulary: I am hungry; I am thirsty; bread; wine; water; hard-boiled egg; omelette; soup; meat; vegetables; salad; potatoes; cheese; fruit; butter; a map.

3 August. Next morning Madame Mounicq gave us a wonderful breakfast of hot chocolate, bread and butter, and masses of honey. She sat over us and spooned honey onto our plates, saying we weren't eating enough. We had a glass of white wine to end up with. It was decided to set off that evening.

We lunched again at the hotel, and spent the afternoon repairing old haversacks which the doctor gave us. I had an old one from the Spanish war, and discarded my black bag and other treasures. I also sold my bicycle for 150 Frs.

We were waiting for the bus at 20.00hrs, but it passed us at 21.00hrs, quite full, with people on the roof, so the doctor's son, who had arrived on leave an hour before, drove us off in the car, which had been laid up and was not licensed.

We drove round the Gendarmes at St-Lary-Soulan, and then waited on the road for the bus, which was now less full. We went on in the bus, slowly up the valley, with a typical marketing crowd, who dropped off at intervals, and kept the bus waiting while they said goodbye to everyone, or slowly got out barrels of wine.

Approx 22.00hrs. Finally the bus turned into a courtyard and we all got out [*most probably at Fabian at 1,182m above sea-level*] the doctor whispering to us not to speak a word. Four Gardes Mobiles were there checking up on people return-ing, and on contraband, but we walked past them in the dark. We went on quietly for some miles, past two lots of douaniers – just going a slight detour to miss them, till we finally turned up a tiny track to avoid the Douane at Le Plan d'Aragnouet.

This track was very difficult, as it was very steep and on the side of a hill, and we could hear a burn roaring down below, while away below us on the other side of the burn we could see the lights of a village, where the douane post was, and hear their dogs. It was pitch dark and we had to use a torch at intervals when crossing burns and rocks. [*On occasions they climbed down the side of the valley, forded the burn, and then up the other side to avoid Frontier Guard posts.*] Some time after mid-night, we crept past a lighted window into a barn in a farm up in the hills. A dog barked and a man came out to see what was up, but didn't see us.

4 August. About an hour and a half later we set off again [*approx. 02.00hrs*] and re-crossed the stream to a better track.

It was still pitch dark, and as the track was rocky, it wasn't easy going. Then the track began to climb steeply up out of a little valley where cows and sheep were feeding.

We began to see something about 04.00hrs but when we stopped to eat and rest at 05.00hrs we couldn't see to distribute food. When we went on again, however, it was quite light. The track climbed on, steeper and steeper – past cartridges, dead mules etc. from the Spanish war – so that we were soon using our hands to help us up and we got very blown.

The valley was very lovely, but rugged and bare. We went on past a bit of snow, and got to the frontier [*Port de Barroude at 2,534m*] at about 07.30hrs, and, looking down into Spain, saw a man down the valley. The Doctor thought he must be a garde, as he was near the old Douane post, and decided we must get over into the next valley to avoid him.

We were up some 9,500ft., and had to go on up to the right over a nasty bit of rock and loose shale, which took us some 3 hours, and was almost too much for my head. It was very hard work with our loads, and Freddie was very done by the time we finished this climb. [*Approx. 10.30hrs.*]

There were quite a lot of gentians, and some small rhodos, violets, colis, iris etc. but they didn't show up much on the rocky ground. We stopped to eat again when we had gone down a bit into the next valley. [*Approx. 12.00hrs.*]

After this the Doctor left us – running off lightly, a good effort as he must have been about 55. He had played rugger against Scotland and the Springboks in 1912, and was very fit. [*Dr Paul (Pierre) Mounicq (1887–1964) played 9 times for France between 1911 and 1913 and was French champion in 1912.*]

We were alone but soon lost our track, which petered out, and so we merely climbed down several thousand feet to the bottom of the valley, where the going looked less awful. It took us much longer than we expected to get down. [*Approx. 15.00hrs. They had climbed around the uppermost slopes of Pic de Troumouse 3,085m and Pic de La Munia, 3,133m, but then descended into the same valley as before, the Cirque de Barrosa, albeit lower down.*]

The mountains looked lovely from the bottom of the valley. After going on for some time, we came to an old vine and worked along the top of a conduit. I wanted to go on along the side of the mountains for some hours, but Freddie's leg was hurting a lot, and the going was very bad – steep hillside, sheer rock or shale – so that we decided to come down on to a track, after we had passed what we thought was the Douane post. [*Approx. 16.00hrs.*]

We had almost got down to the road, when there was a shout behind us and three Gardes Civiles ran along. They came out of a ruined building, inside which a shack had been built, and we, by bad luck, had come down within 100 yards of them. They took us to their post and explained by signs and odd words, that we must go back over the frontier – 'Franco's orders' was the most used phrase.

After some time they got hold of a French speaker, and we told them that we must see an officer. They refused, but after 2 hours argument, we set off for Bielsa. [*Approx. 18.00hrs.*]

Col Edward Bradford's memorandum of the affair, which he recorded after hearing his son's full account, reports in his customary long sentences:

> *The Commander of the post, which consisted of eleven men, at first was for marching them back over the frontier at once, but eventually agreed to take them down to the village below, where there was a 'Maire' who could decide what to do. B. & Fitch had attempted*

during their talk with the Commander of the guard, to bribe him
to let the party through, as they calculated that if they could only
get to a sizeable town they could get hold of a British Consul or
some official who could communicate with the Embassy at Madrid,
which should in a neutral country be able to help them; however the
attempt was unsuccessful, though from their attitude towards it, had
there been a smaller number in the guard B had an idea that it might
have succeeded.[56]

We saw a telephone and asked them to telephone but they
laughed and said that it hadn't worked since 1915 when it was
run by a British Company. On the way down this very rough
road, we had to pass another police post in a half burnt house,
where we should probably have got caught, as you couldn't
tell where the post was going to be.

We went past a village, which was mostly destroyed from
the Civil War, and, after 10km, came to Bielsa, also mainly
burnt. [*On the way down they passed a man who asked them in good*
French what they were and where they were going: they explained the
situation in the hope of getting some help from the Maire; however
their questioner soon destroyed their hopes, saying that the Maire was
a rabid Falangist and very anti-British.[57]] Here we were put in a
room in a house used by the Civil guards and told we should
see the Mayor and the Doctor, and that we should get some
food 'at once'. [*Approx. 20.00hrs.*]

Nothing happened for some hours, except that they gave
us water out of a jar with a long thin spout. You held this
jar six inches or so from your face, and let the water squirt
into your mouth and gurgle down your throat. Everyone was
very pleasant. I had a French-Spanish phrase book, and read
out such phrases as 'Call me at 8 a.m with a good breakfast',
which produced shouts of laughter.

After some time a sort of officer saw us, and gave us to understand that we should be sent on to Saragossa in the morning – just what we wanted. At last, at 23.00hrs, when we were ravenous, we were marched off to the inn, one of the few buildings undamaged. We went into the kitchen – the other room was full – and had an excellent, though oily, meal of soup, tiny trout-like whitebait, potatoes and very oily tomato and pumpkin salad. A youth was singing in the kitchen at the top of his voice the whole time we were there. We had to pay 150 Frs for our meal – a ridiculous price, but we didn't mind as we thought we were going on in the morning.

We got back to the police house about midnight and lay down on very dirty mattresses on the floor, with some blankets. The windows were barred, and we were guarded, but we didn't try to get away, as everything seemed to be going well.

10

Spain to Marseilles:
4 August–November 1940

5 August. Next morning we were got up in rather a hurry and told we were going off soon. The guards seemed less friendly and we were fallen in and marched off.

We found we were being taken the wrong way and expostulated, but we had an escort who spoke no French and you can't argue about your rights with several armed men. We bought some brown bread and cheese at an exorbitant price and were marched back up the road.

Bradford managed to write a half sheet of letter to his parents and gave it to one of the guard to post at the village.

Bielsa Postmark
August 1940
I am posting this in Spain. I managed to cross the frontier with some others, but afterwards we were all caught and are in the process of being marched back through the Pyrenees to France. I hoped to be able to reach Portugal

and get home, but I am afraid I shall probably be interned in France on arrival.

The mountains are lovely and we came across some lovely flowers – little rhodos, iris, gentians, violets. We went up to over 9,000ft. getting across the frontier.

We got a new escort at the first village and another at the last police post. On the way from the last police post to the frontier, a stiff climb of some miles, we saw the man we had seen from the top the day before – a shepherd with his dog, who spoke no French. He had seen us climbing round the day before.

It was raining hard on the way up, and we were in a mist. At about 17.00hrs we got to the top and were told to go down the other side while the guards waited with their rifles. They knew we couldn't hang about long in the hills as we had very little food with us.

A short way down we fell in with a shepherd – it seemed so funny that his opposite number just across the tops couldn't understand French at all. We continued on down with him as it was a bit misty. He was collecting his sheep into groups with a dog, but the mist got too thick and he had had to stop.

At his very simple little cabin he gave us a good hunk of bread and some wine. We went on to the first farm, beside which we had halted two nights before and got there by 20.00hrs, hurrying hard. The woman there knew at once who we were, as Dr Mounicq had looked in on his way down, and was an old friend of theirs. She promised us supper, and later we had a good meal of soup, a bit of sausage, beans and fried potatoes.

They had often had tourists staying there and gave us supper in a separate room. The son came in to discuss what we had better do, and the others decided to go with him over the hill into the next valley, where he would arrange a car to get them past the douane.

I said I would go back the way we came as we at least knew where the police were, and I couldn't see any point in the other scheme. Some time later he asked us how much we would pay him, and it turned out that he was a professional guide, and wanted 100 Frs for the trip, so we all decided to go the ordinary way. Then the woman asked 18 Frs each for the meal – an excessive charge compared with café prices.

We went off soon afterwards, about 23.30hrs, and crept past the first douane post at Fabian – alleged to be 'très méchant'. We didn't dare to go by the hill track, as we weren't certain of it, and passed Fabian about 00.30hrs.

The Battle of Britain started on 5 August.

6 August. We went on a good many miles, through two brightly lit villages, with not a soul about – brightly lit because of the Pyrenees hydro electricity scheme – which made them seem rather ghostly. We had several scares, and once stood still in a ditch for a long time, because a man came out of a house.

We were all very tired, and the night was so dark that we couldn't see a yard, and kept falling over each other and the edge of the road, and finally sat down and dozed for a short time till at 02.20hrs we could see a little.

On entering St-Lary we saw some people coming along, and hid, but they were only coming home late. As we passed the last house, two gendarmes jumped up and stopped us. We told them we were Belgians, who had been on an excursion in the mountains from Pyrenees – a likely story at 03.30hrs. They took us into the police station and woke up the officer. We were so sleepy that we sat on his chair and desk, in the most un-Belgian way. He questioned us and then took down our Belgian names, birthplaces etc. When he came to Sellar, who spoke appalling French with a Glasgow accent, Freddie tried to save him, and said 'Il est cultivateur aussi' but Sellar wasn't to be beaten, and insisted 'Non, je suis etudiant medical'.

After a few more questions, we were told to go. We went on for about half a mile and then we were so tired that we lay down on the edge of a field. After 15 mins, the gendarmes appeared again, and said we must move on or be arrested for loitering.

We moved on, much against our will, and walked till about 05.15hrs with the gendarmes following a few hundred yards behind. By this time they had got tired and had disappeared so we lay down in a field. At 07.00hrs we got permission to sleep in a loft in a village and the woman gave us some wine.

After sleeping for a few hours, we decided that Martin and I had better push off, as four of us were too many together, and the others didn't care much for Martin. It was a great pity having to separate as I wanted to keep with Freddie but if more than two or three arrived together it was difficult to get food and a barn.

We got to the next village for lunch – soup and potatoes at 6 Frs for the two. We went on slowly to Arreau, but didn't go and see the Doctor, although I had left some things there. We went to buy back our bicycles, and found mine had been lent to M Legrand at Sarrancolin 7km on, so I had to walk there, while Martin bicycled.

M. Legrand was a big wine wholesaler, and when I explained to the manager that I had had to walk an extra 7km he immediately offered me a bottle of wine. Then Madame Legrand appeared and offered me another – most excellent white wine from Perpignan, rather heavy.

We stopped in a meadow above the river and had some wine and the remains of the Spanish bread for tea, after which we slept heavily till 18.45hrs.

We turned right off the main road, along one which also led to Montréjeau. After a short time we stopped at a farm, some way off the main road. The people were cutting corn, but said we could sleep in a loft. They were very nice, Monsieur had been a prisoner in the last war, and made us come and have supper in the kitchen.

It was a small farm, and very simple inside, but they gave us a good supper – some soup, two fried-eggs, bread and wine – and wouldn't hear of our paying anything. They also made us take some old sheets when we went up to the loft to sleep. The loft was very stuffy, but we lay near the door and slept well.

7 August. Next morning they gave us some coffee and lots of milk for breakfast. While we were drinking this, a young man came to get milk and was introduced to us, as he spoke English. He asked us to come to listen to his wireless. He was very pro-English, and we heard some news, and also met his uncle, an Abbé, who insisted on giving us 10 Frs each for lunch, although we told him we had a little money – perhaps 60 Frs by then.

We had a wash and a shave and then left. We ate our meal in a field just short of Montréjeau, where we agreed to separate as I had another address I was going to try, and I was also rather bored with Martin.

On getting to Montréjeau, Martin's tyre punctured, so we found a shop, where he bought another. I got a new one too, as one of mine was finished. Another reason I didn't stay with Martin was that he wanted to stay and feed with the French army each day, and I had had enough trouble with them.

Bradford had decided he would have another go at getting into Spain before writing-off that option for escape.

I was making for a place on the frontier, where I thought I might get across, and went past Luscan, where I stopped and washed my feet and then turned up a steep road running about east.

It was a very steep climb, with various good view-points signposted by Michelin and I had to walk for miles pushing my bicycle. Late in the afternoon I came to an Inn, where two teams of men were waiting with loads of tree trunks behind them, and went in for a cup of milk.

They told me that the bicyclists in the Tour de France bicycled all except the top bit of road. I can hardly believe it, and I, at any rate, was reduced to walking 15 minutes at a time and then resting, but of course I was, by then, not very heavy.

I rested at the top [*Col des Ares*] – 796m where there was a deserted café, and then flew down the other side, where there was a succession of hairpin bends. It was as well Martin wasn't with me, as his back-pedalling brake would have been red-hot before long. There was a grand view all down this big valley.

I stopped at the first group of farms, and went into one, but found one slightly mad woman with an awful burnt face, who told me there was no room. But at the next farm, where they were just returning from harvesting, I was welcomed at once. In addition to farming, the man was a wheelwright and blacksmith and had an old lathe turned by a horse from outside. I helped them to cut up some wood for the kitchen fire, which impressed them a great deal. They kept trying to make me rest and do nothing.

At 20.00hrs we sat down to eat in the kitchen, and had some fried onions and tomatoes followed by a bowl of milk. After we had talked for a bit, I told him what I wanted to do and he told me to go to a little village some way down where I might find someone to help me. I went to sleep in a loft above the cow byre, which was so dark that I couldn't find where I was at all, and was frightened of falling down one of the chutes. It was rather smelly but there was plenty of hay.

8 August. Next day I went off early after a glass of milk. They told me I could stay and do a little work in the field, but I thought that once I stopped, I shouldn't get going again.

It was a nice run down for some miles – then I got stopped by a soldier at a gate, but said I was Belgian, and going to St-Girons, so they let me go on. [*Bradford doesn't mention crossing the Col de Portet d'Aspet which is on this road. He does refer to the climb, to over 3,000ft. in his letter from Ch. Las Tronques.*]

I got to -----, the village I had been told of and went to a café, where, after some enquiries, I got in touch with a man who had guided other people over the frontier, and was ready to help me for money. I rested that afternoon, and collected some food; bread, and two tins of sausage meat.

We set off that evening into the hills, and had no trouble with getting round police posts. About midnight we had a short rest, and then pushed on again until dawn, all the time up a track in the hills. By then we were in Spain, and lay down among the rocks till the afternoon, when we pushed on again till evening.

9 August. The track was too bad to try and walk by night – it is much easier going up than down by night – and so we rested. At dawn we went on for a bit, and then the man said he must get back and would point out the way. I had understood he was coming further with me, but I couldn't make him, and went on alone, having little idea of the way, and feeling very much alone.

I came down on a track soon after this, which gradually turned into a road. After a bit I came to a village, which I got through all right, and was feeling quite confident, when a Garde Civile came up behind on a bicycle, and spoke to me. Of course I couldn't say anything except 'Buenos dios' and he made me come back to the police station with him.

After some time I was put in a car and taken to the next village, where there was a French-speaking Garde, but when I explained I was British, and wanted to see some authority, they took no notice, and put me back in the car. I was furious, and determined to be detained, but couldn't make them keep me.

They drove me back a different way, till the track deteriorated too much; then I was marched off by two 'gardes' up a track in the hills. At the top, which was not as far as I expected, and was, presumably, the frontier, they stopped and told me to go on alone.

My watch had stopped, but it must have been after 16.00hrs. I went on down, and fairly soon afterwards came on quite a good track, which led to a village. There was a police post here, but they took no notice of me, and I went on to the next village, which, to my surprise, was the one I had started from and where I had left my bicycle. I am not sure now exactly what route I had taken.

It seems most likely that Bradford's second crossing of the border started from the D618 up the valley of the River Lez and that he left his bike at the village of Lascoux (c.700m). From there he would have continued up the Lez and then over the border at Porte d'Urets (2,522m) and down into Spain to Salardú. The return journey will have started by car from Vaqueira and then by foot from the region of Montgarri to the Port d'Orle (2,363m) and then down the valley of the River Orle to Lascoux.

I collected my bicycle, which I had left at the café, and then pushed on hard to a Château, at Moulis near St-Girons, the address I had been given by the banker in Toulouse.

La Baronne had heard from her cousin, and was very nice, although I suspect she wasn't very pleased to see me. She was one of the smallest and frailest figures one could meet and so was her daughter. Both looked as if they came straight out of the Court at Versailles. They were an ancient royalist family, and hadn't got a penny.

Unfortunately there was a Colonel there, who was billeted nearby, and when he heard who I was, said it was his duty to telephone the authorities. [*He told Bradford that he had an order on his office table saying that all British military personnel in unoccupied France were to be collected with a view to repatriation.*[58]] I ought to have pushed straight on, but I was so tired that I thought I must rest and I hoped nothing would happen. Also I couldn't think where on earth to go, as I didn't want to go near Perpignan because of the Senegali regiment, and had been warned to keep clear of Marseilles.

It was a pity I didn't go to Perpignan, as I should never have been seen, and it turned out later to be the easiest place in the world to get across the frontier.

The Château was an old place, built on the side of a steep hill, so that it looked immense from below, and was one storey less on the other side. I was given an enormous room on the same floor as the entrance, hung with tapestry and with a big four-poster bed. It looked as if it might last have housed Louis XVI, there was a powder closet off it with a very old-fashioned WC built in it.

In 2005 we found Château de Las Tronques. It is clearly still inhabited but it was closed when we visited and couldn't get anyone to answer the door. It is situated on the side of a very steep hill and looks imposing from across the valley but quite modest from the main door.

I can only suppose that Bradford was confused about the date of this next letter as he cannot have reached this address until the evening of 10 August.

August 9 40
chez Mdme la Baronne Gauthier d'Annous
Château de Las Tronques
Moulis, Ariége
When I post this I shall be with the French Army once more as a sort of interned prisoner. I am staying at the moment with a kind Baronnesse (sic) whose address I was given in Toulouse. I met another officer in Toulouse, and by hunting around I got an address of someone who might help me to pass into Spain.

We bicycled down there, about 160km and on arrival I found two more officers, with whom I had already spent several days, and who I knew were going towards Toulouse also. After a day's rest, we set off into the mountains with a guide in the evening. We managed to pass the Douanes & guards by night, and got 2 hours rest in a barn. We went on up a tiny path till we got to the frontier at 2,600m. On looking over we saw what we thought was a Spanish Douane & so decided to climb to nearly 9,000ft into the next valley. It was very hard work carrying our kit etc, and took us hours. We got past the first post, but bumped right into the second, and were taken.

We managed to spend some 30 hours in Spain, but couldn't make any one let us see a mayor or a high-up officer. We had an extraordinary meal in the inn at 11 p.m., with some Spaniards singing hard the whole time.

The meal was good but very expensive. There were only a few houses rebuilt in the whole village.

The next day we were marched back over the pass, & then had to push hard in order to get past all the French guards during the hours of night. We succeeded fairly well, but by the end were absolutely done, as we had been on the go for almost 76 hours with very little rest and a lot of hard climbing & marching. I meant to try again, but I am still exhausted and my boots are cut to pieces. We have all split up again, as it is easier to feed by oneself. I picked an enormous basket of plums this afternoon – all different kinds, yellows, green, big red and little red ones like damsons but quite sweet. Every tree is absolutely loaded with them and they just let masses of them rot on the ground. This year, for lack of sugar, they are drying them off in the sun – like prunes.

This is an old château, standing on the side of a hill & looking straight across a valley at more hills. They are very poor, I think & don't have much to eat, except very filling bread, soup and lots of potatoes. This is much more than I am accustomed to however! There are lovely things in all the rooms, and I sleep in a room which I am sure was exactly the same in Louis XVI's time – it is on the ground floor, is big and has a large double bed in an alcove. I don't believe even the curtains & hangings have been altered. The owners are very Royalist and old-fashioned. Monsieur is away at present.

Have you ever seen the Pyrenees? They are lovely, though no more so than the hills in Scotland. I never thought I should end up down here. Will you again tell Col Barstow (AG2) what has happened to me or anyone else who you think may be able to get me home somehow. I am presuming that you have had some of my previous letters? I shall put an address at the bottom of this, to which I hope you can write. I think the best method is via the Red Cross in Geneva, but the ordinary mail may be working. Try both as I am simply dying to get a letter from you. It is over 3 months now since I heard from you. It is still no good trying to send me any parcels or money. I think they will make some arrangement for me to get my money.

I was always so full of hope that I would be back home fairly soon, but now I am rather disheartened. I thought that once I had got into Spain, I should be taken before a British Consul and he would somehow get me home. I really don't see what else I can try and do now, and I am so tired of walking! I am reporting to the French authorities voluntarily, as I have no longer got the means to live with.

Will you write to Frances Campbell-Preston and ask her to let Patrick know what has happened to me. I left him as a prisoner on 19 June, and I don't know where he is. I should like to know his address and also have some news of him and the others if Frances has any.

I wonder if you ever got any guinea-pigs to keep on the tennis court or any bees? I stayed with a doctor who had lots of bees, and he told me that you never ought to eat the comb, but merely slice off the top and let the honey drain out, and then let the bees refill the comb. The reason being that a bee has to eat ten times as much honey to produce a bit of comb!

I believe Di ought to keep rabbits at home, like all the French do, just for eating. The climate down here is very hot – much too hot for me. We have had a certain amount of rain, and last night we had a heavy thunder-storm, when all the lights fused, and the switches flashed. Now it is lovely and sunny again. I got boiled coming here as the main road goes steeply up to 3,000ft, and it was hard work pushing my bicycle along.

I stayed two nights there, and was made very welcome by the family, but the third day the police arrived and carted me off again to St-Girons. I was told I was going to be sent to Marseilles, where they were collecting British soldiers, with a view to sending them home.

This, and the fact that I was without funds and my boots were hardly usable and again tired out stopped me from making any effort to avoid arrest.

After a night in the cells, I was taken by train, starting at about 05.00hrs to Toulouse, where I was put into a concentration camp in an old barracks. This was being run by the army, and I was given no liberty at all, being shut up in a room with a washing place off it. However, on the third day I was sent down to the Commandant's office, and while interviewing me, the Commandant left the office for a few moments. I seized his rubber stamp, breathed on it and quickly stamped the bottom corner of four bits of paper.

When I went back to my room, I wrote out a 'pass' for myself to go and visit friends in Toulouse for 48 hours. That afternoon, I asked if I could see the Commandant again about a private matter. I asked him something stupid, and then came out of the office, produced my pass to the sentry and walked straight out of the barracks without difficulty.

I went off to a garage, which I had been to a few weeks before and got them to let me sleep the night there.

Two days later when I was wandering around not knowing quite what to do, I was asked for my papers by a gendarme, and as they weren't in order I was taken along to the police station and after some delay, sent by bus under escort to another concentration camp at Monferran-Savès near Auch.

11 August
I reported to the Military Authorities at St-Girons yesterday. Madame kindly came with me and said she would be
pleased to have me till they decided what to do with me. So
I can't give you any other address. Will you write here, and
I will get them to forward the letter. [*This last sentence was
crossed out in pencil.*] They have lent me David Copperfield
which I am reading, as it is a blessing to read something
in English again. There is a Protestant Church some 25km
from here and I shall try and bicycle there next Sunday,
when I have found out when the services are.

   I do wish I could know more what is happening at
home, as the French News is only what the Germans
give out, and the wireless set here is not good enough to
get London.

   I do pray that everything will be all right.
Best love to you all from your loving Ben

Added in pencil squashed into the bottom of the letter:

At a moments notice I was suddenly whisked off to the
Gendarmerie, slept the night there comfortably, and dined
with them in a café at their expense, then left at 4.15 a.m.
by train and bus for here – a prisoner of war camp with one
other officer & about 10 men. We are in a large, newish &
unfurnished château.

   Can you try & send me gradually some pyjamas (1 pr),
a shirt, a tie, some socks, walking shoes (? too heavy) &
above all some tins of jam, some tea, chocolate or sweets,
cakes, tinned margarine. Parcels must not exceed 5 kilos but
number is unlimited. Can you also try & get Punch to me &
any other Reading Matter. I haven't seen Punch since May.

There I found Ian Garrow who had also been at Bélâbre and had left the same day as the rest of us. He had been picked up at Limoges and been there ever since.

This camp, which had been for German officers, was in a Château, a modern palatial building, built by the proprietor of the Bordeaux casino. It was magnificent inside, but was entirely empty of furniture and hideous. There were about 30 soldiers there, several of whom had been at Bélâbre.

We were only allowed out of our rooms for 1½ hours' exercise behind barbed-wire, twice a day, and had nothing on earth to do. However, the food was excellent, as the cook had been chef at a hotel in Nice.

Col Edward Bradford recorded:

> *Depot 602 P.G. where B now found himself consisted of a large modern château with a considerable garden around it; it had until the collapse of France been one of the Depots for German Prisoners of War and the envelopes used by B for his letters from there were the official P of W ones with the instructions on the outside printed in German. It seems rather ironic that soldiers who until a few weeks before were allies of France should be put under restraint in a place intended for enemy prisoners and have to use stationery printed in enemy language.*[59]

The full example is included only once. [Write with pencil, and not between the lines. Leave this letter open. Do not give place names.]

Mit Bleistift und nicht
zwischen den Zeilen
schreiben.
Diesen Brief offen lassen.
Keinen Ortsnamen ange-
ben.

Capt. B Bradford
L'Armée Britannique
Depot 602 P G
Monferran-Savès
(Gers), France
15 August 40

I am in a definite sort of concentration camp here. I gave myself up at St-Girons, because I had heard there was a Collecting Centre for British, and I hoped they might be doing something about getting us exchanged. As there is only one other officer here & twelve men, I don't imagine much will happen for some time. I could not see any other way of getting home to try, and it didn't seem much good wandering about France any longer, and living on other people's charity. Now I am rather sorry I didn't wander on to Perpignan and then along the coast to Marseilles, as it would all have been new country. Also, there were masses of fruit down there, and round here they tell us there is no fruit, or butter or cheese, and a scarcity of vegetables. We are allowed to buy things through a French soldier but the only thing he seems to be able to get is bread. He did manage to get some tomatoes one day, & a little fruit also.

We are limited in the number of letters we write home, and so I shan't write to anyone except you. We are only allowed to write two a month, but I shall see if they won't let me send more, as we oughtn't really to be 'Prisoners of War'. Can you get anything done about my being exchanged from your end – either through the Red Cross or through Col Barstow? We live in a Château [*Ch. d'Envalette at Monferran-Savès*] which was built by the owner of the Bordeaux Casino [*André Delieux*], some 30 to 50 years ago I should think. It is similar to the ordinary Châteaux outside, and most expensively decorated & constructed inside – very

nice inlaid woodwork with little scenes – marble floors etc:
it has been empty for ten years and the rooms only have a
few pieces of typical Army furniture. We have each got a
large room, containing a bed & some chairs, and we have
one table between us for eating on. Our rooms communicate on to a nice toilet-room with twin basins (hot doesn't
work) and a WC. There is a shower-bath in the basement,
but no proper baths. One of our soldiers looks after us and
brings up our meals. We have b'fast of café-au-lait and dry
bread at 8 a.m. – in bed. Lunch – fairly adequate but not
enough vegetables and never a sweet at 12.30, and supper
– rather lighter than lunch – at 7.30 p.m. We get about ½ a
litre of red wine between us at lunch and supper.

The grounds round the house are nicely planted with
trees but we are wired into a small space round the house.
There appears to be no garden, but there is a large high old
conservatory outside our wire. I have asked for leave to go
out into the country for 2 hours at a time on parole, and
they are considering it. I have already got permission to
listen to the wireless and give the men a summary of it,
which cheers them up after the German announcements in
the French papers. I hope to goodness I get leave to go out,
as otherwise there is absolutely nothing to do. I have two
English books which I have almost finished, and they can
only lend us the dullest of French books. I have hopes of
getting more English books from various English ladies I
know in France, but I want to get out and talk to people,
and see things.

How I am longing to hear from you! The wireless said
that bombs had been dropped in rural Hants. I hope none
of them were near you. You must all be having an awful
time now. That was a splendid raid of the RAF's on Italy
the other night, wasn't it?

We had a few days of rain and thunder while I was staying at Las Tronques, which was unfortunate. Now it seems to be set fine again, but we can make little use of the lovely days.

My companion in captivity is a chap, Garrow, I have met before for a few days at Bélâbre, and, unfortunately, do not like very much. However we are both trying hard to get on together. He is a rough sort of chap and was brought up in S Africa. The soldier who looks after us is his batman Glasgow Highlanders (9th Bn HLI *Highland Light Infantry*) but was in The Black Watch from 1918 to 1925.

Time clearly began to hang heavily on their hands as a result of this close imprisonment.

18 August

I got a letter today from the American Quakers in Toulouse to where I had written asking for books. No one had got an answer from anyone in France to whom they had written till yesterday, when one of the men got a letter. This has cheered them up a lot, but of course they are all longing for news from home. The Quakers hope to be able to send us some books. Our food has improved slightly since I have been here. I think they find it easier to dish up 2 rations than 1. We have also been able to buy some tomatoes and pears. I know that food is pretty scarce in France, but we absolutely crave for something sweet! Will you please forward the enclosed letter to Lloyds Bank for me. You mustn't look at it!

I wonder what happened to all my Punches between 9 May and now. Do you think they sent them off somewhere or wisely stopped the subscription for a bit? I don't suppose I shall be able to return any books to England,

but if anyone can send me books or magazines which they
don't want returned, I should be most grateful & so would
the others here. Can you think of anyone who could send
me on The Field or Tatler after they've done with it? I
expect most people have stopped taking them for the war.
I should love to read some Walter Scotts as I have time for
any amount of reading now. I think I can borrow Dickens
without difficulty from an English lady I met in St-Girons.
She is married to a French Doctor aged 80. She is 73 & they
both look 20 years younger. She is a great character, lively
as anything, and doesn't mind what she says to anyone. I
had tea with her one day.

I have asked Lloyds to write to you about investing any
money in my account, & for you to be the authority for
doing it in my name, so can you please put it in whatever
you think best. It seems stupid to worry about little things
like that when Great Britain is being attacked night and
day. I do wish I could get out and do something about it.

I hope to goodness you are both well and not too much
worried by everything. Have you got more evacuees in
the house now? I hope you have managed to get a lot of
fruit and vegetables out of the garden and are storing up
some against the winter. The French are beginning to use
a kind of flower called 'saponeur' for washing things in,
as soap is almost unobtainable. I saw in a paper that there
were several other flowers & plants which you can use as
a substitute for soap. Bye-the-bye in one of the cardboard
boxes of mine over the carpenters shed, you will find
various boot-polishes. Do use them before they dry up
completely. A General has just visited us and asked us how
we were. I mentioned the difficulty of getting soap and his
Staff Officer made a note of it and they say we shall now be
able to get some. We had only a tiny bit left between us. I

told him we had got no books to read & absolutely nothing
to do, & he also made a note about books. So far nothing
has come out of my request to be allowed out for a few
hours on parole. I can't think of anything more to write
about as our life is so very dull.

Best love to you all from

your loving Ben

PS I wonder how these letters go – through Switzerland?

To begin with I was thankful to rest and to have a bed to sleep
on. I was extraordinarily tired, and my boots had rotted away
altogether, so that I only had an old pair of canvas shoes on.

Very soon, however, I wanted to get a move on again, as
nothing seemed to be happening about our being sent home,
although we were definitely told we should be 'any day now'.

*On 24 August the Luftwaffe attacked Central London for the
first time. The following night the RAF retaliated with an attack
on Berlin.*

*Bradford wrote to Lt-Col Stephen who was once more Commanding
Officer of 1st Bn The Black Watch:*

26 August

My dear Colonel,

I thought you might like to know what has happened to
your late Adjutant. As you probably know, what was left of
the Battalion was taken prisoner on 12 June near St-Valery-
en-Caux. By then, we were split up into several groups, and
so we were never very sure what had happened to several
officers and men. Most of the officers met together the first
day as prisoners. Neill Grant-Duff was killed the last day,
I'm afraid – also L/Cpl Gardiner of the Officers' Mess. They
thought Alistair Telfer-Smollett was killed too.

We marched about 32km a day – 2 days we got trucks
and went further – via Doullens, St-Pol, Béthune, towards
Belgium. We had no food at all for the first 36 hrs, and as
we had had practically nothing the day before, we were
nearly starving. I escaped on 19th near La Bassée, when on
the line of march. I couldn't make anyone come away with
me, as they thought it was useless. I think Thomas Rennie
and Col Mackintosh-Walker escaped the same time but I
don't know. I went back to where we were when we left
for the Saar in April, and revisited several places you know
on my way to Boulogne and the coast. Later, when I realised that it was impossible to get a boat across the Channel,
I decided to make for Spain and visited the Café with the
Twins, where we had lunch with Geoff one day.

I got into Spain, but was arrested by the Civil Guards
and, after a day's pause, taken back over the frontier. I am
now in a sort of prison camp in unoccupied France, but
I hope to be let out fairly soon and put on 'Liberté surveillée' in a town near here.

We have no liberty here, but are quite well treated, and
even eat with the French Officers. We are only 2 officers
and 13 men here.

I do wish I could get back home, but I see no prospect
of it at present. I was so tired of walking by the time I had
tried Spain, that I was quite glad to rest here. It was a long
journey down from the North of France and I was never
keen on marching.

I wonder how you are and what you are doing now.
Do write to me and tell me all the news, as I hear nothing
here. I have only been here since 14 August and so I haven't
had time to get a letter from my parents yet. We manage to
listen to the British news every night, and give a summary
of it to the men, so that we are not quite as out of touch

with the situation, as if we only listened to the French or German broadcasts.

Did the 4th Bn get back safely? We were changed to each Bde in turn, and I think they got away in our proper Bde.

I hope you and Mrs Stephen are both very well

Yrs Sincerely, Bill Bradford

When this letter eventually reached its destination, over 3 months later, Col Stephen wrote immediately to his Brigade HQ.

The Headquarters
154 Infantry Brigade

1. I forward three copies of a letter just received by me from Captain B.C. Bradford, The Black Watch, who was my Adjutant from 1.1.39. Captain Bradford was taken prisoner at St-Valerie [*sic*], France on 12.6.40.

2. It will be noted that the letter is dated 26.8.40. Since the events set out in the letter I have heard that Captain Bradford has made further desperate efforts to get away from France.

3. The killed mentioned (marked A) are:-

A/Captain M A M Grant-Duff

2nd-Lt A D Telfer-Smollett

2749396 L/Cpl Gardiner J

all serving in 1st Bn The Black Watch

4. The place meant (marked B) is a village called Bailleul-les-Pernes near Lillers. Captain Bradford left a bag containing clothing in a cellar of a farm there, with the permission of the farmer. I presume he went to fetch his kit.

'The Café with the twins' marked C refers to a café in a small village called Willeman about 12 miles S.W. of St-Pol where the inhabitants were very good to a detachment of the Regiment in April 1940. They were very pleased to have Black Watch soldiers there again as they had them billeted in the area in the war 1914/18 when, apparently very good relations existed.

May this report on Captain Bradford's attempt to escape be sent to the War Office to be placed on record for future reference when this gallant officer eventually returns.

C.G. Stephen, Lt-Col

Commanding 1st Bn The Black Watch (R H R).

Keith 11 Dec 40

The Commandant, Colonel Gradelet, was an Anglophobe, and glad the war was finished for France, but he was strictly correct in his behaviour to us.

I couldn't get much idea of the plan of the building, but assumed that the room under my washing place would be a similar place. The windows were indifferently wired, and I decided to try and get out one night. We were on the first floor, some 30ft off the ground with an area round the house in parts.

Late at night I lowered myself on my sheets from the lavatory window. When I was at the end of the sheets, I was still some way off the ground and had this narrow area below me. I was wondering how to get clear, when I noticed a bed in the room, whose windows I was level with, and at that moment the Colonel, who couldn't sleep, jumped up and shouted.

I jumped clear, and made off, but before I was half-way through the barbed-wire fence I was caught by the guard and taken back.

A few days later, a general visited the camp. No action had been taken as a result of my effort, and the general told us that arrangements were in hand for our being sent home and that meanwhile we could go out on parole. [*It appears that this*

*relaxation of containment was a direct result of Bradford's complaints
to the previous general.*[60]]

We walked out that afternoon, and went over to a
Château, Caumont, not far off. There was a very nice
family there who were charming to us and showed us
round the Château – a lovely old place – and there was also
an English lady, Mrs Curle, staying there. She had got left
in France at the beginning of the war, when she was travelling with her son, and had been ill. Since then she had
kept putting off her journey until now it was very difficult
to arrange.

Depot 602 PG Monferran-Savès (Gers)
28 August 1940
We really are going to be let out and put on 'liberté surveillée' at Auch – the capital of Gers, some 25 miles from
here. Two days ago, they received a letter here which said
that we ought to have been on 'liberté surveillée' all the
time, and so yesterday we were allowed out as much as we
liked. I saw a sign-post in the village which said 'Château
Historique 7km' & so we bicycled off there in the afternoon. When we arrived, we happened to meet the son of
the house, & he invited us in, when we told him who we
were. There was an English lady staying there – Mrs Curle.
She was out here with her son last August. He had just
got into the Diplomatic, but rushed back to join the Irish
Guards, & left her out here, thinking the Channel would
be too dangerous. Now, of course, she is trying hard to get
back & finding it extremely difficult. It was a lovely old
Château, built in 1535 on this plan.

It looked rather Spanish, I thought. It had towers at the
corners, and was on the side of hill, so that there was a big

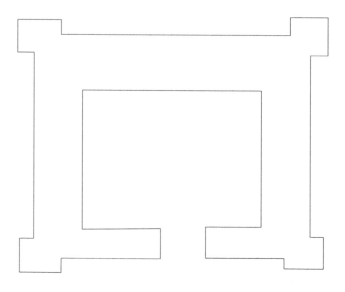

Layout of Château de Caumont.

drop on the far side of the main wing. The de Noirmonts were very kind and showed us masses of lovely rooms, with old pictures, tapestry and furniture. There were sweet little rooms in the turrets and towers.

They all spoke English well, and have always had a lot to do with English people – they have got several old signed photographs of notabilities of some time ago – Lord Cardigan, Duke of Beaufort etc. We had tea and then came back here.

In 2005 we visited Château de Caumont. Madame de Castelbajac allowed us in to take a photograph of the outside of the building but after hearing our story she couldn't have been kinder. We were taken by her on a tour of the castle and shown what, presumably, were the same rooms as Bradford was shown in 1940. After the war the de Noirmonts sold the property and then in the late 1970s it was bought back into the family by their cousins the de Castelbajacs. What with the sales and a subsequent burglary many of the fine objects referred to have disappeared. Nevertheless the interior of the place is spectacular. The association with the British continues. Madame was very proud that one room has been re-named 'The Queen's Room' in honour of a visit to the château by Queen Elizabeth, The Queen Mother. There was a photograph of that occasion too. The château is on a good site – it has a steep drop on three sides and a dry moat protects the entrance where presumably there was once a drawbridge.

There are masses of blackberries in the hedges here, and we picked and eat them – lovely big ripe ones without many pips. It is no good picking them for puddings, as (1) they never have puddings, and (2) they haven't got enough sugar here to sweeten them. For the past few days, before the letter about our freedom arrived, we have been feeding with the French officers in the dining-room, which is much nicer. They are only four, and I couldn't think why they kept us feeding alone. We now get our food nice and hot, and also get much more – in fact as much as we want. We usually have a nice bunch of white grapes each after each meal, as other fruit is scarce here. Don't bother to send me out any food if you haven't already, as we shall be all right when we aren't shut up. I am fairly well off for socks now too. I wrote to the American Quakers in Toulouse and they sent me enough socks, and a cardigan for all of us. They have also sent some books, and so we are very well off. In addition the French General has given me a pair of French Army boots and so you need not worry if my shoes are too heavy to go by post, though I should like to have them. Can you also send me a French Grammar & a small dictionary if you can find them at home – not one of those minute dictionaries. Don't buy one as I can do that at Auch. I think my Grammar is somewhere about at home, and I want to get my French as good as possible. I am reading 'Edward VII et son temps' by André Maurois now and enjoying it very much.

I wandered in the old kitchen-garden here yesterday. It is some way from the house, and completely derelict. The fruit trees haven't got anything at all on them which seems extraordinary after only 10 years. I find the house was only built in 1913 – what a waste of money. I do hope you are both very well at home, and that Di is there looking after you well, too. I will arrange for letters coming to this address to be forwarded to me at Auch. I do hope I get one soon – though Mrs Curle said she hadn't had one since 6 June. Telegrams definitely arrive as she had had two quite lately. The country round here is quite pretty and undulating and on a clear day you can see the Pyrenees. I wish I could have been interned down there as it was much prettier. The farms and houses all have very flat roofs & are built to keep cool in summer so that they too look very Spanish to me. They go in for mixed farming with a good deal of vineyard.

We visited Ch. D'Envalette (formerly Depot 602) in 2005. It is now a reform school. The building burned in 1942 and the roof replaced with a far simpler and even uglier design. The property is large, imposing and, as my father wrote, absolutely hideous. It is in a nice location on rising ground with views to the distant Pyrenees. The grounds have continued the deterioration that Bradford recorded. The interior is still as he describes – a great deal of marble and painted woodwork inlaid with illustrated panels.

3 September 1940

Many happy returns of your birthday – if this arrives in time. We have had a very full week since we got our semi-liberty. A Frenchman, who had heard we were here, came and visited us on Friday, & then invited us to meet him in a town 10km from here & go on to some friends of his. We got a lift to the town & then found we had got to go on 7km, so we had to borrow bicycles. One of these belonged to a one-legged man and only had one pedal, which was most uncomfortable. The people we visited were an Italian, M. Monti, who is a well-known 'cellist, and his English wife, who plays the piano & is awfully nice. We had tea there, and they have invited me to come there temporarily if I can get permission. This would be very nice for me, as they have got a farm of some 75 acres, and a garden, so that I could make myself of some use. I have asked for permission to do this.

On Sunday we again visited one of his friends at a château 17km away. This turned out to be a lovely Georgian house, but everything was neglected. The owner is a bachelor and apparently permanently drunk. However we had an excellent tea – he is half American – with butter – which is almost unobtainable here, and honey. We never get butter or margarine, so it was a great treat.

Yesterday the Frenchman, M. Mark, came over here. He simply won't leave us, and is really most kind, though one gets rather bored with him. He speaks English fairly well. He is a most peculiar little man, as he doesn't belong to this part of the country, and has just firmly got to know as many people as he can. He foists us on them, and I'm sure they don't want to have anything to do with us. This afternoon he has arranged for us to go to another house!

Last Thursday we bicycled off to Gimont – a town about 9km away. We are just about 1/2 way between Gimont and L'Isle-Jourdain. It has an old Church, 1335, which is a rather unusual building with no tower, and also an old covered-in market place, which extends right across the main road. We bought a few things we wanted, and also a small melon, which was lovely and sweet. We are getting much more fruit nowadays, and could get any amount of vegetables, but we usually have those dried white beans or tinned French beans – I suppose because they are less trouble! We are really being fed extremely well.

We suffer badly from fleas here. Apparently the Midi is renowned for fleas, and we seem to pick them up whenever we go outside. It really is rather a trial, so, however carefully you search your clothes before going to bed, you always seem to miss one, which gives a very disturbed night. I have got about fifty new bites from last night, but I caught him at last. Our rooms are beautifully clean and we never had one till we began going out.

The blackberries are really amazing here. It takes you a very short time to collect two pounds of lovely big ones. I made some blackberry fool yesterday, as we never have a pudding. I had no idea how to make it, but it was very good. I didn't use any sugar at all, which shows you what lovely sweet brambles they are. I boiled them all first, and then squeezed all the juice out. Then I boiled the juice again, and poured into it a bowl of milk with the yolks of two eggs mixed up in it! Is that anything like the way?

I have borrowed some more books from the Montis, including 'Waverley' by Walter Scott. They have got a lot of English books and so I shall be quite happy if I get there. They have got a daughter of about 15 I should think. She speaks English, French and Italian and is very fat. I have also borrowed a Bible from them. Haven't you got a Bible in modern English or rewritten? If so, I should love to have it if you can lend it to me.

Several more soldiers have arrived here now, and our strength is something like twenty-seven. I wonder if anyone is going to do something about getting us exchanged? They can't leave us interned indefinitely can they?

On 7 September the London Blitz began in earnest with a raid of 300 bombers escorted by 600 fighters.

Depot 602 P.G.
Monferran-Savès
(Gers) France.
9 September 1940
I am sending this letter via the British Ambassador at Lisbon, and asking him to forward it on by Air-Mail, as I have managed to get 2 Air Mail stamps. If you send yours back by Air Mail to him, and ask him to forward it to me, it may be quicker. We can try at any rate. Will you forward Ian Garrow's on to his home, please.

We went over to Château de Caumont again yesterday. I told you about it in one of my other letters, which may not have arrived. Mrs Curle, an English lady who is staying there, has had a letter from her son by this means which only took 23 days! Goodness knows how long the normal method takes. It wasn't a very nice day yesterday, and we had some rain, so we couldn't do anything at Caumont except talk. We had heard disturbing rumours about the whole of France being occupied in the near future. The de Noirmonts relieved our minds about this, and we came away much more cheerful. They are a most charming family.

Ten of our soldiers ran away a few days ago when on parole. I am furious about it, as I got them their parole, & I'm afraid it may result in all the others being locked up again. Our numbers have increased considerably and at one time we were 29.

The French soldiers here were relieved 3 days ago by a new detachment at about 6 hours notice. The Mess Cook went too, & we all thought we should starve for several days, though he was far from being an expert, having been a butcher till a month ago. However, a man, who had been a chef in several hotels at Cannes, turned up in the new detachment, and our meals are now beautifully cooked and served up. Also the range draws, which it never would do for the previous man, when the kitchen was always full of smoke. I'm sorry my letters always deal so much with food, but our life is somewhat uneventful and we always seem to be hungry – I suppose because we only have two real meals a day!

We went over to the Montis again the other day and had tea there. Afterwards they gave us a short piano and 'cello recital, which was lovely. M. Monti's brother is a well-known sculptor in Italy – have you ever heard of him?

That raid on London on Saturday night must have been frightful. I do hope the weather will soon be too bad for more raids. It is awful being perfectly safe here, and not being able to do anything at all for anyone. I listened to JB Priestley speaking after the wireless news last night. Today I have listened to the wireless a lot as it has been raining, and also because the Colonel is away in Toulouse for the day. The wireless is in his office, and so we cannot normally listen except at certain hours. Ian Garrow has also gone to

Toulouse for the day to see a dentist, and try and buy himself some more clothes. I must go myself one day & get a new pair of trousers. If you get a letter from the American Embassy or International Red Cross asking you if you will pay them a sum of money, which will be passed to me in francs, will you please do it. I am trying to raise some money & I believe they work it like that. It is no good your trying to send me any yourself, as cheques can't be cashed.

The well here has almost dried up and in addition the pump doesn't work very well, so that we haven't been able to get much water for washing, and in addition none of the WCs work. I hope the rain we have had today & yesterday will fill up the well a bit. I don't think it will do much harm to the grape harvest, as the grapes look very small at present and I think this will make them swell.

I am enjoying reading Walter Scott's Waverley very much. I have always wanted to read more of his books and also Dickens but there seemed so little time when I was at home. Now I have got plenty of that at any rate. We are also very lucky in being able to borrow English books from Mme Monti. I must go into Auch one of these days and find out if there are any more English people living there.

10 September I went to Auch today in the army car which had to go. I managed to buy a hairbrush and nail brush, which I have been longing for, and also looked at the Cathedral, which is lovely – sixteenth century. Most of the stained glass had been taken out for the war, but the tracery of the windows was lovely and also the vaulting. The town is very picturesque with steep, narrow streets – many of them with steps every 10ft or so. There are several very old houses – fifteenth century. It was a very pleasant change being allowed to go shopping!

Depot 602 P.G.

Monferran-Savès

(Gers)

19 September 1940

I sent off a telegram to you on the 11th, and was hoping to get one back before I wrote again. It wasn't very expensive, and will be well worth it, if it has arrived. Mrs Curle, whom I have written about before, sent one home and got an answer quite soon. We have been sent some money by the American Embassy, and so are quite all right now. I am hoping to get a regular monthly allowance from now on through the American Consul at Marseilles, as presumably my pay continues to go into my bank. [*This was the first of a monthly allowance of £10.*] I went and bought a pair of corduroy trousers in L'Isle-Jourdain the other day. They have altered them to fit me quite well enough. It had been quite cold for several days when I bought them, but now it is very hot again. My only pair of trousers is practically worn out, and I shall have to get another coat soon, too. It is quite difficult to find any clothes, and mine was the last pair of corduroy trousers for miles round. I can't see a respectable sort of tweed coat anywhere, and very much doubt if they ever have anything I should like.

We have had quite a lot of rain this last week, and the well has filled up a lot. It was then found out that the pump had broken, & when it was mended, we still got no water in our rooms. Finally we found that there was another stop-cock, which someone must have been playing with, and at last we have got water again, which is a blessing.

A wretched Indian soldier arrived here last night. He has lost one arm, and cannot speak a word of English or French. I have forgotten what Urdu I used to know, & so it will be awful for him here. I hope they will put him in a camp reserved for Indians, as there must be several about.

The figs are just beginning to be ripe here, and we have had several. They are good aren't they? There are also masses of melons now, which are beautifully sweet. This is just as well as you can't spare any sugar to put on them.

The Colonel had a friend to lunch last Sunday – a very nice Captain, – and to celebrate this, and the fact that he had been promoted to Officier de Legion d'Honneur, we had a tremendous lunch, which lasted from about 12.50 to 3 p.m. We ended up with Sparkling White Wine and biscuits, and then coffee and Armagnac. We hope the Colonel will have someone else to lunch soon!

I found one of those little green tree frogs the other day. There aren't a great many round here. There used to be some in the greenhouse at Chilworth.

We went over to the Montis for tea again the other day, and borrowed some more books. I have collected 'The Old Curiosity Shop'. I finished 'Waverley' and enjoyed it thoroughly. I shall read one of the other Scotts later, as I think it is better to read something else in between. We have invited the Montis to come over to tea here tomorrow. We now have tea in our room every day – just a cup of tea out of a tin pot-cum-kettle, and some bread and jam. It helps to split up the afternoons, which are otherwise very long. We had a marvellous view of the Pyrenees the other day, just before it began to rain. The visibility was extraordinary and you could see the snow on the peaks.

They have caught the men who escaped when on parole, and are sending them back here. They had got down near to Perpignan. Their breaking of parole has resulted in all the others being deprived of any liberty at all.

Other people arrived in the camp from time to time, including Bob Hodges in the RAF, who had crashed in Brittany on his way back from bombing Stettin or Berlin, and had made his way down to Toulouse with his sergeant-gunner[61] – the rest of the crew had jumped before he force-landed and he hadn't seen them again, so presumed they had ended up in Germany.

On 4 September 1940 Flt Lt Hodges was flying home a Hampden Bomber from No. 49 Squadron when it was damaged by ground fire. His crew-member had not heard his command to bale out.

I was allowed to go for a few days to Raphael Monti, who had an English wife, and who lived nearby. We had made their acquaintance through a Jew, who took us over there and liked them very much. He was a celebrated 'cellist and had to leave Italy because of political trouble, and was now farming in a mild way. They were charming to me and we had lovely concerts every evening.

In 2005 we spent some time looking for this particular house. We followed our usual practice of asking an elderly looking person. After following a few false scents we found a man who remembered going, as a child, to concerts given by the Montis. He directed us to the house, Les Chabries at Pradère-les-Bourguets which is now owned by an English family. I confirmed it was the correct place by speaking to the former owner who now lives in Toulouse and who had known the Montis. It turned out that Raphael Monti was violently anti-fascist and had had to leave Italy as a consequence.

  chez M Monti
  Pradère-les-Bourguets
  Léguevin (Hte Garonne)
  October 8 1940

My darling Mummie

You can't think how excited I was when I got your letter yesterday – the first news I had had from you since the beginning of May. I am sending a telegram today to tell you to continue writing by the same way, and the British Ambassador will forward the letters to me. I do wish I had gone with Thomas Rennie. We left the column at exactly the same place, I believe, though I didn't see him go. Do ask him to write to me and say how he passed. I see no hope of coming his way at present, I'm afraid and am in the depths of despair about the whole thing. Can anyone suggest anything else. You remember 'I'm afraid I can't tell you where I am' out of all my old letters! I am now staying on parole with an English lady whose sister is Miss Johns, Imperial Hotel, Barnstaple, Devon, whom you could write to to find out all about her sister. M Monti is a celebrated violin-cellist. I cannot stay here too long of course and shall return to the camp again – it may be moving elsewhere in the near future. They have given me my parole with the stipulation of going myself to the police force each week. I shall have to correspond with the authorities at Toulouse before changing my place of residence. There have been several changes at the camp. The Colonel has left and been replaced by an elderly Major. All French military have been replaced by gendarmes, and our soldiery do their own cooking. They seem fairly satisfied with this but life is pretty dull (for) them, as they have less liberty than us.

I shall never get over Thomas Rennie getting back when I have failed, though I am awfully glad he did. A Flying-Officer Hodges joined us a week ago, having made a forced landing in Brittany on his way back from Berlin.

I do hope Papa is better again now. Do tell me how you are yourself and give me as much news of everybody as possible, as I am longing to hear of everyone. Don't try and send any parcels as I think they will get lost, though the Red Cross might get things through. I am quite well enough off for food and money at present. I am glad you got my letter with Fitch's. Has his mother had any more news of him? His address was Bank House, Sheringham, Norfolk. Do you think there is any prospect of my being exchanged against a prisoner in England? Don't think I am content to stay out here, as I am nearly desperate with anxiety to return to you all, only I can't think how to.

I wonder how many letters you have had from me as I must have written dozens by now? The Montis have a very nice house right out in the country and a farm, which they run themselves. For the first time for many months I ate butter yesterday, and it was awfully good. They make it themselves here, and they have also made quite a lot of jam with grapes, melons and figs, as they cannot spare any sugar for jams, and these three fruits don't need any. They just finished picking all the grapes before I arrived.

PS I have just learnt that Mrs Monti and her sister lived a long time at Villa Hortensia, Bordighera and knew cousin Charlie Hardy & Katherine very well – Miss Johns being a great friend of hers. Mrs Monti was a VAD at Guildford Hospital in the Great War, and remembers Freda Giradot just (she was Freda Johns). Also she used to walk out to St Martha's often & look down on Chilworth.

Observant readers will of course have spotted the signal in this letter that there is a hidden message.

The Voluntary Aid Detachment was formed by the linking of the British Red Cross and the Order of St John of Jerusalem in 1909.

Mostly they worked as auxiliary nurses but some performed a wider range of tasks including fund-raising and driving.

I went back to the camp for one day, and then left hurriedly for Toulouse, and then took the train for Marseilles. [*Permission for this move had been granted by the Military Authorities in Toulouse and so parole was not broken.*] Ian Garrow and Bob Hodges were on the train too. We went down first class – probably the least noticeable way.

Bradford's father recorded that 'B was feeling very depressed that he could think of no way to get home and in a code which we had luckily arranged with him before he went out he asked whether we can't suggest any means of escape for him and that he is thinking of moving to Marseilles as it may be easier from there.'

Hodges described how the French had taken them to a French Military Headquarters in order to obtain documentation, a 'Feuille de

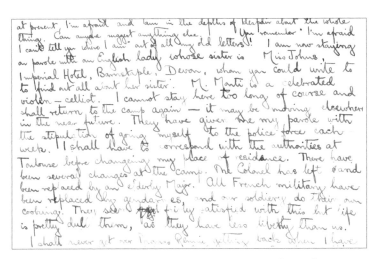

There is a 14-word concealed message in this extract from a letter. Answer at the bottom of Appendix 1.

Demobilisation', which was required in order for men of military age to buy a train ticket. On the way the car ended up in a ditch and when some German troops arrived to assist, their French guards advised them not to say a word. 'We didn't — they pulled us out of the ditch and we were off' he said.[62]

When we were having a meal in a restaurant car, the attendant whispered to me 'Je suis très content d'entendre votre accent, Monsieur'. I was slightly taken aback, as I hoped my accent was less English, but he was very friendly and offered to give us our meal without coupons — you had to give coupons for so many grammes of meat, bread, cooking fats etc. before each meal — and to hide us in his office, when they came to inspect papers etc. Actually I had a set of food coupons, and my false papers were in reasonable order, although unfortunately they were Polish.

We were told we should never be able to find a room in a hotel in Marseilles as the town was packed, but the attendant told us of a small hotel where we could try.

The train got in in the evening, and we got out of the station — where there was a great crowd — and went quickly to the hotel. They gave us two rooms, so Bob Hodges and I had to share one with a very small double bed, in which we slept indifferently.

Next morning we went out, got a cup of coffee and a roll, and walked to the American Consulate (British Branch) which was in the old British Consulate. There we saw Capt. Deane, from Cannes or Nice, who told us he couldn't do anything for us, except give us a little money, and that there were about 150 British soldiers at the Fort St-Jean, who were given every liberty. He told us we had better go down there, and said there was a hope of being repatriated, but didn't sound very optimistic about it. He also told me that Thomas Rennie and Ronnie Mackintosh-Walker had passed through at the beginning of August, and had gone on by train to Spain with visas and passports in order. If only I had found them, I might have been home too.

We walked off to the Vieux Port, and then on to the Fort St-Jean, as we hadn't enough money to stay in the town, and it sounded safe enough to go there – though I was rather dubious.

The fort was an old Vauban-type fortress, built on a rock in the sea with a draw-bridge leading to it, and looked a most unhealthy place to try and escape from. Inside one went up a long flight of steps, and through tunnels but the guarding was very slack.

When I came to the top, the first person I saw was, to my amazement, Freddie Fitch. After various wanderings round Perpignan and the frontier, he had come to Marseilles – I forget whether he had been arrested or not. No one seemed very interested in checking up on us, and Freddie showed us to an untidy room with a stone floor and some eight beds, where five officers were already living.

He was in a great hurry to go off and meet someone, and took me off with him. On our way he told me all the news since we had last met and also what he was up to here. There were about thirteen officers and over one hundred soldiers in the fort, conditions were uncomfortable and dirty, but on the other hand no one bothered about you, you could come and go as you pleased and bed and breakfast was free, which was a great thing.

When he first arrived in Marseilles Bradford expected, in a vague way, that the British Secret Service might be organising some channel by which people could escape. He found however that there was nothing of the sort but that a group of officers, of whom Capt. Fitch was apparently the moving spirit, was busy trying to establish such a channel.[63]

Freddie was trying to get people out of the country and had several plans in hand, and said I should be a great help, as there weren't many officers who spoke French, and he had dozens of people to meet each day with a view to planning something.

We went to two cafés – one at the end of the Canabière and the other facing the Vieux Port, at each of which we met someone – an Italian, who had fought against Franco commanding a Foreign brigade in Spain was one of them – and we rather furtively exchanged news over a Dubonnet.

Freddie said that most meetings were disappointing but that you couldn't afford to let the least chance slip and had to keep your fingers on all the threads. We then went on to the Bar New York, also facing the Vieux Port, which was the main rendez-vous of British officers. There we met Colin Hunter, Adjutant of the Camerons, and several others, who had also drifted to Marseilles and were wealthy enough to live in the town.

After we had talked for a bit Freddie and I went and lunched on bouillabaisse at a cheap café close by.

In the afternoon, I went with some of the others to the Sailors Mission, which Revd Caskie from Paris was running. Here there were a large number of British refugees of all types, whom he was looking after as best he could. I met an Austrian-Jew, Das, and other queer characters, all of whom promised to try and help you get out, but, one felt, must have said the same thing to dozens of others.

There were a few Black Watch soldiers at the fort, Monaghan, Price, Clartain etc. who I knew quite well, but whom I couldn't help much. Two of them told me that I had been mainly responsible for their escape as I had gone over to them at one of our camps, and said 'for heavens sake, try and make a break for it before they get you into a train', but I don't remember doing it at all.

Most of the officers at the Fort didn't seem to be very active in their efforts to find ways of getting away, and spent much of their time and limited money enjoying themselves. I had got a few thousand francs together by the time I came to Marseilles, from the American Embassy at Vichy and various other sources, but was keeping it carefully.

Very soon I was as much involved as Freddie in plots and plans, and had a mass of meetings each day. One thought one was leaving the next day on several occasions, but then a mass of things intervened, boat's sailings were cancelled etc. and one's plans came to naught.

Doubtless these failures had made many people almost give up trying, and if one hadn't been such an impossible optimist one would have done the same.

Various projects were on foot for getting away in a small sailing boat, and one night I was meant to be going in place of someone who had ratted at the last moment – a Gunner. I couldn't find the party in time, and they went off. There was an awful gale a few days later, and presumably they were drowned, as they were never heard of again. However, we all thought they had got away to Gibraltar at the time.

Other plans were to get on a steamer going to North Africa, Syria, Greece or Dakar – I could have made one for Greece, which wasn't in the war, but I wasn't sure that I would be any further forward. Various people had gone over to North Africa, but nothing had since been heard of them, although they had promised to get word back; there were rumours that they had been arrested and were now breaking stones in the Sahara. It was not very difficult to get on a boat either as a stowaway with the help of a sailor, or disguised among a Foreign Legion draft.

On one occasion Bradford managed greatly to surprise his parents by telephoning them from Marseilles.[64]

I had got fairly good at cutting stamps out of lino, and then, with a purple ink pad, forging an official looking document, which the French fonctionnaire loves. I made one saying I was British and had authority to travel to Perpignan for 48 hours, and stamped it with a copy of the American Consulate General's Seal, complete with eagles, and also with 'Securité Générale Bouches-du-Rhone', which may have meant nothing at all. Armed with this, I took a small party of men to Perpignan, and handed them to a guide, who promised to get them into Spain.

Several parties went down this way, but the majority were returned to France, and we stopped any more going down when we heard that the Spaniards were handing them over to the Germans at Biarritz.

I didn't go over myself again, as I thought I ought to try and get, or help some of the men away. I could speak French well compared to them and could help Freddie quite a lot in this way.

One night Freddie and I went to the Splendide, the best hotel in the town, to meet an American, and arrange a money transaction, as a big scheme of Freddie's was about to come into operation. It was rather queer sitting in the lounge on a sofa with some of the German Armistice Commission on one side and Italians on the other. They could hardly have realised that two British officers were so near them. When we came to discussing our plan, he took us up into his room, and then into the bathroom. He was a born conspirator, and turned on the taps so that we shouldn't be overheard, and enjoyed himself enormously.

The scheme was due to come off the next night, and included the purchase of a large boat, which could carry about 150, arranging to get the men to a place on the coast and then embarking them. Only the final purchase of the ship needed fixing up and was being done by Freddie with a gang of gangsters. I went down that morning to see the Italian about something else, and while talking to him, found that he was trying to get about eighty men away that night and could also take some of ours. On going into his plan we discovered that he had been sold a number of places in our scheme by the same gang, and our scheme began to look less certain.

At about 18.00hrs a strong wind got up and soon a full gale was blowing. However, all arrangements had been made, and at 22.00hrs men in small parties left the fort, and made their way to a small cove just out of the town on the opposite side of the port.

By 23.30hrs our complete party was assembled, over 100 soldiers and some thirty important foreigners, including Italians and Germans, some of whom had several suitcases as baggage. Sentries were posted on the approaches, and we met part of the gang who were organising the ship.

Col Edward Bradford recorded: 'B said that the police could not have helped noticing this unusual flow of people carrying suitcases and other impedimenta at such an hour of the night but they turned a blind eye to it and asked no questions.' [65]

It was blowing like blazes and as we depended on getting people out to the ship in small boats it looked rather hopeless. The gangsters were all for continuing, but said that the boat wouldn't put out until we handed over the money – about 300,000 Frs, which Freddie and I were carrying in our pockets. We didn't want to let the least chance slip, and finally handed over the cash through an American doctor, who was also involved, and was certain all was well.

We waited for some hours with various alarms, but with nothing happening, and everyone getting very cold. Finally at 03.00hrs we decided to call the whole thing off and to try again another night.

Everyone started off together back into the town and the scene was rather like a railway station when the last train has just come in. There were no police about, and all returned safely to the Fort. That day we got hold of the chief of the gang, a Rumanian I think, and he promised that everything would be all right for the night after, but said that he couldn't give us the money back, as it had had to be paid out.

The next night, we went through the same performance again, without success. There was no wind but the boat never turned up, and we had to disperse again. After this we got hold of the chief gangster in a café and Freddie tried to get the money out of him, while six of us sat downstairs to stop him getting away and to prevent anyone interfering. Later Freddie got hold of several of the gang and prosecuted them in the normal way, saying that they had promised to get him out of the country and had stolen the money.

The three gangsters were a Rumanian, a Jew and a Levantine called Ostenga, Guichard and Figuere.[66] *After the abortive escape attempt Capt. Fitch, Bradford and other leaders of the group spent several days searching Marseilles for them. Eventually they found the Levantine in an estaminet. They took him outside and demanded the money. While frightened he inevitably said that his other conspirators had the money. The British, numbering about 10, forced him to take them to the others. As they entered the café to meet the Jew and Rumanian they saw the barman handing over revolvers. Some rapid action ensured that the two were hustled outside without a shot being fired. The money was demanded and, as before, not forthcoming. Determined that these rascals did not go unpunished the British took them back to their barracks at Fort St-Jean and effectively imprisoned them on a bread and water diet for 3 days. The Superintendent of Police, who was pro-British,*

*advised that this imprisonment could not continue and that prosecu-
tion through the civil court would be a wise course of action. It turned
out that the three were well known to the police who were keen to get
them on a charge. When Fitch pointed out that it would be awkward
if questions of what the money was for and where it came from were
raised during the case the Inspector told him not to worry about that as
the Judge would be told all about it beforehand and the defence wouldn't
be allowed to go into the matter. The case was taken to court and went
exactly as the Police had said!*[67]

*No action was taken against Freddie, but three gangsters got
about three years hard labour and turned up in the same prison as
Bob Hodges.*

*Flt Lt Hodges had made an attempt to escape by stowing away on a
ship to Oran but had been detected and imprisoned. Hodges remained
in jail until after Bradford had left Marseilles. They did meet once
more at an investiture at Buckingham Palace where both were receiving gallantry medals. In 1941 Hodges escaped via Perpignan and his
later wartime flying activities, often delivering or collecting SOE oper-
atives in Lysander aircraft are legendary. Escaping was clearly a good
career move, for Hodges rose to become Air Chief Marshal Sir Lewis
Hodges, KCB, CBE, DSO and Bar, DFC and Bar.*

When I first got to Marseilles, I wrote to the Eire Embassy
under another name, Patrick Koe, to ask for a passport. I
said I had been on a small ship, bringing lorries up the
Seine to Paris, and had had to run for it when the Germans
arrived. The story about the ship, including the ship's name,
was true, and two of the crew had only been signed on at
the last moment.

After a few days some papers arrived, and I returned them
with two photos. I didn't hear again for some time, and
thought they were not going to play. Actually the passport
came a few days after I had left, and an RAF chap got a hold

of it, got the necessary visas and was home in a fortnight. I got this cheering news when I was languishing in prison.

Two ships came in with French sailors from England, while I was there, and of course everyone had the idea of getting hidden on board, as they were going back for more Frenchmen. It seems extraordinary that we were so soft as to send back all those French men, while they were keeping all of us locked up.

Freddie managed to arrange a sack full of letters on board, and we told everyone to have letters for home in by a certain time. He and I then went down with a large sack of mail to a café, where we handed it over. The letters got home, uncensored, fairly soon.

On one occasion Bradford went to tea with a lady to whom he had an introduction from the Montis. It was as Col Edward Bradford recorded 'somewhat trying as the lady was a rabid Anglophobe, or had become so, and kept on about the British who she was convinced had deserted France in her hour of need and to whom she put down France's collapse entirely.'

I was getting impatient with hanging about. We didn't seem to be having much success with getting people away, and so a small party was going over to Algiers to see how the land lay, and try and arrange for trans-shipping of others who came to Tangier. W-, who spoke French well enough to pass off as a Frenchman, was going, but wouldn't go at the last minute, so I said I would go with Burn [*Capt. H.B. Burn, 7th Northumberland Fusiliers*], who spoke no French, but had been going with W---.

It was a pity Freddie and I couldn't go together, as we got on very well, and he spoke French better than me and was a great plotter. However we decided it was his job to stay and try to get people out of Marseilles, as other officers weren't doing much for the men and he had his fingers in a hundred pies.

I had made the arrangements necessary with the 'Rumanian' (another one), who was very 'windy' and was frightened of being seen with one at all. He was a most annoying chap to do a rendezvous with, as three times out of four he didn't turn up, and when he did, was so furtive that he would never stay in the same place for more than a few minutes.

Captain B.C. Bradford
c/o Rev: Caskie
Sailors Mission
36, rue Forbin
Marseilles
23 October 1940

My darling Mummie

I think this letter may reach you, as it is going another way. I have come down here now, and only wish I had done so right at the beginning when it was easy to move on. Now, I fear, it is almost impossible, but we all live in an atmosphere of hope. In many ways I was very sorry to leave the Montis, as they were the most charming people, but I thought it was the best thing to do.

There are quite a lot of British people collected in Marseilles from all over France and Italy. I met an Ionidas whose nephews I knew at Eton, and I am going to tea with him tomorrow. One meets a great many people all the time. I haven't had another letter from you yet, but I am hoping to any day now. I'm afraid it isn't much good my writing regularly as I am almost certain that most of my letters don't get anywhere.

We are quartered in the Foreign Legion Barracks here, and are well treated and have plenty of liberty. There are five of us in a fairly small, dark and dirty room with no furniture except beds, so that writing is not too easy. We have black coffee at 7.00 a.m., lunch at 11.30 a.m. & supper at 5.30 p.m. – lunch & supper usually consist of stew and we always want something else in the town before going to bed. Somebody managed to get a wireless yesterday, and so I hope we shall be able to get the news again.

This town is absolutely crowded with people – I have never seen streets and pavements so full. The food in this town does not appear to be too scarce, though naturally there is not a great variety.

Before leaving the Montis, we had some lovely musical evenings. He played some pieces by de Falla and Boccherini which I liked very much.

I went to a cinema with Ian Garrow last night. We couldn't get into the one we meant to go to and saw rather a rotten film – a life of Chopin. There was also a news film of Mers-el-Kebir which was received without any demonstrations of feelings at all. [*The showing of this news-reel was undoubtedly a ploy by the Vichy Government to try and stir up anti-British feelings. Bradford's report of the audience reaction confirmed his general impression of the French attitude as a whole towards the British which was decidedly friendly.*]

I'm afraid I can't tell you when we are likely to move at all! I only wish I could. There is a performance of Gounod's Faust on Friday, which I think I am going to. I am told it is a very good company.

You can address any letters for me as above and I will keep the Padré in touch if we are moved on. He is the Church of Scotland Chaplain from Paris and is in charge here as all the other British ones have returned to England from Paris and everywhere. He is an awfully nice man, and we all went up to the Service in the Mission last Sunday afternoon.

Revd Donald Caskie commandeered the British Seamen's Mission in Marseilles and was conscripted to service by Allied Intelligence. The Mission became a vital link on the escape route for POWs and Caskie fed, clothed and gave men shelter before sending them through the Pyrenees with forged papers. Unfortunately this escape route, in which Bradford was involved in establishing, did not become fully operational until after he left Marseilles. Caskie became known as 'The Tartan Pimpernel'.

In the above letter of 23 October, is another hidden message. 'Going Oran.' Bradford has used a simple Caesar shift code to disguise the 'go' part of his message. The plain text of the paragraph gives the additional message 'I think I am going on Friday'.

Clockwise from top:
Col Sir Edward R.C. Bradford
(1836–1911).
Col Sir Evelyn Bradford (1869–1914).
Capt. Ronnie Hardy (1882–1915).
Commissioning photo of 2nd Lt Bill
Bradford in 1932.

*(Unless otherwise detailed, all photos are
from the author's archive)*

Bradford's introduction to sailing was with fellow Black Watch subalterns Mick Baker-Baker, Michael Young and Bernard Fergusson at West Mersea.

Bill Bradford with his parents Col Edward A. Bradford DSO (1879–1859) and Margaret L. Bradford (1878–1972) in Mull, 1934.

Bill Bradford and his sister Felicity sailing at Loch Ken, Dumfriesshire in 1934. Note the jury-rig.

The Officers of 1st Bn The Black Watch on going to war, September 1939.

Insets: 2nd Lt A.D. Telfer-Smollett, Lt and QMS Allison, Maj. R.H.C. Drummond-Wolff, Lt C.L. Melville, Capt. M. McPhail (Padre), Lt Maiden (Medical Officer).

Back row: Lt R.U.A. Sandford, 2nd Lt J.R.P. Moon, Lt P.S. Douglas, 2nd Lt E.F.D. Campbell, 2nd Lt J. Graham, Capt. G.C. Howard, Lt R.N. Jardine-Paterson, 2nd Lt S.A.V. Russell, 2nd Lt A.D. Rowan-Hamilton, 2nd Lt A.D.H. Irwin, Lt A.M. Grant-Duff, 2nd Lt N.G.A. Noble, 2nd Lt J.E.K. Spratt.

Front row: Capt. G.P. Campbell-Preston, Capt. J.A. Hopwood, Maj. N.D. Stevenson, Maj. M.A. Carthew-Yorston, Lt-Col. C.G. Stephen, Lt B.C. Bradford (Adjutant), Maj. W.F. Dundas, Maj. G.H. Milne, Maj. O.G.H. Russell. *(Photo by kind permission of The Black Watch Regimental Museum)*

Inspection of the 1st Bn Black Watch by the King and Queen, 27 September 1939. From left to right in inspection party: Lt Bill Bradford, Capt Pat Campbell-Preston and Lt-Col C.G. Stephen, HM King George VI, HM Queen Elizabeth. Lt Noel Jardine-Paterson is the officer nearest the camera and L/Cpl Gardiner is front left marker.

RMS *Mona's Queen* carried the 1st Bn Black Watch to Cherbourg on 5-6 October 1939. She was sunk at Dunkirk. *(By kind permission of John & Marion Clarkson, Ships in Focus)*

Château de Mantenay. where Bradford sought refuge on 24 June 1940.

Bradford walked over 600 miles as a fugitive, mostly on minor roads and tracks. This section is between the Loire and the Cher.

Château de Nanteuil, where Bradford was a student in 1930 and arrived as a fugitive on 7 July 1940.

Mme Théry, seated (*née* Betty Gardnor Beard) with, left to right: Andrew and Nicola Bradford and Frédéric Théry at Château De Nanteuil in 2002.

Les Sicaudières, where Bradford spent his first night in unoccupied France on 9 July 1940. The farmer's granddaughter-in-law points out the stable where he slept.

Above: Dr Paul Mounicq, the French Rugby International who guided Bradford over the Pyrenees. *(By kind permission of Midi-Olympique, France)*

Left: Château de las Tronques.at Moulis. After his second crossing into Spain, Bradford reached this château hungry, exhausted, impoverished and with worn-out boots.

The Pyrenees looking north-west from Spain towards Pic de Troumouse and Pic de la Mounia. Bradford and his companions skirted the summits of these mountains before descending into this valley.

Château d'Envalette at Monferran-Savès. Depot 602. Three barbed-wire fences encircled this French POW camp intended for German prisoners-of-war.

Fl. Lt Bob Hodges (later Air Chief Marshall Sir Lewis Hodges, KCB, CBE, DSO, DFC). A fellow prisoner at Depot 602, Monferran-Savès. *(From Sir Lewis Hodges' collection by kind permission of Lady Hodges)*

Château de Caumont, Cazaux-Savès in Gers. Bradford visited this château on parole during his imprisonment at Depot 602.

Les Chabries at Pradère-les-Bourguets in Haut-Gauronne, Midi, the home of Raphael Monti, a refugee from the Italian fascist regime. Bradford visited several times while on parole from Depot 602.

Fort St-Jean, Marseilles. A French Foreign Legion barracks, it formed an open prison for British military personnel in 1940. Unlike most, Bradford never gave his parole.

Carte d'Alimentation issued at Monferran-Savès, 27 August 1940.

Above: Maj. R.N. Brinckman, Grenadier Guards, from a portrait by Maurice Codner dated 1941. *(With kind permission of Sir Theodore Brinckman).*

Left: Capt. Freddie Fitch (Royal Norfolk Regt, senior British officer at Fort St-Jean, Marseilles) and Capt. Ian Garrow (Highland Light Infantry) in Marseilles in 1940. *(From Sir Lewis Hodges' collection by kind permission of Lady Hodges)*

The *Djebel Nador* on which Bradford stowed away at Marseilles for Algiers. *(By kind permission of Photo Marius Bar, Toulon)*

US Foreign Service ID issued in Marseilles, 21 October 1940.

Emergency Certificate issued by the US Consulate in Algiers on 5 November 1940.

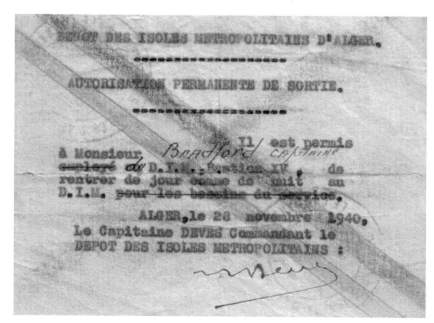

Permit issued in Algiers on 28 November 1940.

Above left: Capt. B.C. Bradford; ID photo taken in Algiers, 1940.

Above right: Permis de Sejour issued to Bradford in Algiers, November 1940.

Left: Message contained within the envelope lining sent to Bradford's parents. The instruction to 'look inside envelope' was contained in a coded message within the letter.

The Yacht Club at Algiers in 1955, apparently little changed since 1940. The unskilled crew of *L'Odetic* sailed off these moorings in a strong wind. *(By kind permission of Pierre Plevan)*

Sayonara, originally constructed as Archduke Charles Stephen of Austria's private yacht, was converted to a Royal Naval Armed Boarding Vessel. *(By kind permission of Beken of Cowes)*

t-Col. B.C. Bradford, DSO, MBE, MC, representing the 51st Highland Division, ys a wreath at the war cemetery in St-Valery-en-Caux, 2 September 1944.

t-Col. B.C. Bradford, DSO and bar, 1BE, MC, CO of the 5th Black Watch, ads the Roll of Honour at Drumhead ervice, 10 June 1945.

Lt-Col. B.C. Bradford, MBE, MC, in 1944.

HM Queen Elizabeth, The Queen Mother inspecting the 2nd Bn Black Watch in Dortmund in 1954. Maj.-Gen. Neil McMicking, CB, CBE, DSO, MC and Lt-Col B.C. Bradford, DSO, MBE, MC. *(By kind permission of the* Dundee Courier*)*

Telegram from Bradford to his parents arrouncing his arrival in Gibraltar.

Bill Bradford in 1990. *(By kind permission of Katy Bradford)*

11

On the Home Front (2)

At home we had left Bradford's parents back in the middle of July, desperate for news of their son. They had no idea whether he had been killed, injured or captured. Eventually, over six weeks after St-Valery, they received the first definite news.

POST OFFICE
TELEGRAM

Received: 7.57
26 July 40
PRIORITY – MRS E A BRADFORD, EMPSHOTT
LODGE, LISS, HANTS
INFORMATION RECEIVED FROM THE MILITARY
ATTACHE MADRID REPORTS THAT CAPT B.C.
BRADFORD BLACK WATCH IS ALIVE IN FRANCE
LETTER FOLLOWS =
Under Secretary of State
For War

The letter to which this telegram referred shed no further light on the situation.

A week later Bradford's letter, sent from Bélâbre on 14 July, reached home to the very obvious delight of his mother.

Empshott Lodge
Liss, Hants

3 August 1940
My own beloved boy,
Thank God you are alive and well and we have got a letter from you at last. God has been with you all the way as He always is, and has given you strength and a great courage darling – so many have been praying for you daily and have written telling me so – besides every member of the family, including Spicers and Fyffes, Cousin Dorothy Knight – Kitty – Cecil – The Willmotts – Sargeants – The dear Graces – Miss Keane – and many other true friends – and I know He will never leave you, and will guide us in the way to keep you best.

We are doing everything possible as you will feel sure, and have many irons in the fire – we got your letter yesterday – what you have accomplished is truly wonderful – God bless you. I am glad and thankful for the Kind American – perhaps he can help you further? – We are all flourishing and most peaceful here, except that Papa has been in bed again – This long anxiety has been a great strain on him but now the blessed Knowledge of your safety will soon put him right again I trust.

We heard from Adela that she is going to have another baby! Isn't it amazing? She is trying to book a passage home this month, but I doubt if she will be allowed to – she is expecting the babe in Decr. So are Peggie Tweddell, Betty Rose and Peggie Knight, aren't they all gallant?!

We have had the Rices here for 9 weeks, as they wanted to leave Danefield – They were a great strain as they are both rather dotty on close acquaintance and insist on doing exactly what they like, always! They have gone on to Maimie and Bill now. We have got a very nice new Vicar, isn't it a blessing. The garden is simply packed with vegetables. I gave heaps to At. Norah who came over 2 days ago – and the potato patch has grown a splendid crop, but we must cut some more to the south when you come home as it is rather shady and draws them up rather.

David did so well in cricket this half, and in the finals which they won, made 72 not out and got 4 catches – he is head of his house – games and library next half, isn't it splendid? Di is at home and doing lots of useful things – making lots of jam etc. – she went up to London to Grannie E for 2 nights this week for a dance and much enjoyed herself, at a very amusing Play and bathing at Roehampton. F [Felicity] asked me to give you her hugging love, on the 'phone, & Papa and Di send theirs too, in huge masses. Sir Arthur [Sir Arthur Wauchope, Colonel of the Black Watch] thinks they may be able to send you a little parcel from Perth, he goes up there tonight. It is simply glorious being able to write and hear from you again my darling, tho' I daresay you may not be able to again just yet. God Bless you all the time – we too Thank Him continually – that His is the power and the glory –
Your always loving proud Mother

This letter never reached Bradford as, by the time it arrived in Bélâbre, he had moved on. It is an astonishing reflection of how some facets of normal peacetime life still operated that Mrs Bradford's letter was returned-to-sender by M. Surreaux, was delivered back to Hampshire and thus survived for posterity.

As instructed Bradford's parents communicated the information to the War Office and the Red Cross. There was inevitably confusion and a dearth of information for, by the time the letter had been received Bradford had moved on from Bélâbre and was actually making his first attempt to cross the Pyrenees. On 6 August the Red Cross wrote:

Dear Mrs Bradford,

Miss Thornton has passed on to me your letter of August 3. enclosing a portion of one from your husband [sic] Captain B.C. Bradford, 1st Battalion, Black Watch, giving a very interesting account of how he escaped and made his way to unoccupied France.

Since you saw Miss Thornton on Friday, we have received a cable from the International Red Cross Committee at Geneva reporting him as a Prisoner of War in unoccupied French territory.

We do not at present know what the position is likely to be for British Officers in this part of France but as soon as the situation is clearer we will, of course, let you know at once.

As his mother had indicated, many members of the family were trying to help and in any way they could. Bradford's step-grandmother Edith Mary, Lady Bradford, widow of Sir Edward, late of Scotland Yard, joined in. She had taken an active part in public life after Sir Edward's death and had been Chairman of Westminster City Council. It seems today that some of these efforts were, at best, fruitless or even counter-productive by adding to the confusion but at the time everyone was clutching at straws.

BRITISH EMBASSY
MADRID

9 August 1940

Dear Lady Bradford

I am answering your letter on behalf of the Ambassador.

Your grandson Captain Bradford is not in German-occupied France, but at Bélâbre [Indre], where with others he is detained by the French Authorities. As you know, the USA are now in charge of the affairs of British subjects in France, and there is an English official working with the American Consulate at Marseilles, to whom your grandson's situation has been reported.

I am afraid that getting English soldiers out of France is not at all an easy matter, but if and when it is possible arrangements have been made for providing visas and money.

I would suggest that Colonel Bradford should approach the American Embassy in London with a view to getting into touch with his son and possibly providing him with funds.
Yours sincerely
Alan Lubbock
Major R A
Assistant Military Attaché
P.S. I should be grateful if you would remember me to your brothers, Col Nicholson & Reggie. You will not remember me, but we have met at Bereleigh. I hope all is well there. AL

Of course some efforts were clearly wasted as by the time Lady Bradford wrote to his mother Bradford was, once again, detained by the French and several hundred miles from Bélâbre.

12 August 1940
My dearest Maggie,
You will be pleased to have this – giving a prospect of help if possible to Berenger.
I wrote a few days ago to the Vicomtesse de la Ganmse – as their home in France is a few miles North of Tours & Nelly & I lunched with them there 3 years ago – & Godfrey very often stays with them. It is now a Hospital during War.
I thought she would be able to get her letters to France and might have friends in the neighbourhood of Bélâbre.
Love from yr. Affectionate
E.M. Bradford

Mrs Bradford wrote on 15 August to the War Office:

On 3 August I had the honour to inform you that I had received certain information regarding my son Capt. B.C. Bradford, Adjt., 1st Battn. The Black Watch, who had been reported to me as 'believed missing' on 26 July.

As I have received no acknowledgement of my letter I presume it has not reached you and therefore repeat the information, communicated by my son. His letter was dated 14 July from Bélâbre – Indre – Chez. M. Surreaux – Villa Bellevue. He was taken prisoner on 12 June escaped on 19 & after trying to cross the Channel, walked to unoccupied France where he is now detained at the above address. He was in civilian clothes and it seems most unjust that we should repatriate French soldiers instead of exchanging them for British detained in unoccupied France.

Advice started flooding in and it is interesting to glean from them the somewhat unorthodox wartime arrangements for dealing with correspondence. The following is an extract from a letter to Dorothea Brinton, a friend of Mrs Bradford, from Mrs Wyndham Tour wife of Brigadier Tour, Military Attaché at Madrid:

17 August 1940
I am writing this letter for Wyndham, who asks me to beg your forgiveness for not doing so himself. But we never know when a 'bag' is going to England, and therefore he has much official stuff to get off at short notice, today – so I am doing his private letters for him. He says that Major Dodds [Late HBM Consul, Nice] is now working with the USA Consulate at Marseilles, on Captain Bradford's case, and is hoping to get his release. Wyndham's assistant MA Major Lubbock has already written to Mrs Bradford to suggest that she should get in touch with the USA Embassy, London and ask them to help as a channel of communication, with Capt. Bradford in France.
I do hope she has got this letter safely. All goes by Air now, & several planes have had trouble tho' I believe only one has been lost.
We have just come back here from Lisbon, which is crowded with refugees from France, & Wyndham's office is working day and night, getting soldiers over the Frontier – British, Polish, French.

Such fantastic stories of escapes and hardships and all with one idea only, and that is, to get to grips again with the Germans.

If there is anything more we can do, do please write; — if we get further news, I'll write to Mrs Bradford.

Frustratingly the advice, even when no doubt 'steered' by British Embassy staff, was not always helpful as this reply from the splendidly named official relates:

THE FOREIGN SERVICE
OF THE UNITED STATES OF AMERICA
AMERICAN EMBASSY
LONDON

22 August 1940

Madam,

The Embassy has received your letter of August 15 1940 enclosing one addressed to your son in France. As the Embassy has no means of forwarding your letter other than through the regular post, it is returned to you herewith.

You may be confident that the American Consul General at Marseille will do everything he properly can to assist your son. The Embassy is unable to send funds to him for you but the Consul General at Marseille has British official funds which he can advance to your son.

Yours very truly

For the Ambassador

Theodore C Achilles

Third Secretary of Embassy

Theodore Carter Achilles, 1905–86, while serving as director of the State Department's Division of Western European Affairs in 1947–49, was one of the main architects of the North Atlantic Treaty, the founding document of NATO. He was also US Ambassador to Peru, 1956–60.

Other advice gave a word of caution that ill-advised communication with Bradford might place him in greater jeopardy. On 24 August the Red Cross wrote:

> *Dear Mrs Bradford,*
> *I have received your letter of 7 August, asking us to forward one to Captain Bradford.*
> *The position with regard to officers in unoccupied France is extremely delicate at the moment, and we think it very inadvisable that any steps should be taken which might draw attention to their whereabouts. We are, therefore, returning the letter which you sent for Capt. Bradford, but of course, if you yourself wish to send it, there is nothing to prevent you from doing so, as postal communications have been re-established with unoccupied France, and the letter can be posted in the ordinary way.*

Bradford was finally able to bring the situation up to date with a telegram on 16 September after many weeks of imprisonment at Monferran-Savès.

AT MONFERRAN SAVES GERS WRITE AIRMAIL
AMBASSADOR LISBONNE WELL = BRADFORD

The telegram didn't explain much and during this time letters from Bradford were arriving from previous locations in France. The situation at home must have remained confusing. On 18 September Lady Ampthill, Chairman of the War Organisation of the Red Cross, wrote:

> *Dear Mrs Bradford,*
> *Thank you very much for your letter about your son. It is most kind of you to have sent me an extract of the letter and I am sending it on to the Foreign Office to see whether anything can be done.*

I do hope you will get news of him soon, and I shall be most grateful if you will let me know at once if you do.

Two days later Alan Lubbock wrote from the British Embassy, Madrid with a rather accurate guess.

I have today got your letter dated 11 September and was very much interested and extremely sorry to hear about your son. I heard recently that a Captain Garrow, who previously was at Bélâbre too, was later at Monferran–Savès [Gers], and it is possible that your son may be there too; but this is only a guess. Efforts are being made to locate and help officers and soldiers confined in France but it is a difficult business. As soon as I hear anything further I will let you know.

All of these somewhat informal means of communication appear to have been well ahead of the officials, however, for on 23 September 1940 the Casualty Branch of the War Office wrote:

Madam,
I am directed to acknowledge your letter dated 12 September 1940, and to inform you that the first official notification concerning Lieutenant B.C. Bradford, The Black Watch, that this Department received, was 'alive in France', at the end of July.

Since then, no further information has been received other than that contained in your previous communications.

I am to add that if any immediately further information is available, it will be transmitted to you, and to ask that you will forward any address of Lieutenant Bradford or other information of importance which may come into your possession.

A note on this letter indicates that on this occasion Mrs Bradford had been tardy in reporting Bradford's own telegram of 16 September as their letters had crossed.

Bradford's parents kept up the pressure. There is a hint of frustration in this reply from Lady Ampthill at the Red Cross dated 27 September 1940:

Dear Mrs Bradford,
Thank you so much for your letter. It is most kind of you to give us the information you received from your son at once, and I am sending this on immediately to the Foreign Office so that they might know. They are very much exercised about Capt. Bradford, and I know will do all they can.

On 30 September Mrs Bradford replied seeking to clarify how she might communicate with her son:

Dear Lady Ampthill
Many thanks for your kind letter of 22 September and I hope you will forgive my troubling you again. Naturally we are very anxious to communicate with our son, but the letter from your dept. dated 24 August ref: [MS/JW – A/O 947] says 'The position with regard to Officers in unoccupied France is extremely delicate at the moment, and we think it very inadvisable that any steps should be taken to draw attention to their whereabouts.' Will you very kindly let me know if this advice still holds good or whether it is now considered safe to write to individuals situated as he is?

As it happened detailed advice came from another and what must have been a surprising quarter. While Bradford paid a visit to Revd Donald Caskie soon after his arrival in Marseilles this was actually some days after the following letter was written. It seems that Bradford's co-escapee Freddie Fitch's parents had arranged for this letter to be forwarded to Colonel Bradford. This seems likely since mention is made in Bradford's letter of 8 October of a letter being sent with one of Fitch's. This would have been sent at some point

*between their meeting at Bélâbre and their parting after their first
attempt for Spain.*

From THE CHURCH OF SCOTLAND, OVERSEAS
DEPT
Office 121 George Street
Edinburgh 2
4 October 1940
Dear Sir,
*I am very pleased to be able to let you have a piece of information
which without doubt will bring you cheer and comfort.*

*The Revd Donald C Caskie, formerly Church of Scotland minister
in Paris, after much trial and privation, managed to reach Marseilles,
where he has now been for some time as a refugee. A considerable time
ago Mr Caskie took over charge of a large hostel for other British refugees who have been and still are under his care. He has sent me a
number of cablegrams giving me the names and addresses of relatives of
men whom he is looking after. His most recent telegram gives me your
address and asks me to let you have the following message —*

FITCH BANKHOUSE SHERINGHAM NORFOLK
FREDERICK HERE
In another cable Mr Caskie says —

'*Refugees here would value news from home by telegram or airmail, two words would suffice to bring them happiness.*'

*So I give you information about the methods of communication.
There are various means: a] you may dispatch an ordinary letter, the
postage being 3d for the first ounce, and 1½d for every additional oz.
b] you may send an airmail letter, the postage being 5d for the first
oz. and 3d for every additional oz.; or, c] you may send a cablegram.
Letters must be brief, contain no enclosures of any kind, deal solely
with personal matters and make no reference whatsoever to the fact
of your relative being a soldier [if he is one], but simply use his full
name on the envelope; nor should any reference be made of his rank*

or military attachment in the letter itself, and no reference at all be made to war affairs. Letters, however, sent by ordinary mail take a very long time to go – perhaps two months or more. Airmail may be somewhat delayed, but it is certainly speedier. The address is –

Full name of relative [thus, Frederick Fitch]
Care Reverend Caskie
36 Rue de Forbin
Marseilles.
Some of those who have already had information about their men have inquired of me whether they should endeavour to send out money to them or clothing etc. Nothing, however, of that nature should be attempted. I understand that our British Government has made an arrangement with the American Embassy and American Consuls to provide relief for British subjects in need in the area covered by unoccupied France and probably in other parts as well.
With all good wishes
Yours sincerely
[signed] J. Macdonald Webster.

It certainly can't have helped when on 6 October the Bradfords received this message from their son indicating another change of address:

TELEGRAPHIEZ VOS NOUVELLES CURLE CAUMONT SAMATAN GERS

This was followed 3 days later by a partly encouraging but somewhat enigmatic wire:

LETTRE RECU ECRIVEZ MEME ROUTE DEMANDEZ RENNIE ECRIRE ATMMENT ACHEVE = BRADFORD

On 8 October Bradford had received his mother's letter and in it news of Rennie's escape. Slow as these communications must have been it was contact of a sort. Ian Garrow who was also imprisoned at Monferran-Savès was so frustrated that he inserted a letter home in one of Bradford's. Garrow wrote:

> *I have tried many different ways of getting letters to you & I hope at least one of them has reached you.*
>
> *However I will presume that you have received nothing & give you a short précis of my adventures up to the present. My wanderings began on 17 June when we were surrounded by the Germans. Myself and 8 men started off to find the British lines & travelling mostly by night and across country. The roads during all this time were crowded with German troops and we had some narrow escapes from capture.*
>
> *About 27 June we heard the French had packed up. We didn't know in which direction to turn. Finally I decided to make for the Channel Islands but when we came within about 60 miles of St-Malo we heard the Germans were there.*
>
> *Nothing for it but to retrace our steps & try for the unoccupied zone. After much walking we reached the Loire when I had to spend 24 hours scouring the neighbourhood for a boat. Found a friendly fisherman who took us across in early morning of July 16. There was only the Cher now to pass, but we did that in style in the ferry.*
>
> *But I soon found out our troubles were by no means at an end. Apart from one or two individuals the French authorities were by no means pleased to see us. After a couple of days in Châteauroux we were taken to Bélâbre – Indre where we found more British soldiers and five officers. When we had been there 10 days rumours were flying around about concentration camps, & we decided to make a dash for it, & try to cross into Spain.*
>
> *I got as far as Cahors where I was arrested. There followed several days in a prison cell until we were moved to this derelict*

château formerly used as prison camp for Germans, all nicely laid out with triple barbed wire fences and sentries. If I could see the slightest chance of escape I would have refused my parole and tried to escape but now that Spain is also interning British soldiers all ways seem closed. In former letters I have asked for food, but that is now unnecessary. Our great needs are soap, sweets and if possible razor blades.

Garrow's parents did receive this for they wrote from Glasgow on 12 October:

Dear Mrs Bradford

Many thanks for your letter with the enclosed letter from our son. A few days ago we had our first letter from him since he was reported missing in the middle of June. It is dated 9 July and written from Monferran. Three weeks ago we had a cable from him giving his address, and we wrote at once, but our letters had evidently not reached him because we had a telegram this week asking us to tele-graph our news.

I am very glad that you have had satisfactory news from your son also. It makes such a difference after the long period of waiting.

It is very difficult to understand why repatriation appears to be altogether one-sided. We read of French soldiers being sent back from England to France if they do not wish to join the forces of De Gaulle.

With every good wish

I am

Yours sincerely

M. Garrow

Meanwhile the Bradfords kept informing the War Office of develop-ments. On 15 October 1940 Mrs Bradford wrote:

Sir,

Since my letter of 24 September I have received a further letter from my son Capt. B.C. Bradford, Black Watch, dated September 9 [received by me on 10 October] giving as his address Depot 602, P G Monferron- Savès, Gers, France – and saying they are interned in a derelict château surrounded by barbed wire with sentries, which recently contained German prisoners. He apparently enjoys a certain amount of liberty as he speaks of going to tea with M & Mme de Noirmont at Château de Caumont, Samatan – so the camp must be in this neighbourhood.

I see Samatan is about 30 miles SW of Toulouse and 20 miles SE of Auch where Capt. Bradford speaks of. He says he is sending his letters to the British Embassy, Lisbon to be forwarded.

Mrs Bradford clearly tried to send more than a letter:

BRITISH EMBASSY
LISBON

30 October 1940

Madam

The Ambassador has asked me to reply to your letter of the 18 October asking whether the Embassy would forward a parcel to your son. The position is as follows: – parcels for prisoners of war cannot be sent from England to Portugal by diplomatic bag, and by ordinary post they take a long time. There is, however, a very efficient organisation in Lisbon instituted by Mrs Ian Campbell, which will arrange for parcels to be sent from Portugal to prisoners of war, payment being made to Mrs Campbell's account at the Westminster Bank, New Oxford Street branch. We have therefore informed Mrs Campbell of your request, but until it is known where your son is at present it will not be possible to despatch a parcel.

The address of Mrs Campbell's organisation is:

JARDIM NOVE DE ABRIL, 5: LISBON

After Bradford had been many weeks at Monferran-Savès the International Red Cross Committee advised:

> *Geneva 30 October 1940*
> *Dear Sir*
> *According to private information received from the Brit. Consulate in Geneva we beg to advise you that*
> *Capt. Bradford B C 1 Bat. Black Watch was in good health at: Depot 602 PG Monferran-Savès, [Gers] France*
> *This information was wired by us on 30 July 1940 to the Prisoners of War Information Bureau*

By early November Colonel Edward Bradford was clearly frustrated by the lack of progress. On 5 November he wrote to Sir Reginald Dorman Smith his MP. Dorman Smith had been Minister for Agriculture from 1939 but was not reappointed by Churchill after Chamberlain's resignation.

> *5 November 1940*
> *Dear Sir Reginald,*
> *As the Member for this Division may I bring to your notice the following facts in regard to my son Capt. B.C. Bradford; he was Adjutant of the 1st Bn Black Watch and was captured by the Germans with most of the 51st Highland Division at St-Valery on 12 June.*
> *On 19 June he escaped and after various adventures reached unoccupied France early in July. There he was detained by the French Military Authorities; after resting a few days he again escaped and made his way over the Pyrenees to Spain by 5 August when the Spanish Authorities apprehended him and sent him and other British soldiers back into France.*
> *On 10 September, the date of his last letter he with one other officer and a few men were accommodated in a Prisoner of War*

Camp, lately used for Germans; they are not really treated as Prisoners as they are on 'liberté surveillé' and are allowed considerable freedom of movement.

I give you these details in the hope that it be brought to the notice of the Government so that steps to obtain the release of these men may be taken.

One hears of Frenchmen being repatriated yet our men are wrongfully detained in France.

No doubt the situation between the two governments is difficult, but if Frenchmen desirous of returning to France were detained here instead of being sent home one would have thought that an exchange might have been practicable.

Regular Officers of several years service and war experience are I am sure badly needed for training our new armies and it seems a waste that any of them should be doing nothing in France if it is possible to extricate them.

Yours very truly

E.A. Bradford [Lt-Col]

Meanwhile the wheels of bureaucracy ground slowly onwards. The War Organisation of the British Red Cross Society wrote on 5 November:

It has recently been arranged that this Department should take over correspondence concerning members of our British Forces who are in unoccupied France. Lady Ampthill therefore passed to us the correspondence she had with you concerning your son.

We have been informed by the French Department of the Foreign Office that, provided a definite camp address is known, there is no reason why people in England should not write to their relatives in unoccupied France.

We have just heard from the Foreign Office that Captain Bradford's address is as follows:-

Depot 602 P.G., Monferron Savès.

It is not quite clear from their letter whether this information has been sent to you, so we thought it better to let you know, even though you may have already received this information.

With regard to parcels, there is at present no parcel post service to unoccupied France. Later on, however, when the position of these men has been clarified, we hope to make some special arrangement by which they may receive parcels, and will not fail to let you know.

It seemed that any attempt by Bradford's parents to get wheels moving merely added to the churn of paperwork.

HOME DEFENCE EXECUTIVE
C/o Mr Rance
Office of Works
Storey's Gate,
SW 1
11 November 1940
My dear Colonel,
Thank you for your letter of 5 November.

I was extremely sorry to hear that your son has had the bad luck to be interned in France, especially as he had evidently so nearly managed to get away. Obviously every effort will have to be made to try and get him repatriated to this country. I am taking the point up with the Foreign Office in the first place, as a matter of urgency, and I hope to be able to write to you very shortly with good, or at least, hopeful news.
Yours ever
R. Dorman-Smith

It is probable that Bradford knew little if anything of these efforts to get 'something done' about his plight. He was clearly of the view that he had to take action rather than to wait for rescue. We rejoin him in Marseilles.

12

Marseilles and North Africa: November 1940-May 1941

They were beginning to try and tighten things up at Fort St-Jean, but we weren't playing much. Officers were sent for and asked to give their parole, but I did not go and nothing happened. Those that did give their parole were told that they could come and take back their parole at any time and that they would then be given 48 hours grace to get clear in.

The Captain, who was responsible for us, was very friendly, and even offered to lend officers 100 Frs, if it was any use to them.

29 October 1940. Almost the last day I was there, McKay and Bernardi arrived, and I had a long talk with them. They said that at St-Léger that day in July they had seen the Germans stopping a certain number of people in the street at the No Entry sign and had not liked to come past. So they had gone back a bit to a farm, where they had stayed for about 2½ months.

Then they had heard that the Germans were coming further South, and had moved on again. They weren't awfully keen on walking too hard, and their attitude was well expressed by McKay – 'Well Sir, we've got here just the same as you in spite of your hurry' to which I was fortunately able to answer, 'Yes, but you haven't been into Spain, and you're not leaving for North Africa tonight.'

[*As it turned out Bernardi and McKay may have had the last laugh as it seems they returned home in April 1941 some 3 months ahead of Bradford.*[68]]

On my way out of the fort for the last time, I heard some-one say, 'Here's the Adjutant,' and found a man, who had been in the Carriers, being brought in by two gendarmes – Clarkin I think it was. I hadn't much time to talk to him then.

That evening I went to Snappy's Bar with Freddie, a place we used to meet some odd types in occasionally, and then had dinner with Burn. We had a good farewell dinner, and a bottle of cheap champagne and then said goodbye to Freddie and went off to meet the Rumanian at an Hotel.

He took us to a room, and we waited until midnight, in the worst quarter of Marseilles, where anything might have hap-pened. Then we walked down to the side of the docks, and waited again in the shadow of a wall, till we were sure that there were no police about. Then up the steps of a railway bridge near a corner of the dock walls, across on to the wall and a jump down the far side, where we lay in shadow, feeling we had made an awful noise.

We had picked up Das, the Austrian Jew, who had helped make a lot of the arrangements, we were helping him across, thinking he would be useful in making enquiries in the docks of Algiers etc.

When we found no one had heard anything, we crept for-ward among carts, barrows and large packages and wine barrels. We had to lie still once, as a Police patrol came up. Then we got quite near the ship, and dashed across an open lighted space up a gangway, and into the side of the ship, the *Djebel Nador*.

[*The* Djebel Nador, *3,168 tons gross, was built by the International Shipbuilding & Engineering Co. Ltd in Danzig, Poland, completed in February 1938. Length 324ft 8in, breadth 35ft 6in, draught 26ft 5in. She was propelled by a two-cylinder Oil Engine, [MAN] and was registered to Marseilles. Her owners were Cie. De Nanigation Mixte. In 1942 her name was changed to NOTO when she was siezed by the Italians. She was sunk by RAF bombs on 30 January 1943 at Bizerta.*]

A man met us there in the darkness, it was a smelly place, where horses and cattle were carried, he took us aft, up a ladder into quite a nice cabin – the steward's I think!

We had to leave our haversacks with the Rumanian as he said we would never get over things with them, but he promised to get them to us in the morning. When mine came, all the useful things had gone, including some tins of pâté – one of them an enormous tin which I had been looking forward to for a long time.

We had always understood that we should be travelling in a cabin and having ordinary food etc. We slept on the floor and couch quite comfortably, but very early in the morning the sailor, whom we had met on board, came in and said we must come out and be hidden at once, as they were searching the ship.

All ships were searched three times to try and catch people who were getting away – by French representatives, then by members of the Italian Armistice Commission and finally by the Germans. We were hurried out and put in the bread store, a small place with a port hole, right in the stern of the ship. It was full of long loaves of bread, which we sat on and among.

To begin with we hid ourselves, but then got careless, and as a result couldn't get hidden again in time when we heard someone coming. It was only another sailor who didn't seem to worry much.

We were there for some hours, till about 13.00hrs the ship sailed and later we saw Fort St-Jean astern of us, and wondered if the others were watching us sail. Our sailing was delayed because they were suspicious that someone was on board and searched very thoroughly. We had been unable to go to the WC and I had some tummy trouble for a few days previously and was longing to go.

We ate some bread and then the sailor came and took us back to the cabin, but after a short time, came again and said we must hide once more, as the Captain was suspicious that there were stowaways, and was going to have another search.

We went up on deck and followed him by short rushes to the bows where we went down a hatch, hurried past the end of the sailors mess – several looked up as we passed – then down a ladder into a store, where there was another trapdoor and ladder going down into the bowels of the ship, where some canvas awnings were stored round the sides and where the anchor chain came down in the middle. It was a horrible place, wet and hot.

We had some bread and half a bottle of water, and later the sailor brought in some cold meat. We merely lay in this place among the canvas – by day, with the sun beating on the sides of the ship, the temperature was terrific and we sweated through everything we had got. The sides of the ship were far too hot to touch and were all round us.

2 November 1940. We got to Algiers about 13.00hrs on the fourth day, I think – it may have been the third, but merely stayed below until about 18.00hrs when the sailor came along and told us to follow him. We did so, along the deck, down the gangway and off along the quay.

As we neared the gates there were quite a lot of people leaving – sailors, labourers etc. and the police stopped and checked some of these including our guide, who was carrying a parcel, but didn't happen to touch us. We went up the steps on to the esplanade, where I paid over the other half of the money, 5,000 Frs each, to the sailor, who had fulfilled his part of the agreement by getting us ashore clear of the police.

I had no idea of the size of Algiers and had pictured a small-ish port and town rather Arab in appearance, whereas actually it is a very big town, modern and typically French.

You can imagine us in this town, having absolutely no idea of where to go, how the place was laid out or anything. It was getting dusk, and we settled to find somewhere to eat, and then ask about my various addresses. I had got the names of various Czechs, Poles, Rumanians etc who might be able to help us, but after having a meal for Frs 9, in a rather dirty restaurant, I found out that three of my addresses were non-existent, one was a poste-restante and so we set off to find the fourth.

We went by tram right up the rue Michelet to near the Hotel St-George and then found the right address, a house divided into three apartments, but no one had heard of my Czech.

I thought we had better get in somewhere, and said I should knock at one of the doors. Burn and Das didn't agree and wanted to go off to a hotel or sleep outside, so I went in alone. I found a door with a visiting card 'M le Conte de C' and knocked. Monsieur came out himself, and I explained who I was and my predicament. He spoke English well and was very pleasant, so was his wife.

After that, I called in the others, and de C said he'd drive us off to the golf club where there was an English woman. He would have put me up if I had been alone, but Das was too much for him. We went off in his Citroen. It was good of him to take us as petrol was non-existent for private motorists.

At the golf club, Miss May was a little overcome, but very glad to meet us. Again Das was rather putting off – he was

very large and thin and very Jewish looking – and she had
a P.G. [*Paying Guest*] staying, a Frenchman, so that she was
dubious about keeping us. Her own position, like that of
all English residents, was not too certain, and also depended
entirely on her position as Secretary of the Club, which
might be closed at any moment.

However, she said we could sleep on sofas downstairs and I
went off with de C to the American Consul-General's house.
Mr Cole was in, and I told him all about us. He then drove back
in the car with us to see the others. After talking for a little
while, they left, and said a car would come in the morning.

*Felix Cole [1887–1969] was the US Consul in Algiers. He became
US Ambassador to Ceylon in 1948.*

3 November 1940. We had a good night as Miss May made us
really comfortable. She got us up fairly early so that we could
wash and then slip up-stairs and be out of the way of the P.G.
Then we had an enormous breakfast with eggs and bacon,
marmalade and every sort of thing.

Taft [*Mr Orray Taft, Jr.*], the Vice-Consul, came in his car
during the morning, and after giving us a shirt and some
underclothes, took us down to the Consulate. We were given
a Certificate stating who we were, and some money, but
Mr Cole said he could do nothing for us, and ought really to
inform the authorities that we were here.

We hadn't expected him to do much, but hoped that he
would be able to drop a hint as to what to do or whom to see.
Taft drove us down to the town and then left us.

Once again we had no idea what to do, but realised, from
what Taft had said, that we were going to have a difficult time
and shouldn't get away easily ourselves, let alone arranging
to help others through. Mr Cole had told us that there were

about 100 British soldiers interned at a place on the coast, who had been on ships in Algiers at the Armistice. Some soldiers, who had drifted over from time to time in Foreign Legion drafts had been locked up too. (I had formed up with one draft at Fort St-Jean, but had been picked out.) However, he didn't tell us that they were just going to be sent home, and didn't suggest that we might be sent there as seamen too.

Actually two Welsh soldiers, who came over after us, and were arrested at once, as they got drunk, were sent down to this place, and the whole lot were sent home via Casablanca about 10 days after our arrival.

We fixed a daily rendezvous with Das, as he wanted us to come and live in the Arab quarter, where I should have been much more conspicuous. Actually he was arrested a few days later. We met various people that day, including a young American with plenty of money, Thiers, who had been in the Foreign Legion for the war. He helped us meet some of the others, including Eichner, who was something to do with the police. [*For Bradford's comments on Michael Eichner see his report to MI in the Post Script, p332–3.*]

We were on dangerous ground, as Thiers was in the Hotel Aletti, where the German and Italian Commissioners both lived and which was full of spies and detectives. Thiers was longing to help and full of ideas, but he talked rather too much, and in 'Le Club' a smart bar, introduced us loudly to different people, although one of the barmen turned out to be a detective. It was all very difficult.

We met several people and hoped we were on to something. That night we slept in the flat of Jean, a French officer. It was a lovely flat, but filthily dirty, and the light had been cut off. Obviously no servant had been near the place for weeks, and Jean merely got into his unmade bed again in the evening – probably drunk.

4 November 1940. We continued trying to make contacts and
get something going, but on the third day, on getting out of a
tram, we were tapped on the shoulder and asked for our papers
by a plain-clothes man. For a moment I hesitated whether to
produce my forged French papers but as I was with Burn, produced the one from the Consul, which wasn't enough.

The detective was quite friendly and uncertain what to do.
He questioned us a bit and we told him we were British civilians, and gave him various particulars. Then he asked where
we were living – to which I had no answer; nor could we
tell him were we had spent the night. Finally he took us to a
cheap hotel nearby, and made us book a room and told us to
stay there till we heard from him.

Soon after he had gone, I went out to try and find Eichner,
but quickly discovered I was being followed. I didn't show
that I knew and went off to the Post Office where I lost the
man. Then I telephoned Eichner, and got him to meet me at
a little café, where I told him what had happened. I met him
and others at intervals trying to fix to hurry up the plans for
moving on somewhere. I sent a postcard to Freddie Fitch telling him that I wasn't feeling too well – we had arranged an
easy code in illnesses.

In the afternoon or evening, when we thought that things
were almost arranged, I was talking to Eichner in the lounge
of the Aletti. He went upstairs to get hold of Thiers or someone, and immediately afterwards two plain clothes men
appeared and said, 'Come along with us please'. I said I must
wait a moment as I wanted to see a friend, but they wouldn't
wait, wouldn't let me see their warrant or tell me what it was
about. Burn was with me, I remember, chiefly because he had
got bored with sitting alone anywhere else, as he wasn't much
use in taking part in any discussions.

I was frightened by this arrest as I couldn't think how
anyone would know what had happened to us. We were

hustled out to a car – it was almost dark – and pushed in and driven off. I then noticed that the driver was a man I had already met several times. It was obvious that this was a plant of some kind, but I couldn't tell how it would end.

On arrival at the Police HQ we were taken to a room, and then I was questioned by an Inspector on my own. Another Inspector, whom I knew by sight, was there. I told them a lot of nonsense about myself, refusing to admit that I was a soldier – I had been locked up too often in France for that.

After that Burn was taken in. We hadn't had time to agree as to what we were going to say but I whispered to him 'You can't speak any French'. I heard from outside that they were in difficulties, and offered to help by translating, so I was able to let Burn give them the same dates and particulars as I had. After waiting a bit longer we were told to go back to our hotel and to return in 2 days' time. Later I got a chit from Eichner and met him at another café, where he told me my arrest was all part of the plan, and I should go by train tomorrow. I wish I had been told this earlier – it would have been far less worrying.

5 November 1940. Next day, I got instructions to go to a certain café and sit in a corner. The hotel we were in was far from clean, by the way, and we killed various types of bugs in our beds, and in the woodwork round it. I waited for hours in this café, dallying over my drinks, and feeling I must have gone to the wrong place.

Finally a man turned up and, after talking for a bit, asked me for enough money to pay for our tickets to Oran, and told me to be at another café in the afternoon. Burn and I went to this café and again had to wait for a long time. We played some game with cards, which he taught me.

The man came at last, gave us our tickets etc. and later that evening we went down to the station, accompanied by himself. No one took any notice of us – we had heard that everyone's papers were looked at and that you had to have a permit to travel at all. Someone was in the next carriage to see that we didn't get into trouble, but his presence wasn't necessary, as no one troubled us except for tickets.

We were in a fairly full second-class cabin with a most annoying and rather smelly priest who would keep putting his feet up on my lap and who snored loudly.

6 November 1940. We got to Oran early in the morning [*7 a.m.*[69]] and walked down the street till we found a café open. Then we got a shave and left our haversacks in the shop. After that I went on alone to see the Netherlands Consul [*referred to as M.G. in a very water-damaged notebook of Bradford's*] who was in charge of British and German interests – a charming man who, before I had told him my name said, 'I suppose you are a seaman, who has got stranded. Well, they are sending those ones home from Algiers in a few days.' I told him I was Hardy and all about myself and he told me to get photos for papers.

I collected Burn and told him this. Then we went down to the shipping port to try and contact someone. We met two or three Englishmen but no one who could help or suggest anything or anyone to meet even.

Then, stupidly, we went and lunched with one of them in a good restaurant. I ought to have refused to go but didn't. After lunch at which Burn and the other man had had a good deal to drink, we got into a taxi, and then Burn disappeared. I went off to look for him, but couldn't find him anywhere. (Later I found out that he had wandered into a house and made his way to the roof to sleep it off. Someone had seen him and notified the police who had arrested him.) If this had not happened, my whole story might have been changed.

After looking for him for sometime, I went and saw the Consul again, as we had a date with him, and then booked two rooms at a hotel, where I had told Burn I would go. Later I went along to the Englishman's office [*a Mr Walton* [70]] to see if he knew where Burn was. After that I again went down to the port area to try and find something out about getting to Tangier or to Casablanca.

7 November. [*A brief entry in Bradford's notebook reads: 'Shaved off my moustache and had my photo taken for new papers.'*] Next morning I wandered round again, and then, in the afternoon, when I wandered into a café, I walked straight into Das, whom I thought was in prison in Algiers. He had been arrested, fined for landing without permission, and then released, largely through, I think, the man whom I had told about him [*Eichner*], but I hadn't meant him to send Das to Oran after me.

I couldn't avoid him, and told him what had happened to Burn, as far as I knew. While I was talking to him I noticed a man whom I had seen in Algiers and who I thought was a detective, so we moved away and after some time, threw him off. However I wasn't very pleased at this, and when later on I saw Das talking to this detective I was far from pleased.

That evening, Das came round to find me, and told me it was most dangerous to stay in the hotel, and that I was going to be arrested that night. He also said he had a friend down in the port who was ready to hide us, and had got a small ship sailing for Spain either tomorrow or the next day. He promised he had got this all fixed up.

I went off with him, and down to the port. He soon lost his way and had to ask where this man lived. Someone took us to a house, and Das started talking to a man in the passage. Later I found out that he had never met this 'friend' but that someone had told him about a man with some queer Italian name – there happened to be about twenty with the same name – and he had dragged me off to find him, inventing the story about the ship being ready to sail. The worst of Das was that he would tell a mass of lies with an air of sincerity. This man expostulated badly that he had no knowledge of what Das was talking about and recommended us to try someone else.

When we came out, there was a small group of men, who closed round us, and told us to come quietly. I asked them who they were and asked them to show their badge or papers but was told to shut up and two men seized me. Apparently no one was allowed where we were after 20.00hrs.

We were marched up to the Police station, and then they started questioning me – three detectives or inspectors. I told them that I was a Belgian – I had some Belgian papers – and answered some questions hoping to be let out.

Then they seized my pocket book and found a paper saying I was Hardy, a British seaman. I tried to explain this away, and said that I had only said I was a Belgian, as I thought I should be left alone more easily. These three had been firing questions at me continuously and after finding this paper, started being far more unpleasant and threatening. They let me go to the WC after some time and I got rid of some papers with Bradford on them and one of my identity discs but couldn't get rid of much as they were watching me all the time.

They were trying to make me confess I was an 'Agent Provocateur', which of course I wasn't, and went to the extent of firing off a revolver to frighten me – one bullet hit a water pipe in the corner which caused a temporary delay, while we moved to another room.

Later they searched me twice more, each time finding another identity paper hidden in the linings of my clothes – I had a Polish and a French set. I tried to explain it all away, but it got more and more compliqué and when the paper that the Consul in Marseilles had given me came out, it was beyond explanation, and nothing would make them believe the truth – I still refused to tell them I was a soldier.

8 November. About 03.00hrs, after hours of questioning, I was thrown into a cell, underground. I really couldn't believe that they were going to put me in this place, when I was led down a dripping and stinking passage. I had demanded that they should ring up the American representative and the British one, as soon as British papers were found on me, but they refused to do anything about it.

I was put in a cell 4 yards by 2 yards in which there were nineteen Arabs, two Germans, one French, Das and me. The police cleared a small space into which I could squeeze, shoved me in and slammed the door, then the light was turned off. The stench was perfectly awful, and I didn't think I should be able to breathe. There was only room to squat down, jammed between the wall and men. The floor was an inch deep in slimy filth, and the only ventilation was by a small grille in the door. There was a blocked drain in one corner, but it obviously hadn't worked for days. They told me that some of these people had been in here for 5 days without being let out for any purpose and without their having even been tried. The French really don't seem fit to administer anything.

Later, a guard brought in some food in a bucket. One fell into a sort of stupor and just squatted in one's place in a daze. I had never imagined being thrown in such a place, and could hardly believe it was me.

That day, one of the inspectors told me that he knew I was a British officer – they had found my haversack in a café, and the hotel people had rung up because I had booked two rooms in the hotel and my friend had never turned up. Burn, having been arrested, was connected with this enquiry, and though he had been released for the moment, it had made them realise we were together, and they already knew he was a soldier.

This was a nuisance as I was still hoping not to be thought military, but I asked them why I was still being kept locked up in this filth. The man just laughed and said I would stay there as long as he pleased – I was furious.

I began to itch, as there were lice etc. about. It was too dark to see anything. I lay there all that day.

10 November. After I had been there 2½ days, I was taken away in a car, to another Police HQ, and confronted with Burn in a room, and asked if I knew anything of him. I hadn't mentioned him at all, and had said the room was for Das, so I looked at Burn to try and see what he wanted me to say. He couldn't help me and so I said that I did know him.

All that day and till next afternoon, 11 November, they went on questioning us alternately, putting us back with Das in a common cell in between. This cell was filthy too, and full of bugs and lice, but there was some air and one could see.

Later on I wasn't sure that being able to see was such a good thing, as one could see the bugs and lice coming for you in little lines. This got on one's mind, and one kept turning over, feeling they were probably just getting to you behind. Also one fought against going to sleep, feeling they would get you – although actually one was so covered with them already that it didn't really matter.

That evening the Inspector in charge of the prison threatened to release us unless some charge was preferred against us – but unfortunately didn't do so. They sent in quite a good meal from a café, which we paid for.

12 November. Next day, I got very angry when I was being asked the same questions yet again, and let the Inspector know exactly how I felt being treated – an officer – like this by our former allies. I took off my shirt and shook it over him and his desk. This only resulted in me being locked up again, but I also said I would see that they got it in the neck when I did get out.

Later that day, they told us that we were to be taken to the military, but, as a final indignity, we were taken to the Criminal Registration Department, made to strip in front of several natives, and were then photographed and measured all over, ten sets of finger-prints were taken. When they had blacked my hands completely for the ninth time I very nearly planted it in the man's face I was so angry.

After this, we were taken to the barracks overlooking the harbour, and handed over. As the Inspector was leaving, he said to me: 'Please don't think this was all our fault Monsieur. We wanted to do our best for you but could not help ourselves.' I was still too angry to do other than say that I hoped they would get into trouble, and I should do my best to see that they did.

I talked for a bit to a Captain in the 2eme Bureau, who seemed very nice, apologised for the treatment we had received, and said that we should be sent to Casablanca in a few days for repatriation with some sailors. Meanwhile we should have to be confined in the barracks.

We were taken by an English-speaking Sergeant to a NCO's room in the barracks, with a basin and beds in it, and then started getting clean with the help of a hot shower about half a mile away. Actually it was 2 or 3 days before our clothes were completely clean.

We were fed the same as the NCOs and allowed to walk in a courtyard. Some of the NCO's were very friendly, and brought us wine, 'C'est très bon, c'est quatorze dégrées' – their sole measure of excellence seemed to be the wine's strength, as it was so harsh as to be almost undrinkable.

We got them to send the British representative (i.e. the Dutch Consul) up to us, and asked him if he could help us at all. They told him we were going to be sent home too. I saw the 2eme Bureau officer about every other day, but he always said the same thing, and said he must wait orders from Algiers.

About 21 November. One morning, about the ninth day I should think, we were told we were going and must report to the 2eme Bureau at once. We went up, greatly excited, and found two police officers, who took charge of us and took us to another office. There we were told we were not going to Casablanca at all, but back to Algiers – an awful blow. So we were taken to the station and back by train to Algiers escorted by police.

Left on train at 11.30 a.m. First Class. Fed on train and arrived at 8.15 p.m. When we went up to D.I.M. [*Director of Military Intelligence*] no one knew anything about our coming. We eventually slept on mattresses on the floor in a senior N.C.O.'s room. He gave us bread and sardines at midnight.

There followed a period of several months which are not covered in any but the sketchiest of detail in the diary. The letters do, however, give an idea of events.

25 November 1940

I haven't heard from you for a long time and I don't suppose any of my letters reach you.

I am in Algiers at the moment and am quite all right. Will you address your answer to
Revd H.W. Cummin, c/o Mr T. Warren, British Post Office, Tangier.

The cost is 4*d* per ½oz by air mail. You could put for Mr B. Bradford inside before you write 'Dear Ben', – not on envelope.

I have had many adventures again lately, and am dying to get back and tell you all about them. I never seem to get any nearer home though, which is most disappointing.

I have met several friends here – there was a large colony before the war. I had not met Mr Cummin till today, so I did not know there was a Church. I shall go next Sunday however.

A telegram message re-established communications:

BRADFORD – HOTEL ROYALE – ALGIERS
BRAVO TOUS BIEN ICI BRADFORD

And again on 4 December.
TELEGRAPHIEZ ET ECRIVEZ PAR AVION HOTEL
ROYAL ALGER = BRADFORD

15 December 1940
Royal Hotel,
Algiers
You can imagine how pleased I was at getting your telegram. It arrived at 8.30 a.m. on 3 Dec, only about 20 hours after you had sent it.

I am now living here 'liberté surveillée' with H B Burn 7th Bn 5th Fusiliers. We tried to get home but were caught and imprisoned at Oran – a filthy prison full of lice. We are completely free but cannot get any further. We have applied to the French Authorities to be repatriated in exchange for French Officers, and the American Consul-General here looks after our interests, but it doesn't look to me as if anything will happen for months. Can you try and get something done from your end. Possibly Col J.A. Barstow, War Office, may be able to help. Do ask him at any rate, as you can imagine how I am dying to get home. They have sent back others from here so it is possible. Will you also ask Col C.G. Stephen if he can't do something.

I am hoping to get this letter off by someone so it may miss the French censorship. French people here are most friendly except for navy. I meet lots of army officers and talk to them.

I met six of Ridley's [*a cousin*] friends who came down near here last Monday. They gave me all the latest news from home. Unfortunately they have gone to a place about 70 miles from here.

There are at least forty British people here and many of them have been very kind to us. The Church is open here, and I have been up every Sunday. There isn't a very big congregation, but it is very nice having a service at all.

We have been having quite a lot of rain here lately, and it hasn't been too warm. In fact the regular inhabitants are complaining like anything of the climate.

Best love and very happy Christmas to you all from

Your loving Ben

30 December 40

Hotel Royale

I got your letter of 2 December this evening and it was a joy to get it. Funnily enough, I got letters from Aunt Norah and Grannie Edith [*Edith, Lady Bradford, his step-grandmother*], posted on 5th, on the 27th. Aunt Norah's only had 5d in stamps. Perhaps it is better if you don't put 'Africa'. I also got your letter of 10 October, a few days ago. It had been following me all over the place. I'm afraid I can still see small chance of getting home for some time. One cannot move at all in this country. I am writing this in bed where I have been since Christmas evening with a sort of gastric-flu. I saw a Doctor, who only made me more sick.

3 January. I haven't been able to finish this up till now. I have been moved to a good nursing home, through the care of friends and am much better though I still can't eat

anything. I have had a sort of jaundice. I got another letter from you of 6 Nov, so am now well up on your news.

You ask about Neill Grant-Duff in your letter. I am very much afraid he was killed, also Alistair Telfer-Smollett. I can't swear to either. Has no casualty list ever been issued? I wrote to Col Stephen in October telling him who I thought killed and prisoner. He went home in May as he was sick.

Very best love and God bless you all

From your loving

Ben

12 January 1941

I am now quite recovered, and am leaving this nursing-home tomorrow. An old English lady, who is also here, had been very kind in lending me her wireless from time to time, and so I have been able to listen to the news and all sorts of nice things from home, and to know that you were also listening to the 9 p.m. news. I listened to a very nice service from Edinburgh this morning.

We have moved to a very much cheaper hotel, but I have not slept there yet. It looks very nice. It has been an unusually cold winter here, and there has even been some snow. Today it is beautifully sunny, and nice and warm in the sun. There are roses coming out in sheltered corners, and of course all the orange trees are lovely with their fruit. But how I am longing to leave it all and get home, and I can't see any means still. All the news has been excellent lately, hasn't it? I hope you will write via Mr Warren at Tangier in future – if my letter telling you how to has arrived! It seems to be a very quick way.

I can't think of any news from here as I haven't been doing much!

*It was on 3 February 1941 that Major R.N. 'Naps' Brinckman,
Grenadier Guards, arrived in Algiers. He had been wounded in
action on 27 May 1940 (for which he subsequently was awarded a
DSO) and taken prisoner. He had escaped from a temporary prison
camp at Malines in November and, having been hidden for some
weeks, travelled by train to Marseilles and thence by boat to Tunis.
Brinckman's account of his escape covers part of the time spent by
Bradford in Algeria.*

*The manner in which Brinckman's journal came to light is worth
recording. In 2004 Freddie Burnaby-Atkins, a fellow officer in 1st
Black Watch who had been captured at St-Valery with Bradford, was
staying with friends in England. They went to dinner with neighbours
and, spotting some Second World War medals in a frame on the wall,
Freddie asked about them. They were his host's father's medals and
Freddie heard the tale of fighting in May 1940, wounding and subsequent escape. 'Did he write a diary?' asked Freddie, who went home
with a copy that very evening. A few days later Freddie wrote to me
in great excitement saying he'd found many mentions of my father in
Naps Brinckman's diary. Until that moment I had no idea of its existence. Brinckman's son Sir Theodore Brinckman kindly let me have
sight of the diary for this account.*

*On arrival in Algiers Brinckman, still suffering from his wounds,
met the American Vice-Consul Felix Cole. He wrote:*

> *Felix Cole was about fifty-five years of age and very charming. He
> asked me up to dinner that night in his beautiful villa, 400ft above
> the city, and sent his car for me. He explained the whole situation to
> me, and that he thought I stood a very good chance of being repatri-
> ated. He also informed me that there were two other British officers
> in the town, at present on parole, and who had not been interned
> so far, owing to the fact that they had been very ill. The following
> day I found these two, Captains Bradford of the Black Watch and
> Burn of the Northumberland Fusiliers. They had both been in*

Algiers about 3 months, had both tried to escape twice, and had both been re-arrested. I gathered from them that the whole thing, as far as they were concerned, had been a light-hearted game of hide-and-seek with the Sûreté; that in fact, the last time they had both been allowed to get as far as Oran, but had been arrested there, and sent back to Algiers. It was on Friday, 7 February that Burn, although on parole at this time, again escaped, which escape immediately got to the ears of the French authority which was not friendly to the British. A slight glimmering of the diplomatic-cum-international layout of the place became apparent to me when, on returning to my room that night, I found M. Lalanne awaiting me in a some-what excited state. He produced a stout walking-stick for me, and said: 'There is a danger of your being arrested under orders from the Italian Commission. M. Hasciari has arranged that you be taken to the Clinique des Glycines before breakfast tomorrow morning on account of the sudden aggravation of your war injuries. Mr Cole has placed his car at your disposal for this journey, and I have much pleasure in presenting to you for your health, two bottles of Johnny Walker whisky.

Brinckman was taken to the clinique where Bill Bradford had a room on the floor below him. Brinckman writes:

> *We began by taking life very easily, sunning ourselves on the ter-race in the mornings (breakfast of course, always being in bed) with dejeuner at twelve, followed by a siesta.*
>
> *Bill, who had been in Algiers for some time, knew all the locals, and I soon found myself taking part in an absolute orgy of teas with what was left of the English colony, and one or two of the well-meaning old French ladies who had pro-English sentiments, or English connections.*

Bradford wrote again:

Alger

10 February 1941

Thank you very much for your letters of 10 and 17 January The latter only took 13 days – very quick. Now you know where I am at any rate. Papa's letter was very cut [*censored*] in parts – I can't guess for what I must wait. [*Here is evidence of advice to wait for 'something to be done' and to refrain from making an escape attempt. See also 'On the Home Front – 3'.*] I hate waiting in boredom here; in any case I must be thankful that I am able to have letters from you. I have managed to hear the news quite a lot lately, and listened to the P-M's speech last night. How wonderfully Archie W is doing. I wish to goodness I was with him. [*Gen. Sir Archibald Wavell, Black Watch. Bradford was referring to the rout of the Italians from Cyrenacia.*]

My friend, Burn, who came over with me has been arrested and will probably be returned to France – I have been ill again the last few days, but not seriously, and am well looked after. A telegram from the F.O. came out to the American Consul about my being ill before. I suppose you asked them to do something. Can't Grannie Edith get on to someone important at the F.O. or somewhere, as another chap arrived has wired to D Cooper and is expected to get a personal exchange to the U.S.A. The new chap who has come a few days ago is Brinckman, GGs.

It isn't much good my writing often as I haven't much to say.

The hidden message in this letter reads 'trying for Gib in small boat'.

17 February 1941

I got Poppa's of 29th a few days ago via Mr C. so I have been very lucky. At any rate you now know where I am! I will try to write more often, as luckily the mail is not so slow. It is extraordinary really that they manage under very difficult conditions. I hope things get better soon.

Will you please try and get in touch with Commandant Mieczystaw NIEMIEC of the Polish Army at home, whose wife's name is Elslietta, and tell him that his sister-in-law is now at the Hotel Aletti, Alger. Will you also try and communicate with Mrs Magdalene Eales, 109 Park St and tell her that her brother is at same hotel. They are both longing to have a letter. Let me know if you get into touch with either of them.

The quickest way of letters getting here would still seem to be addressed to Mr C. It doesn't matter how many you send that way, as I pay the other man in Tangier.

Brinckman, who is also here has wired to Duff-Cooper and expects to be got home by him somehow. I hope always. Can you send the enclosed letter to my bank please. [*Alfred Duff Cooper [1890–1954] later 1st Viscount Norwich, was Minister of Information 1940–41.*]

The hidden message in this letter reads 'look inside envelope' and within the lining of this letter's envelope was written the following message:

Message to be dropped in Northern France as Tracts particularly in area where I was when I came on leave – also give out on wireless in French hour.

'Aux Gueux de Vlandres.

Mes amis – votre commandant est toujours avec vous avec notre fière devise.

J'ecris – Vivre sur mon drapeau la liberté, l'amour at la lumière de tendresse, et ma peau premiere d'Acier et ma seconde Jean.

Vive les Gueux de Vlandre

Le Commandant LA TAVERNE

Money is also urgently required in that area to help away a lot of my fellows. Please forward this to D.M.I. [*Director of Military Intelligence*]. Let me know if you get this by saying 'Cassandra arrived safely'.

Army and Air Force all very friendly here. Navy not so friendly. German Commission control petrol supplies, and many other supplies so that they can't do much. I cannot get in touch with any quick means of comn home. Can anyone assist. BCB.

Brinckman again wrote:

Bill introduced me to the most extraordinary couple I have ever met. Mr Eichner was an Austrian, who had fought for his country in the last war, and afterwards had served in the French Foreign Legion, subsequently becoming a naturalized Frenchman. He had worked for some time in the French Bankers' Intelligence Service in Paris. He knew all the old haunts, and some of my Ritz Bar friends, such as Erskine Gwynne. Michael Eichner was a little blonde man, always very well turned out, exuding pro-British sentiments, and frequently addressing me as, 'old man'.

I became pretty sure, after some time, that he was playing a double game, but that he really was working for the French Deuxieme Bureau. I met him several times in Commandant Duriot's office; he always wore plain clothes, and I think his function was to pose in the Hotel Aletti as a sort of elderly playboy, exuding pro-Nazi sentiments, thereby hoping to gain information from the Italian Commission and the German agents for the Deuxieme Bureau. Madame Eichner was certainly a most striking woman. She was a Pole by birth, very dark in appearance, good-looking in a sort of horsy way, and standing about six foot one in her socks. She had very expensive furs, clothes and jewellery – was a terrific snob, and evidently had all the money. Michael

used even to have to ask her for his taxi fare, on the rare occasions
that he was allowed out of her sight on some errand. The Eichners
also had a most cantankerous French bulldog bitch called Dolly,
who always had to be given a chair at their table in whatever restaurant they happened to be feeding. Nevertheless, whatever game
the Eichners were playing, it would be true to say that they were
very good friends to Bill Bradford and myself, and there was little
doubt that Bill and I were able to circulate freely in Algiers, owing
to the combined 'protection' of Eichner, Hasciari, ★ and Duriot.
For some time, of course, Bill and I were very much 'en residence
surveille [sic]' and we were shadowed by Hasciari's dicks, but this
did not worry us very much, as in the evenings, when we used to go
to the Casino Bar, the dicks used to come and drink with us, so that
we got to know them quite well. It was really a very funny set-up.'

[★*Brinckman reported that Hasciari was working with a number of
Frenchmen who were secretly working for British interests.*]

25 February 1941
I have been ill again for some time now with tummy trouble. Don't worry about me as I am in the very best hospital
and have the best doctor. The American Consul-General
has looked after me. It is probably due to my having had
dysentery and they say I never really got rid of it, so my
inside is all wrong. I might even be sent home as 'unfit'!
Do pray for that to happen.

I have bought a tiny New Testament, and have also borrowed a New Testament in Modern language, which I like
rather, as it explains some things differently. Oh, I do wish
I was able to talk to you about everything, as I have found
out so many things during the last 8 months.

I have just bought a lovely cyclamen from a friend to
cheer up my little room here – an almost white one but just

pink. It has eight flowers and masses of buds. The weather has been lovely here the last few days, and we have been sitting out in the sun.

9 March 1941
Algiers
I have no news at all to tell you, as I never do anything at all interesting. I still keep hoping now to be sent home as unfit; do not worry about me as I am very well cared for at a good nursing-home. I hope to goodness I am sent home soon as I am sure another climate would be much better for me, and might help me to get better. There are quite a lot of flowering trees and creepers out which look very pretty – wisteria has been out for about a week now. A cyclamen which I have got in my room has now got twenty-one flowers fully out, and looks lovely. In spite of all these attractions I loathe the place!

Brinckman recorded:

About the middle of March, Bill and I appeared before our first 'commission of reform.' This had been laid on by the American Consul-General, in conjunction with the French military authority, with the object of getting us passed 'unfit for further military service'. Bill had been very ill before I came to Algiers, having had something wrong with his liver. The Commission consisted of three doctors – Dr Binet, representing British interests, having been chosen by Mr Cole; a second doctor representing the French military authorities, whilst a third doctor, who should have represented the German and Italian Armistice Commissions, was actually chosen by the Duriot-Eichner combination, and had obviously been fixed.

We were both passed as being unfit for further military service but before the American Consulate-General could take any steps to

*have us repatriated, the proceedings had to be forwarded to Vichy,
and their final approval received.*

Algiers,
St Patrick's Eve [*16 March 1941*]
Brinckman and I both went before a medical board last
Weds: and were both passed unfit for further service, so
ought to be sent home fairly soon, they say. I will send you
a wire when we start or get somewhere else, as I'm afraid
things may not go very quickly in this place. I hope to
goodness something does happen quickly. Meanwhile I am
still in the nursing-home.

Yes, there are a lot of flowers out here now, and the
place looks quite pretty. It has been nice and sunny, but
also we seem to have a certain amount of rain. The wisteria
has come out everywhere during the past week, and is a
mass of flower – perfectly lovely. There are also some other
very pretty creepers on houses – one with bright red trum-
pet flowers – vigandia? And another with bright orange
flowers. Anemones, iris, pansies, nasturtium, stocks, lilies
and cyclamen are all out too. However, I've got no desire
to stay here! I have been reading quite a lot, and we were
lent some American magazines lately, which were very
interesting. Also the *Illustrated London News*. I saw a book
published by Victor Gollancz by Hudson [?] about the war
in France up to June, which it said would be particularly
interesting to people having anything to do with the B.W.
[*Black Watch*], but I've forgotten the name of the book! I
also read Sense & Sensibility lately, and enjoyed it thoroughly. There is absolutely nothing to do except read, as
we neither of us feel fit enough to do much else. Please
give my best love to everyone, and thank them awfully for
their letters. Do pray for me to come home quickly.

Brinckman writes:

> *Time began to hang very heavily on our hands and I realised that it was no good counting on repatriation, so Bill and I began to make plans to escape. This was obviously not going to be easy, because to travel by train, all sorts of papers had to be obtained, and formalities gone through. We were also watched all the time, and, in addition, both the railway trains and stations were very heavily policed by the Sûreté, and although Hasciari himself and a lot of his men would undoubtedly have helped us to escape, no two people in this country could ever trust each other, and Hasciari would never have dared commit himself, in case he was given away by one of his underlings. In addition, from our point of view, it was necessary to find a Frenchman or an Algerian, whom one could trust, and who would be prepared to help us. We knew, of course, that we could count on the two Americans, and Dashiel, in particular, had been in Algiers a very long time, and we accepted his word as to what Frenchmen were reliable, and those that weren't. It must be realized that Algiers was a seething mass of secret service agents, agents provo-cateurs, plain-clothes detectives employed by the Government, in addition to the Sûreté dicks who always appeared to be friendly to us, but whom, of course, we could not trust. I mention this because we were continually being approached by apparently 100 per cent de Gaullists, who professed tremendous keenness on the idea of getting to England. Bill and I became very bored waiting for the results of our medical commission, and we used to go down to the town fairly frequently before lunch, and met our friends at the little bar behind the Brasserie Terminus, and in cautious undertones discuss ways and means of escaping from this awful country.*
>
> *Six weeks after our appearance before the Medical Board word came to us, through Mr Cole, that Vichy had annulled the whole proceedings because it was claimed that the third doctor on the Board had not been chosen by the Armistice Commission and this was very*

depressing, and Bill and I went off straight away to see our friend Eichner, who promised faithfully that he would get Commandant Duriot to arrange another Board. Bill was very depressed about this, as he felt sure that he would never pass a properly constituted one, as by this time he had recovered from his attack of jaundice, which he had had during the winter, and, of course, he had never been wounded. So we began looking around very seriously for means of escaping.

About this time, a cabaret was opened at the Hotel Aletti, which was run by a French boy who had played in Hollywood. Dancing was not allowed in Algiers, or elsewhere, for that matter, by the order of Petain; but this boy used to sing American songs. As it was the only form of night-life in Algiers, Bill and I decided to try it one night, with our American friends. But we chose the night when members of both the German and Italian Commissions were having a night out, and they were furious at our presence.

In his letter home from Algiers of 27 March, Bradford has heard news of Freddie Fitch's successful escape from Marseilles and that he had visited his parents. He wrote:

I am glad Freddie Fitch came over to see you. He is an awfully nice chap, isn't he. I haven't had a letter from him yet. I wish I had stayed with him after all, but at the time it seemed best to do what I did.

Whenever possible Bradford was sending home information. The hidden message in this letter says 'look inside envelope' and within the lining a slip of tissue paper contained the following message:

Germans take 75 per cent of food etc. arriving at Marseilles from N. Africa. Considerable quantities of tin ore, & other metals also crossing to France for Germans. A method of making cotton for munitions from alfa-alfa [*sic*] grass has been discovered. Alfa-alfa grass may soon be exported to France for German use. Number of Germans here & in Tunisia increasing steadily.

15 April 1941

We have got to go before another Doctors' Board, as apparently the other one was wrongly constituted. It is supposed to take place the day after tomorrow, but nothing seems to be arranged properly. I have met a couple of American journalists lately, who have only arrived here a short time ago, and are quite interesting. Did you understand about 'inside the lining of' in my last letters – or perhaps they never arrived – the mail is still somewhat uncertain. I may telegraph the result of my board to you, if it is exciting.

The journalists were Bill MacGuffin and Dashiel whom Brinckman described as very nice and extremely sympathetic.

The second medical board took place towards the end of April and was a very much more serious affair than the first. Brinckman wrote:

I had been studiously nursing my bad leg, in the reverse manner, and by bathing it in cold water daily, never putting my weight on it, if I could help it, and discontinuing my treatment, which might have done it too much good, I was able to keep it in a fairly atrophied state; this, coupled with the fact that there was still no nerve reaction in the lower half of my leg, enabled me to be passed once more unfit for further military service. Bill was not so lucky, and became terribly depressed, as he did not want to be sent to the concentration camp. However Dr Binet gave him some sick-making medicine which enabled him to stay on with me in the Clinique.

21 April 1941

My darling Mummie

At the present moment I am in the depths of despair, as the Medical Board hasn't passed me unfit, and therefore there is no hope of my being sent home. I had pinned all my hope on this board, as I had already been certified unfit by the previous board, which turned out to be improperly constituted. I just don't know what to do. Brinckman has been passed unfit, which is something. It is awful when all your hopes tumble to the ground like that, and you have nothing to look forward to. I am so miserable here, although I realise I could be a lot worse off, and am grateful for that.

The weather has been rotten lately, with a lot of rain, but I expect it is good for the harvest. Small parties of Trouter's friends continue to come and we have already had the first strawberries!! [*'Trouter's friends' was a codeword for Germans and Bradford was indicating a build-up of troops. The meaning of 'strawberries' is unclear but Col Bradford deduced that Algiers was now experiencing the first fruits of the German's increased presence.*]

Do you know if anyone has managed to do anything about me at home at all? If so, do send me a wire (Night Letter Telegrams are quite cheap), as I may do something foolish otherwise. One can't have patience for ever!

Patience, however, was just what was going to be needed. As the letters indicate, this was the start of a period of deep despair.

28 April 1941

I am still miserable about my Board, as they haven't passed me unfit, and nothing else seems to be happening. The American Consul won't push at all here, and I am really desperate, as the future doesn't seem to hold out much hope for me. Can't they hold up someone at your end to exchange me against? I often listen to the news at 9 p.m. and think of you sitting in the library at home at the same time. Everyone here tells me to have patience, not to worry and to trust in God, but I cannot just go on and on sitting here in comfort. Also I am certain I shan't get well in this climate and with this food. I haven't been at all well again lately, though I have the best medical attention that can be procured for me.

I am afraid this letter is full of my own worries and sounds very selfish, when you have all got much more to worry about, but you know what I mean.

We listened to Winston Churchill's speech last night, and could hear it very clearly. He is marvellous, isn't he?

Churchill addressed the nation on the BBC. He closed with the words 'Westward, Look, the land is bright.'

5 May 1941

As you know, I do not need much money at present. Would be of any help to you if I tell my bank to send any balance to you? If so, you know I shall be thankful to do that instead of putting it into War Savings. Please don't say to yourselves that I had much better save it for the future, as I would much rather you had it if you need it. At any rate do please stop my allowance, as I am sure you are finding life very expensive now.

Brinckman has had several letters from his wife in Canada. He expects to be allowed to leave quite soon now, so I shall be very much alone then. I saw a telegram about us both from the FO inspired by you, but I am afraid that the representatives here will never take drastic action, and are terribly correct and diplomatic, so nothing will be done about me.

Particularly E & W, Trouters friends are on the increase, Here; what a marvel it was that so many were got away from Greece. [*Here is another message about the increase in German numbers.*]

12 May 1941

I saw five RAFs who came in from their internment camp to buy clothes the other day. It was very nice talking to them, and we heard some recent news as some of them have only been interned a few weeks. We were all at Church together on Sunday (7 of us that is) and made quite a good choir, though the psalms and hymns were too high a key as usual. I will remember your little text 'In quietness and confidence', but I do find it so hard to go on being patient and I seem to have so little to look forward to or live for at this moment.

18 May 1941

I got my first letter from Freddie Fitch of 27 February How I wish I had stayed with him!

How lovely everything must be at home now. I wonder when I shall ever see it again.

The news hasn't been very good lately, has it? I'm rather worried about the future in the Middle East, and also on the West Coast of Africa. The papers here are completely under German control and are not worth reading.

His parents clearly appreciated the sense of despair and strove in their letters to keep his spirits up and gradually they succeeded.

28 May 1941

Thank you very much for your letter of 9 May which helps me not to be too discouraged. I know you understand how miserable I feel doing nothing.

What fun it would be up in Mull at the moment with all those birds and ducks. I often think of Mull when I am really feeling desperate. Brinckman knows a lot of Scotland very well. He expects to go any time now as he has got his visa.

I read lately 'The £200 Millionaire' by Weston Martyr – a book about sailing, which was very nice.

We were all thankful to hear about the Bismarck yesterday. I am afraid things in Crete are not going too well at present. I listen sometimes to an American from Ankara giving his report to the New York Times in New York. It is usually a most interesting résumé and quite unbiased.

2 June 1941

No, I hadn't realised that my letters were censored at both ends, but I don't think I ever say anything censorable!

I loved your letter and Mummie's of the week before, which have helped cheer me up.

13

On the Home Front (3)

At home Bradford's parents heard of his move to Algiers and his mother immediately reported this to the authorities:

> With reference to previous correspondence I have now to inform you that on the second inst. I received a cable from my son [Capt. B.C. Bradford, The Black Watch] giving his address as Hotel Royale, Algiers. I had last heard from him from Marseilles in a letter dated 23 October where he had gone with the permission of the French Authorities. I do not know if this latest move has been carried out with their sanction or not. I rather think not.

While hopes might have been raised by the change of continent the next letter will quickly have dashed them. Mrs Brinton again wrote with news from the Embassy at Madrid:

> 12 December 1940
> Dear Maggie
> We have received the enclosed letter from Mrs Tour from Madrid this morning. I expect you will have heard from Major Lubbock,

before this reaches you, but in case not, I am forwarding it to you at once. May I have it back. It is maddening that so few letters seem to have got through to Ben, and I expect he had no idea that people are working for his discovery and release.

Madrid,
December 5
Drummond-Wolff had hopes of getting Ben out — heard on 4 that 2 officers stowed away on ship for Oran — only 1 in prison there — D-W considers only hope of escape stowing away again very anti-Br. feeling at Oran.

On 29 December Alan Lubbock wrote from the Embassy in Madrid:

Dear Mrs Bradford
I am so sorry to have been so long in answering your letter, but I have been away on a holiday in the country, your letter arrived just after I left.

From what you say it seems that your son cannot have been the officer imprisoned at Oran. The news that we had came from an officer who arrived here on 4 December from Marseilles: he had heard the news there, & must have left Marseilles well before 30 Nov., when your son telegraphed from Algiers. We were rather doubtful about the reliability of that information.

I am so glad that he is all right. If only he could have got here, he wd. probably be home by now, even if he had had an unpleasant time, for a few weeks, in a Spanish concentration camp. His being sent back over the frontier was an extraordinary thing that, as far as we know, has never happened on any other occasion.

I am no longer actually doing the work connected with escaped prisoners of war myself. Another A.M.A. has been posted here and is doing it, curiously a man in your son's regiment, Robin Drummond-Wolff; but he had left the battalion some months before *the fighting began & was in another unit, so had not seen your son for some time before he was captured. [Maj. R H C Drummond-Wolff was appointed Assistant Military Attaché, Madrid, on 20/10/1940.]*

I do hope that you will soon have further, better news: I know that some people have already managed to reach home from N. Africa & I expect your son will in the end. If only we could occupy all Libia [sic] the problem wd. I suppose be much simpler.

P.S. Since writing this an officer has arrived from Marseilles who says that the news there is that both your son and the other officer are at Algiers, under 'liberté surveillé', i.e. on parole.

At about this time Bradford's father started trying to get things moving using contacts in the army. Col C.G. Stephen had commanded 1st Black Watch in 1938–40 and knew Bradford well. He had fallen ill and had been sent home early in May 1940. He now proved to be a most enthusiastic and encouraging contact. It would have greatly helped Bradford's spirits if he had known of this at the time.

Ernam,
Keith,
Banffshire
8 January 1941
Dear Col Bradford,

It was kind of you to write and I am so glad to hear news of Bill. About three weeks ago a letter came from him dated 26 August telling of his escape & recapture he was then in unoccupied France it was then of course too late for me to get help to him.

Fancy him being in Algiers in November he is a marvel. I feel sure he will get back somehow.

Have you reported his whereabouts to the War Office? I sent a copy of his letter to me with details of his escape to be filed with his records at the War Office in order that he may be suitably rewarded when he returns.

Bill was a first class adjutant — no one could have done better. We had some hard and difficult times together but he was always cheerful and a great support. His ability to give out orders quickly and exactly, from very sketchy information from me was uncanny. I trust he was happy with me.

I put his name forward for an award which he so thoroughly deserves but nothing came of it. Our fate was sealed the day we entered the 51 Div and left our old 4th Division. Everything went to the Territorials and we had to do all the work and stand the racket.

I also put Bill's name in for the Staff College and if he gets back he must go there it is the only hope of getting on now. If & when he gets back will you let me know immediately as he should make every effort to get in touch with me in order that I can arrange for a staff college case for him — that is most important.

As you say I was a lucky man but I feel things might have been different had one been there. The disaster should never have occurred & history will have some very pointed remarks to make.

I have now reformed the 1st Battalion out of nothing, it has been an uphill business, we are not what we were but can give an account of ourselves when the time comes.

Please remember me to Mrs Bradford. I am sure we will see Bill again before long

Col Stephen's letter commenting on Bradford's of 26 August 1940 moved up the chain of command to the War Office:

From:- Major General i/c Administration, SCOTTISH COMMAND
To:- The Under Secretary of State, THE WAR OFFICE, LONDON S.W.1

Edinburgh,
5 January 1941
Sir,
I have the honour to forward a copy of a communication from the
O.C. 1st Battalion The Black Watch referring to Captain B.C.
Bradford of that battalion, who appears to be an escaped prisoner
somewhere in France.
It seems that this communication may be of interest to the Intelligence
Branch and that it should also be placed with the Officer's records
with a view to commendation for good work at the end of the war.
I have the honour to be,
Sir
Your obedient Servant
J.P. Duke, Col A.W.9
Major General i/c Administration, SCOTTISH COMMAND

For Bradford's parents news sometimes came from the most unlikely
quarters:

Box 113,
Kano. Nigeria
16 January 1941
Dear Mrs Bradford
My wife and I have just returned from Algiers where we met
your son.

I promised before leaving that as soon as we arrived back in
British Territory I would write you to give an outsider's report
on your son's condition, in order to relieve your mind of worry on
the subject.

Your son and another British Officer, Captain Burn, are held
in Algiers by the French Authorities after having arrived there from
France. They are living in the Royal Hotel, but have been required
to give their parole that they would not attempt to escape. The only

alternative to this would have been confinement in surroundings which are not very comfortable to say the least.

The American Consul is providing them with money but is only allowed by the British Government to advance them £10 per month. This whilst providing them with the necessities of life does not allow them anything over for luxuries. At the same time you can rest assured that they are not starving or anything like that. There are still a few British families left in Algiers and your son and his companion are invited to these houses and the tedium of their existence is in some measure relieved in this manner.

I understand that there is some movement afoot to exchange British soldiers in French Territory for French soldiers in British Territory so that your son may in the near future be included in such exchange. The American Consulate have the matter in hand and are doing everything in their power to get a move on. There has already been an exchange of sailors.

My wife and I were exchanged through the good offices of our Resident at Kano working in conjunction with the Free French. I don't know whether it is possible for you to get the Free French Bureau in London interested in your son's case. I understand that there are French subjects in the French Equatorial Africa Territory who are desirous of returning to France and it is possible that they might be able to effect an exchange for your son. In our case it was an Administrator and his wife who were in Free French hands, whilst we were in the hands of the Vichy authorities. Of course it may be that as I am over military age the exchange may have been effected more easily. Anyway, it would be worth your while I think to approach the Free French in London to see what they can do in the matter. If I can find out anything from this end I will certainly do so as I know how tedious it is to be held against one's will, we had 6 months in this way in Algiers. We were caught by events in June when passing through Algiers on our way home to England.

*If there is any further information that I can give you I shall be
only too pleased to do so.
Yours sincerely
J. Ashton*

Other advice came by unofficial channels:

*Ernam
Keith
Banffshire
20 January 1941
Dear Mrs Bradford
Today my husband received a letter from Colonel Bradford giving
details about Bill's whereabouts and his difficulty in getting back to
this Country from Algiers. My husband will at once communicate
with the War Office and try and get them to take action.*

*He is only permitted to work things through the 'usual channels'
— this takes time and Bill's rescue is very urgent, if it is to be effected
at all.*

*Such the usual lethargy of the powers that be, I feel that any
effort being made by my husband will be very late in taking effect.
As I said before the matter is very urgent, therefore, I suggest to you
that either you or Colonel Bradford should write direct to
The Private Secretary
To Her Majesty The Queen
Buckingham Palace
London
giving details of Bill's predicament and asking him with humble
respect etc. to bring the matter to the notice of Her Majesty the
Queen as Colonel-in-Chief The Black Watch RHR to use her
good offices for the rescue of Bill and his companions. A short résumé
of Bill's original escape should be sent.*

*You might think this is rather an unorthodox and drastic method
but I can assure you that Her Majesty takes a very personal interest
in the Black Watch, more especially as her nephew [Hon John A
Elphinstone, later 17th Lord Elphinstone] is a prisoner with the 1st
Batt. and a letter from you to the Private Secretary on the above
lines, will have instant and surprising effects.*

*We do think it is so splendid the way he has struggled to escape
and do think he deserves all the help he can get.*

*With our kindest regards to you both, hoping you will soon have
good news and Bill home with you.*

Yours sincerely

Mary Stephen

Col Stephen wrote again the following day. In this letter to Bradford's
father it can be seen that Stephen greatly exceeded his duty by offering
to bribe the French authorities in Algiers and even offering a substantial personal guarantee to this effect:

21 January 1941

Dear Col Bradford

*Your letter arrived at lunchtime yesterday having taken 4 days, but we
are snowed up all roads being blocked, we therefore have to dig out to
get mail etc. through.*

*I wrote and dispatched a letter in triplicate to higher authority and
that within an hour of your letter arriving. I have marked it 'very
urgent' and asked the powers that be to make every effort to rescue Bill.
I have backed it up by offering to bribe the French officials in Algiers.
I am certain that money will do anything. I have therefore guaranteed
a substantial sum.*

*I am sure if you or Mrs Bradford communicate with the Queen's
Private Secretary as my wife suggests all will be well. You have no
idea how people are made to 'jump to it' when one goes to the fountain
head but of course I am not allowed to do such a thing.*

So far as I can see we are terrified of the Spaniards and are afraid of hurting further the feelings of our dear! ally the French. But this sort of thing is all rubbish compared to the safety of British officers.

Mrs Bradford took Mrs Stephen's advice and wrote to the Queen:

EMPSHOTT LODGE
LISS
HANTS
TEL. BLACKMOOR 281
To The Private Secretary,
To Her Majesty the Queen
23 January 1941
Sir
I write to ask that you will with humble respect bring to the notice of Her Majesty the Queen, as Colonel in Chief of the Black Watch, RHR, the following details with regard to my son Captain Berenger C Bradford, who is now detained by the French in Algiers, in the hope that she may be graciously pleased to used her good offices towards his release. He was Adjt. 1st Battn. The Black Watch & was taken prisoner with the Highland Divn. at St-Valery on 12 June. He escaped on 19 June and after trying the Channel Ports walked over 300 miles into unoccupied France, where he was detained by the French. He again escaped and after many hardships climbed over a 9,000ft. pass into Spain where he was taken prisoner by the Spanish Frontier Guards and turned back into France on August 5.

After some months under 'liberté surveillée' in the Toulouse district he got to Marseilles and 'stowed away' on a ship to Algiers in Octr.

He was again caught, trying to get into Morocco, and detained in a verminous prison in Oran. Since Decr. 15 he has been at Hotel Royale, Algiers under 'liberté surveillé' and when I heard from him today, dated Jany 3 was ill with jaundice and gastric influenza.

He says that he doesn't see any chance of getting away from Algiers and in view of his struggles to return home during the past 7 months I trust that Her Majesty may feel it is very urgent that if possible he should be rescued quickly.

Your obedient servant

Margaret L. Bradford

By this time Mrs Bradford had heard that her son was in hospital and was concerned about his health. She wrote to the Red Cross and received this response, dated 27 January 1941.

Dear Mrs Bradford,

Mrs Campion has passed to me your letter of 25 January, as I happen to be dealing with the case of your son, Captain Berenger Bradford, and upon reading the letter I immediately rang up the department of the Foreign Office who deal with the members of the British forces at present in unoccupied French territory and Colonies. They promised immediately to instruct the United States Consul-General in Algiers [the US being our Protecting Power in such territories] to see that your son received proper medical attention and the necessary diet to help him get over his gastric 'flu and jaundice. I am sure the US Consul-General will render every assistance he probably can, and I very much hope that the next letter you receive from your son will be to tell you that he has recovered.

Hopes were raised when Col Stephen wrote forwarding a message from Gen Neil Ritchie, another Black Watch officer:

Keith

28 January 1941

Dear Colonel Bradford

My letter about Bill has been sent direct from Divisional Headquarters to the C in C, Sir Allan Brooke. This has cut out the 'news-channel??' and the War Office.

Sir Allan knows me well as he was our Corps Commander in France till we went to the ill-fated 51st Division.

As I write this the enclosed was handed to me. So it looks as if something is moving. I know Sir Allan very well he is a thruster so I expect people are jumping about.

It is unfortunate we allow the Foreign Office to deal with such matters in war, they will never act quickly.

Let us hope for good news very soon. I for my part am determined to continue to make myself a nuisance till Bill is rescued.

Will you please return the enclosed in due course.

Yours sincerely

C.G. Stephen

From Major General N M Ritchie, CBE, DSO, MC

Headquarters

51st [H] Division

Home Forces

27 January 1941

Dear Steve

I am sending you the attached extract from a letter received by me from Ronnie Strangforth who is Sir Allan Brooke's personal assistant, concerning Bill Bradford. It looks as though something may be done to get him out of the French clutches in North Africa.

I hope I will be hearing more about it in the course of the next day or two and will let you know how the matter is progressing.

Yours ever

Neil Ritchie

Extract referred to in this letter:

The C-in-C was very interested in your letter of 21st which I got this morning.

I rang up a friend of mine in the Foreign Office, to find out who dealt with these sort of things, and he told me that he knew of

Bradford and all about him and that a certain amount of action had already been taken in this matter. It so happens that I am going to see my friend this week-end, and he has promised to bring me up-to-date information of what has happened to date as far as the F.O. are concerned. I will write to you again directly I get this.

The C-in-C will, I know, do everything that is possible to help.

On 4 February Col Stephen again wrote with encouraging news.

Keith

Dear Colonel Bradford

I have just had a telephone conversation with a very senior officer about Bill.

Action is being taken to rescue him, and the other officers with him, in a manner that cannot be disclosed. I asked permission to tell you this, which was given, with the proviso that you told nobody except of course Mrs Bradford.

It is most essential that no one gets to know what is happening and nothing gets out when Bill arrives. If anything gets out we will all get into trouble so I trust you will keep everything quiet.

I am delighted and so must you be and trust that you will see him home safe and sound before very long.

Again, on 6 February came reassurance from Claude Jacob that matters were in the right hands:

Dear Bradford,

I have been some time answering your letter of 28 January, but I had to make enquiries which were not too helpful in answers. I then got my son, who is one of the secretaries of the War Cabinet, to take the matter up. He did so and asked me to tell you that your son's case is being dealt with. The right people are in charge of it and they hope all will come right soon. He cannot tell me any more, but he says the case has been properly dealt with. I feel sure all will be well in the near future.

It is very difficult in these days of strict censorship to get any news of what is being done about our people who have escaped into French territory.

He should be able to get away from Algiers very soon, as there will be ructions over the German demands on Petain for the French fleet and the port of Bizerta. If the French fleet sails from France and takes refuge in French North African ports I should think your son will be released at once! But one never knows what the French will be up to next.

About this time Bradford had started sending home information that was of potential interest to Military Intelligence. Col Bradford wrote:

Dear Major Irham
Thank you very much for your letter MI.9/E/13/2218 of the 13th inst. and its enclosures which naturally interested us considerably.

I am afraid that we know nothing whatever about the Commandant or about Mrs Eales as my son has never mentioned them before; I imagine that he has come across the relations he mentions out there and that they have been unable to get letters to England so asked him to convey the information of their whereabouts in his letter.

I will not communicate with the persons referred to until I hear from you as requested.

The further message probably conveys more to you than to me. If there is any doubt in your mind about it, I suggest that Capt. F Fitch, Norfolk Regt. who was with my son at Marseilles & got home a few weeks ago might be able to clear it up.

One gathers that there are a large number of British personnel still hiding in N France and presumably 'to my fellows' in the message refers to these.

In case it is of interest my son mentioned in a letter received about 10 days ago that Capt. Burn, 5th Fusiliers, who went with him to Algiers had been arrested and was being sent back to France.

I do not know if your official views are that he is doing useful work in sending messages such as these back but if not we should like to tell him not to do so as by doing so he will if discovered render himself liable to all kinds of penalties I imagine; perhaps you will be kind enough to let me know.

On 7 February the Red Cross wrote with further good news:

The Foreign Office have telephoned to us this morning, and have asked us to pass on to you the following information. They have received a cable, dated February 3, from the United States Consul General, Algiers, which reads as follows:-

'Bradford now good health never in danger, left Clinique in which placed solely for convenience two weeks ago. Have written. Has been maintained comfortably adequately since first arrival.'

We think you will be very pleased to have this news.

On 12 February a response came from Buckingham Palace. The long sentence in the third paragraph is a masterful display of English usage of the time:

12 February 1941
Dear Mrs Bradford,
I owe you an apology for not having sent an earlier reply to your letter of 23 January. I deferred sending a mere acknowledgement in the first instance, because I hoped earlier than now to have been able to give you information of more value, but the delay has been greater than I expected, with the result, I fear, that you may have thought that your letter was not receiving the attention it deserved.

I have been in communication with the War Office, and I heard from the Secretary of State today that the Foreign Office is doing its best on behalf of your son and other Officers and N.C.O.s in like cases.

I understand that a proposition has been put forward to the Vichy Government whereby the exchange of these prisoners may be arranged for certain French personnel. No reply from Vichy has yet been received, and, as you may suppose, it is impossible, with the present confusion which exists across the Channel, to forecast when developments may be expected or what may be their nature, but it will, I hope, encourage you to learn that the matter has not been forgotten, and I have The Queen's command to assure you of Her Majesty's sympathy in your anxiety, with a hope that your son may be duly restored to you.

I am glad to learn from General Wauchope that your son is reasonably comfortable in Algiers, though comfort is, at the best, a poor substitute for home.

Yours sincerely
Arthur Penn
Acting Private Secretary to The Queen

Lady Bradford was still active:

20 February 1941
Dearest Maggie,
I have had the Jacobs lunching with me today – he has written he says to Edward but begged me to say all will be done for Berenger that can be. He was certainly the right person to go to – as his son is now in the War Council – so knows the right person to go to for everything.

They will try to get an exchange for him – and if Petain's Government remains in power it is likely to be carried out – if not – and if Weygand joins us there will be no difficulties in getting him to Gibraltar. The War Office is seeing to these prisoners of the French

– their chief difficulty are the 300 prisoners near Marseilles – some of them sometimes escape – and a blind eye is turned.

Lady Jacob read me a letter from a man their son wrote to about Berenger. Her nephew escaped from the Germans 4 times and eventually got across the Pyrenees and is now home.

I ordered you 2 doz. Oranges for marmalade and I hope you get them.

Col Stephen again wrote on 12 March with advice:

Dear Colonel Bradford,
I must apologise for not writing earlier but I have just handed over command on promotion and have a job here. It was all very sudden and so you can imagine there was not a moment to spare.

On no account go near the Free French people in England they will be certain to make a mess of things.

Efforts are certainly being made through Vichy but I don't trust them a yard. Other matters are also being employed from which I hope for much better results.

I am afraid it is now a matter of patience which is easy to say but hard to bear.

The Germans unfortunately have a 'mission' in Algiers and things are rather difficult there just now.

Believe me although I have left the Regiment I will continue to do all I can for Bill. I hope you will let me know if you hear anything.

Col Bradford was in frequent communication with MI9:

20 March 1941
Dear Capt.
Please forgive me for writing to you about my son again but we had a letter from him yesterday dated 27 February in

which he said he was in hospital again and evidently feeling very depressed.

He tells us that the Doctor says that his present condition is due to his never having properly recovered from dysentery which he first had in India in 1936 and then in the Sudan in 1937–8 and the hardships which he has undergone since making his escape from the Germans in June have no doubt aggravated matters. He was in a Nursing Home in Algiers in January with gastric influenza and jaundice brought on by bad food according to the Doctor and has written since that his 'inside' was out of order so I imagine that his condition has now become much worse.

He says something about possibly being sent home as an invalid on account of his health; can anything be done for this end so as to expedite this, as we are naturally very anxious about him as long-standing troubles of his nature are apt to become very serious.

As was Capt. Irham of MI9 with him:

E/13/2369
C/o P A to DMI
Room 321
WAR OFFICE
Whitehall
London SW1
20 March 1941
Dear Colonel
Very many thanks for your letter of 15 March.

We are extremely interested in your details and will continue to follow up the question of your son's position.

I hope to be able to write to you again soon after our investigations.

> *Your information about Capt. Burn is disappointing. We have asked for confirmation of this.*

In fact Burn, while Bradford was ill, was having his own adventures. He had notified the Chief of Police that he intended to get away. He was arrested and feigned madness while in the concentration camp at Carnot. After transfer to a hospital he was certified insane and unfit for further military service. He was taken back to Carnot from which he escaped, took a train to the border and continued west on foot into Spanish Morocco. He was eventually released on the intervention of the British Consul, taken to Tangiers and repatriated.[71] *Again on 21 March Irham wrote:*

> *I am in receipt of your letter of 20 March and have represented the circumstances of your son's state of health to the appropriate department.*
>
> *All I can say is that we will do all we can towards his situation but it is naturally very difficult to make any promises of a definite nature.*
>
> *The politics as between Vichy and our own Govt. play a big part.*
>
> *Very many thanks for keeping us informed.*

Clearly the information that Bradford was sending home was of some interest to MI9 for on 31 March Irham again wrote to Col Bradford:

> *Dear Colonel,*
> *Further to my letters dated 13 and 20 March we are now in a position to reply more fully to your letter of 15 March.*
>
> *There is no harm in your transmitting the several messages to the persons named in your son's letter dated 17 February. If*

you are not able to convey the message to Commandant Niemiec, we will forward your letter if you will be good enough to send it to us.

The matter of dropping the message as your son requested is delicate in that it may not improve the chances of evasion if, as it is thought certain, the Germans get to know this intention. There has recently been an instance of arrest resulting from too much publicity being given to a leading individual and his efforts.

The sending of money is difficult for the same kind of reasons.

We have not yet heard any further news from the people dealing with the question of your son's case being put on to a medical basis, but we are pursuing the matter.

Col Bradford relayed information to MI9 about Bradford's attempts to get home by seeking repatriation on grounds of his ill health and being passed as unfit for future combat. The War Office took some comfort in this, presumably as it would save them having to effect a rescue. Messages from Bradford hidden in the letters home continued to reach their destination.

17 April 1941
Dear Colonel
I must thank you for your letter of 14 April enclosing copy of the message which your son sent in his letter to you date 27 March.

We have transmitted this message to the various persons concerned.
Yours sincerely
C A A Irham

By May Colonel Bradford was clearly exasperated. His draft letter of 9 May ends somewhat enigmatically, conveying yet another message from Bradford:

SECRET AND CONFIDENTIAL

Dear Maj. Irham

A letter from my son dated April reached me today; he says that the Medical Board which passed him unfit was apparently not properly constituted and that he had to go before another Board the other day, which reversed the previous Board's findings; he has therefore no chance of being sent home as a medical case.

 He sounds rather desperate poor fellow and thinks that, unless we can give him some hope of being got home by official action, he had better try and make a 'get away' himself though he doesn't feel much hope of being successful I gather.

 Until now I have advised him to be patient and wait for some action to get him away as I had hopes that some steps were being taken from England to help him but I am uncertain what advice to give him now.

 I should be very grateful to you if you would give me privately what counsel to give him i.e. whether to wait patiently or to try and escape; I could, I feel, only honestly ask him to wait if steps are really being taken here to get him home which give a reasonable hope of success before very long. I would undertake not to divulge anything which you may tell me.

 Small parties of G continue to come there and we have had the first strawberries already which I understand to mean the first fruits of the presence of these Germans there.

In North Africa Bradford had some inkling that plans were being made. I recollect him telling how he waited on a beach for several days after he'd received a message that a submarine would collect him and some other officers. He expressed exasperation at the fact that, the night after he'd given this plan up as yet another failure, two officers who waited on were rescued and got medals, he said, for a scheme that he'd somehow been instrumental in organising! I haven't attempted to follow this story up. However from the following letter it is evident that rescue attempts were being planned:

S E C R E T
The War Office
C/o Room 321
LONDON, SW1
11 May 1941
M.I.9.b/E/13/32/2599
Dear Colonel
Very many thanks for your letter of the 9 May giving the latest information about your son.

We are in the process of ascertaining the exact position in which he now is, since an unofficial report was received, which I did not pass on to you until confirmed, to the effect that he had been granted some form of sick leave but had not been passed as permanently unfit. We will advise you as soon as we know more.

I think there also is some other effort being made which would include as many of the others as possible. I do not think there is anything that you can do yourself, and in view of what might be happening I think it would be safer for you to have as little contact with him as possible, at any rate for a time.
Yours sincerely
CAA Irham

This didn't go down well with Col Bradford for written in his hand on this letter: 'advised not write each other for some weeks – some hope'.

Raised hopes were dashed once again.

CONFIDENTIAL
2 June 1941
Dear Colonel,
Thank you for your letter of 28 May which I have delayed answering while enquiries were being made.

The temporary ban on communicating with your son can be relaxed. I am afraid this will mean to you — what in fact is the case — that immediate prospects have again been postponed, and fresh ideas developed.

This must be realised as likely to go on happening and is of course very disappointing for you, but in a sense it is one of the dangers of my periodical reports.

I am always anxious to tell you what I can if you will not count too much on things projected working every time on schedule.

The sick-leave is of a weak kind only as you infer.

I will keep you informed if any further news comes in.

Yours sincerely

C.A.A. Irham

Almost a year had now passed between Bradford's capture at St-Valery on 12 June 1940. At home one can only imagine the frustration and sense of futility. Every avenue that Bradford's parents tried seemed to lead to false hopes or dead ends.

Bradford takes up the story once more.

14

From Algiers to Gibraltar: June 1941

At the beginning of 1941 I was in Algiers, having come over from France, as I thought it would be an easier place from which to get home. Wherever one was at the time, all reports lead one to think that everything was only too easy somewhere else, and it was most disconcerting to arrive in Algiers to find that people there thought that Marseilles, from which I had just come, was the place to go if you wanted to get back to England.

After several months during which I had travelled to Tunis and Morocco, and had been in a variety of prisons, I did not seem to be any nearer getting away. I had been in on several abortive schemes, including an attempt to snaffle the ordinary French Airliner, which nearly succeeded. I had had a job as valet to a senior officer in the German Armistice Commission – in fact I had tried everything.

During April and May I had been living in a smart French maternity home, pretending to be ill, as other British chaps were all interned in a camp inland which was a hopeless place from which to make any plans.

By May I was getting desperate as it had been made clear by the authorities that I should not be allowed to remain as I was for much longer.

Todo Le Briers a French friend of mine, who had lived a long time in England and was half English had been planning several schemes with me before. About 10 May we heard of a boat for sale for 18,000 Frs, and, finding it was suitable, tried to form a syndicate with Lieutenant Jean de Vaisseau Moreau, a French naval officer, and some of his friends.

Brinckman describes Moreau as 'a stout-hearted chap who was leaving his wife and planning to join the Free French in England. He was one of the few discreet Frenchmen I have ever met; he would not disclose his plan to us, but he did introduce us to a Frenchman (Thomas) who owned a small sailing dinghy, but who was very hard-up.'

Several times we thought we had got everything fixed up, but Moreau put forward new objections, and finally on 1 June, said he would not come in unless we got an engine. This would involve a considerable delay and in any case only boats without engines and which the French Authorities considered incapable of making a sea passage were allowed to sail outside the port and in the Bay.

Next day I heard down in the Bal d'Or, where we usually met for coffee in the morning, that Moreau's friends were planning to buy the boat on their own and have an engine fitted. I made Todo rush off to Thomas the owner and get an option on the boat, while I tried to find someone else to join us with the necessary money.

I managed during the day to raise 7,000 Frs from a friend of mine [*it was Brinckman who had been able to receive funds from his wife in Canada via the US Consulate*], and another 3,000 from someone else – a thing one might find difficult in doing at any time. A friend also said he would introduce a 'Riche de Gaulliste' who wished to escape – next day, when I met him, he turned out to be a poor engineer [*Botton*] with 2,000 Frs, but he did want to come away and he was prepared to take risks.

About 8 June, Thomas said we must decide definitely one way or the other. We were in despair, as we could not raise the money, and we also heard that Thomas had been broadcasting about the place that someone was going to buy his boat to get away in, so it was essential not to excite suspicion by changing the name of the owner till the last moment. I had to keep out of the negotiations as Thomas would have got windy and blown the whole story.

Next day Thomas suggested to Le Briers that he should buy half the boat and share it with him. This was almost too good to be true and we agreed at once. It meant that no change of the owner's name was necessary, and that Le Briers and Botton, the engineer, only had to get 'permits to sail' from the Marine Police, after putting themselves on the ship's roll. Better still Thomas wanted to get things arranged quickly, as he was going off on holiday next day.

The boat, *L'Odetic*, [72] was lying among a mass of small boats near the Yacht Club, and Todo and I looked at her from a distance, but I wasn't really sure which she was.

Thomas did not go off on his holiday, and we wondered if he had become suspicious. However, on 14 June, there was a really good North East wind, and I got hold of Todo, and arranged to sail that afternoon. He was to get hold of Botton, and we would meet at the café at 14.00hrs. Todo also had to buy the other half of the boat – this being covered by a clause in the agreement – so that, what with collecting food, water etc. there was a good deal to do.

To complicate matters, I had been asked to move out of the Clinique that day and go to the British Hospital, as the other authorities were getting troublesome. So I had to go through with my move, although I hoped I shouldn't sleep there that night.

Brinckman wrote from the British Cottage Hospital:

I forgot to say before, that this dear little hospital had been re-opened about 10 days previous at the special request of the American Consulate, and with the approval of the French military authorities for the benefit of any sick or wounded British who should be in the camp at Aumalle. Bill and I had been kicked out of the Clinique about a week before owing to a sudden rush of expectant mothers.

We met as arranged, and walked down to the Yacht Club, trying to look inconspicuous, although we had tins of water, and our food wrapped up in coats under our arms.

Tins or containers of any sort were difficult to get, but a friend of mine had made two 5-litre tins for water. When I went to get them, I found he had filled one with petrol and the other with water. It was too late to more than wash it out and refill with water.

We had to walk through the Yacht Club – one of the smartest places in Algiers, which I had never been in before – and picked up a dinghy there to get out to the boat. People looked a bit surprised as we went through. We asked the boatman to take us out to M. Thomas's boat, and hoped he would know it as we didn't.

Todo and I got on board, and started getting things ready. Botton was to follow half an hour later. After some time, the dinghy came alongside with a stranger, who said that Thomas had asked him to come for a sail this afternoon. This was a bit disconcerting, as the last person we wanted to see was Thomas. We told him there must have been some mistake and he went off.

By about 15.30hrs Botton had not turned up, and we were getting anxious, but soon afterwards he came along with several bundles of food and clothing – just what we had tried to stop him doing but actually it didn't matter at all, and the food was invaluable.

I had only seen the boat once before – she was about 18ft long, very beamy, with a big centre board and decked over with a sort of small cabin. She had a tall mast and was Bermuda rigged.

By this time it was blowing really hard, and as Botton had never been on a boat in his life before, and neither Todo nor I knew much about sailing, we decided to get out of the lines of the yachts moored before getting the sails up. The wind was so strong however that we got it all wrong, and couldn't do much with an oar at the stern.

After crashing stem on into several boats we eventually got into clear water and hoisted the sail. At this moment, all the ropes got inextricably muddled, and the sail, which was almost fully hoisted, wouldn't move in either direction.

By this time we were almost into the quay where the liners berth, but we came up into the wind, and eventually got things sorted out, although the mainsail was not too well reefed and the end of the boom touched the water when she heeled over.

To get out of the harbour we had to go through a narrow gap in the boom and show sailing permits to the police stationed there. Obviously I had to hide below, and down I went under some spare sails.

Todo was at the helm and tacked backwards and forwards, never seeming to get much closer. I kept seeing the same marks astern on each tack. About 16.30hrs we got out of the entrance and started on a long tack across the bay.

People with sailing permits were allowed to sail in the bay till sunset, when they must be back at their moorings. Our plan was to get right across the other side of the bay and then to begin coming back just before sunset, and to go straight out to sea as it got dark. Everything depended on the wind keeping up all night – it nearly always dropped at sunset – and on our not being noticed, and someone sending a boat out for us.

Out in the bay there was quite a sea running and within ten minutes Botton and I were being very sick, and Todo soon followed our example. We were keeping as near the wind as possible, and waves came right over the bow. Within fifteen minutes none of us had a dry stitch left and we had to bail fairly steadily. We drew slowly away from Algiers – she wouldn't sail very near the wind, as the sail was badly rolled – and continued tacking. About 19.00hrs we talked seriously about the advisability of putting back, as the bay was really rough and it would obviously be much worse outside. The wind hadn't gone down at all but Todo and I were absolutely decided to go on, as we might get a week of still evenings afterwards.

Half an hour later we completed a tack in towards the shore by the race course and wondered if we could just sail straight out. However, it was still very light, and we had to tack twice more before deciding that it was dark enough to go out.

We passed the line of the bay about 21.00hrs and found the sea quite rough enough outside. There were really big rollers coming on, and every so often one would break right over the ship and fairly fill her up. What with being sick and bailing almost continuously, it was really most unpleasant.

I took the helm for short intervals, but there was such a heavy sea running that I was far from happy steering her, as I know next to nothing about sailing. Todo therefore had to steer practically the whole night and he was magnificent.

Brinckman, who was just about to embark on his long journey home for repatriation, noted: 'I began now going around and saying good-bye to as many of my friends as I could find time to. For me, the excitement was considerably increased by the fact that Bill failed to sleep in the British Cottage Hospital that night.'

As mentioned in the preface, Bradford's sailing experience amounted to a day on a river estuary in England and a day in a jury-rigged rowing boat on a Scottish loch. 'I was quite useless' he said. Botton had never sailed before and Le Briers' experience was really no greater than Bradford's.

15 June. We were sailing on a course of NNW to get as far away from the coast as possible by dawn the next day. The lights of Algiers and Cape Matifou lighthouse gradually grew fainter and soon after midnight the wind dropped slightly and the sea got a bit easier.

At 03.00hrs the wind was much less and I took the helm for a long spell to give Todo a rest – on the cabin floor which was sopping. By about 06.00hrs Todo was too cold to lie down any longer. I was frozen too, as I had only my shirt and a thin coat and trousers on. We were longing for the sun to come up and warm us.

Soon after this we heard an engine and an aeroplane flew directly over us. Of course we thought it was looking for us, but it flew straight on and disappeared to the NE; Todo said 'We're caught now' as soon as it appeared, but was all the happier when it flew away.

There was a nice sailing breeze by now, and we unrolled the whole mainsail and hoisted our large jib. The sea was uncomfortable, as we were running parallel to the big rollers, but we were sailing nice and fast and no land or ships were visible. It was a lovely day and we sailed on all day under a boiling sun.

Everything, including food, was spread out to dry. Our food was adequate but not over plentiful, and consisted of ten small tins of assorted pâté, sardines etc. one loaf of bread, three packets of biscuits, six ginger breads, some chocolate and ten pounds of dates. Practically everything was sodden with sea-water.

This was easily enough for 10 days, if carefully rationed out. On Sunday evening the breeze almost died away at sunset, but sprung up again some 2 hours later. We had been sailing since noon on an almost Westerly course, which I didn't exactly agree with, as I wanted to go more north.

We took 3-hour watches during the night, giving Botton the helm for 3 hours, as the breeze was very moderate and he couldn't gybe. During the day we had seen quite a few turtles about.

16 June. On Monday morning there was a good fresh East wind blowing, and we rigged the jib out on an oar and sailed along very fast. We had to pull up the centre board, as there was a lot of play in it, and its knocking shook the whole boat, and looked like tearing away the casing. The cables for raising it were almost worn through, only held by about two strands, so we tried to avoid moving it too often.

[*The boat also leaked around the centreboard casing. Bradford later mentioned that Botton let fly a halyard to the masthead which caused some problems.*[73]]

Todo and I had great differences about the speed – he maintained we were doing 8 or 9 knots and I saying 4 or 5. When we were eventually towed in by a tug at Gib. at 6 knots, he agreed with my estimate.

Todo and I had to steer all day and the night as we couldn't trust Botton with a following wind. By the evening the breeze was strong, and the big rollers following us looked as if they must break on the boat. We thought seriously about taking down the 'contraption' as we called it, but decided to go on under all sail, although she was burying her nose a bit in the waves.

17 June. On Tuesday, the wind was still favourable and we raced on, but at about 10.00hrs Todo sighted land to the SW of us. We were expecting to hit the Spanish coast first and this rather worried us. We changed course to NW, setting the contraption on the other side. It was very hot by day, and poor Todo got terribly thirsty, although we had three good drinks a day.

There were a lot of porpoises about to keep us interested by day, and by night the sea was all phosphorescent and we left a lovely wake. The wind continued East all day and night; Wednesday, 18 June, was just the same, and about 16.00hrs Todo sighted land to the NNW.

We weren't at all certain where we should first sight Spain, but thought it would probably be near Cartagena. Our very small compass had been bought for 30 Frs and it was almost impossible to tell if you were within ten degrees either side of your course. We tried to estimate longitude and latitude but without much success. We gradually approached the coast and by sunset were able to identify it fairly certainly as Cape Gata, which was encouraging.

[*When asked about navigation Bradford replied, 'I had a small map – I merely headed north and then west.'*]

We were now sailing west again, and at dawn, 19 June, we could see the Sierra Nevada very clear to the North. In spite of a good breeze all night, we hadn't gone as far as we hoped, and during the morning the breeze died away gradually so that at 15.00hrs we were absolutely stationary and could not even keep our stern to the rollers. The boat was rolling like anything and to avoid damage to the mast and rigging we finally lowered the mainsail and drifted. In the late afternoon I had a very pleasant bathe.

In the evening we heard a diesel-engined ship coming towards us, and as it got dark we saw her lights coming straight for us. We thought we must have been seen from the coast, though we were some twenty miles out and imagined she was looking for us. One always thinks everyone is trying to pick you up, when actually no one is taking the least interest in you. She carried steadily on, and poor Todo got desperate. She passed us so close that we could hear the crew talking on board, and finally disappeared into the night.

We had hoisted our sails again at sunset and were steering SSW to get further from the coast. The breeze was practically non-existent and we could hardly see any movement through the glassy sea. By dawn on Thursday we were still lying off the Sierra Nevada, though the coast was further off. There was practically no breeze at all, and I bathed twice. We got very hot and bored and a little short with each other. Todo tried fishing, with a bent pin to pass the day, but had no luck. Late that evening, after sunset, a breeze sprung up, still easterly. The sky had looked so threatening that we had hoisted the small jib, to avoid getting caught out at night by a squall. As it turned out it was a very nice breeze.

While I was at the helm from 22.00hrs to 02.00hrs a big school of porpoises chased us and carried out continuous torpedo attacks from all angles. It was a dark night and you could see these luminous shapes dashing at you about 50 yards away. They came so close that it seemed impossible for them to avoid the boat. By day they always kept their distance from us, but at night I suppose they could only see our luminous wake.

20 June. Soon after daybreak, the wind dropped again till we were scarcely moving. We were getting very fed up with this calm, as we had covered such a big distance in the first 3 days and with a decent breeze we would have been at Gib. by now.

The only good part was that Botton was able to take the helm as he would usually day dream and wake up to find the boat pointing in any direction. He was a Communist and rather a useless man. There was no land visible and we set a course of WNW – but hardly moving.

I had a bathe, and after some time a faint breeze came up. By about 16.00hrs the breeze had got stronger and we were sailing along well. About 19.30hrs Todo again sighted land and soon afterwards we could see points of land to the NW, W and SW of us. It was difficult to decide where we were and Todo at last convinced me that we were up North of Gib. When I said that it might be the Moroccan coast he got rather annoyed and started on his long arguments against this again. I was at the helm and told him to try and see what the light house ahead might be from our chart, but he couldn't find it.

It was too late to try and get in now, especially as we thought there was a strong tide from the Mediterranean into the Atlantic and that we might be carried through during the night. We settled to cruise up and down until dawn.

Before this at about 17.00hrs we came through an extraordinary belt of water which was bubbling up quite high, just like boiling water. It was obviously some tide set, and was an extraordinary sight from a small boat.

21 June. There was a good breeze all night, and about midnight we hove to till 03.30hrs when we set off again towards

the light house, about NW of us now after our manoeuvres of the night. About 05.00hrs the wind dropped again, and there was almost a flat calm.

As soon as it was light, I got out the chart and saw that only Ceuta lighthouse was visible at a great distance, and as its flashes agreed with those we had seen, I was convinced that it was Ceuta.

We had obviously come too far south in to the bay near the Moroccan coast the previous evening, and seen the Ceuta to the NW of us at first. We ought to have guessed this at once, especially as we had seen a big ship to the NW, just before dusk. Todo still wasn't convinced but agreed to sail north, 'in case my theory was right'.

After a time he began to be more convinced, when we had taken some bearings with a protractor on points on the coast. It was almost a dead calm, and we worried about being too near the Ceuta.

About noon a slight breeze sprang up and we were soon sailing along well. Soon after 13.00hrs we could see Gib. in the distance. We also saw a French destroyer, escorting two cargo ships through the straits close to the Moroccan coast. We were still keeping well out from the coast, to avoid the tide set, and about 14.30hrs we saw a ship coming out from Ceuta – as it looked to us – and heading straight for us.

Todo suggested letting down our sails in case we hadn't been seen, but it obviously wasn't worthwhile. She came nearer rapidly, and Todo kept saying 'I know we are going to be caught now, just when we are nearly home' and other depressing things. Finally I said 'for heavens sake, shut up' as I was getting apprehensive too. The ship came up to leeward of us, but we still couldn't see the ensign.

Suddenly a voice boomed out 'Is that Captain Bradford?' and we knew we were safe. I answered 'yes' and we were then told to come along side. I shouted back 'I'm afraid we are not very capable of handling this boat' which caused some amusement.

A boat was lowered and came alongside whereupon the lieutenant, beautifully dressed, stood up and, saluting smartly, said 'May I come aboard your ship, Sir?' This to a very untidy tramp with a week's growth of beard.

Two officers took over the yacht and we got into the boat. I was asked to take the tiller, but refused, as I didn't want to make a nonsense of coming alongside. I took an oar instead (stroke, actually), and we rowed over to the ship and climbed on board.

I was taken up to the Captain, Comdr Harry Hamilton – who welcomed us, and said they had had a signal to look out for us. While I was talking to him, the same lieutenant came up and said 'What would you like me to do with your ship now, Sir?' Comdr Hamilton kindly took charge and had her hoisted on his davits, mast and all.

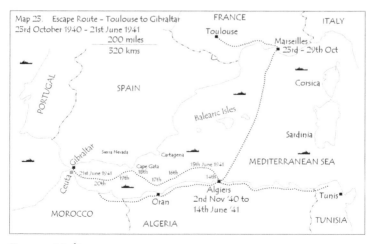

Escape - Mediterranean 40-10-20.

We went below, had a drink, bath and shave. She was the *Sayonara*, a luxury yacht of some 800 tons. The owner's state room was large and luxurious and had a lovely green marble bath room, even the lavatory paper matched. After this we had an enormous mixed grill, bread, butter and coffee which was excellent.

The vessel was originally named UL, *constructed in 1911 by Ramage and Ferguson Ltd of Leith; she had a gross tonnage of 854.43, length 185ft, breadth 29ft, draught 16ft and her original registered owner was HIH the Archduke Charles Stephen of Austria (1860–1933). The yacht was removed from Lloyd's Register of Yachts after 1915 but re-installed in 1927 under the name* Vanduara *and her owner was R.G. Fothergill of Buenos Aires but her port of registry was Dover. In 1930 her ownership changed to Anthony J. Drexel Jr. of Paris, who re-registered the vessel in Philadelphia, USA and renamed her* Sayonara. *Drexel was the son of Anthony J. Drexel who was the financier who turned J.P. Morgan from an under-achiever into a wizard of high finance. Drexel, according to Rottenberg, was the 'Man who made Wall Street.'*

In 1935 Sayonara *was sold to Major Ralph S. Grigg of London and re-registered in Southampton. In 1939 she was acquired by the Admiralty for use as an armed boarding vessel (ABV) and they eventually purchased her in 1941. She served under pennant number 4.72. After the war she was laid up and then sold in 1946 to J. Bruce Kellock of Southampton who renamed her* Barcarolle. *In 1948 the owner was recorded as D.H.C. Wright of Bournemouth, Hants. At this point she disappears from the Register of Yachts.*

I heard that the 4th Bn [*The Black Watch*] was at Gib. which was welcome news. [*The 4th Black Watch had, of course, been part of Ark Force and had embarked at Le Havre on the day that the rearguard of the 51st Highland Division had been captured at St-Valery.*]

I went up on the bridge and talked to Comdr Hamilton again. He said we were looking suspiciously innocent when he sighted us. I had actually put on my tie so as to be able to argue better with a Spaniard, if they tried to pick us up.

They said we shouldn't have got in under sail until the next day, as the current was set easterly and not as we had been told.

After the war Commander Harry Hamilton became an apple farmer in Kent and until his death sent Bradford a case of apples every Christmas.

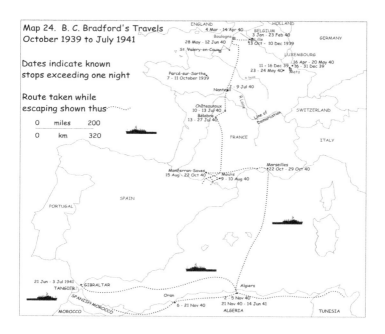

Whole Route.

Bradford was now back with British forces 374 days after St-Valery
and 367 days since he first escaped from the Germans. From St-Valery,
excluding daily trips in Bélâbre, Depot 602, Marseilles and Algiers, he
had walked over 620 miles; bicycled 506 miles; and travelled 283 miles by
vehicle; 2,216 miles by train; 469 miles by ship and around 700 miles by
small boat. The total journey covered some 4,795 miles of which 183 were
as prisoner of the Germans. He had escaped once from the Germans and
got away from French hands at least six times. His brushes with authori-
ties, German, French and Spanish, are too numerous to list.

On arrival off Gib. we were met by a tug, the yacht was lowered into the water and taken in tow, and we transferred to
the tug. At the quay we were met by Duncan Stewart, who
was on the Intelligence Staff and soon afterwards by Rory
Macpherson, who took me away to his house.

Todo and Botton were taken away by the Free French, but
later that evening Todo came up to have a drink with us after
dinner and was got away from them.

I was lent some respectable clothes, as mine had rotted
away with sea water and were only fit for burning. I found
it very difficult to remain steady on my feet after a week of
movement and was just like a drunken man for 48 hours.

Naps Brinckman, who had been in the Clinique in Algiers
for 5 months and was being sent back officially as unfit for
service, arrived 3 days later and I met him at the quay. He
had lent me half the money for buying the boat, which he
had never seen, and without him I might never have raised
enough cash.

Brinckman recorded:

On Tuesday, 24 June I went across the Straits of Gibraltar in the
Admiralty tug and set foot on British territory for the first time since

13 February 1940. As the tug came alongside the jetty, I saw Bill Bradford standing there to greet me. We had become so French that we practically embraced each other. Bill and I sold the 'yacht' and in the end we were exactly square on the deal. Fat Boy* was very impressed by Bill's performance and even suggested that we should both sail back to Algiers and bring some more Englishmen over.

[**General, The Viscount Gort, VC, DSO, MC had been Commader-in-Chief of the BEF in 1939–40 and was, in 1941, Governor of Gibraltar.*]

At home after the many despondent letters from their son the sudden arrival of the following telegram must have come as a wonderful surprise to Bradford's parents:

Telegram stamped Petersfield, Hants, 26 June 1941
CC 1123 25 GIBRALTAR 14
BRADFORD LISS HANTS =
ARRIVED BIG [sic] SATURDAY STOP EXPECT COME ON HOME
SHORTLY LOVE = BEN BRADFORD +++

Post Script:
July 1941–June 1945

Bradford left Gibraltar on 3 July and arrived in Glasgow on the 11th. After an extensive debriefing which included the provision of various reports for Military Intelligence he went home to his parents. On 15 July he wrote to the Under-Secretary of the War Office:

> *Sir,*
> *I have the honour to report that I have now returned to the United Kingdom, as an escaped prisoner-of-war.*
> *I have already been in touch with M.I.(9) and am required for further questioning by other branches of M.I. during this week.*
> *I have also reported myself to the Officer Commanding, I.T.C. The Black Watch by letter, and am awaiting instructions.*
> *I have the honour to be, Sir,*
> *Your obedient servant*
> *B.C. Bradford, Captain,*
> *The Black Watch*

Lt-Col Vesey Holt, the Commanding Officer referred to in his letter, responded. The reply from Col Holt reflects the mood of euphoria at Bradford's escape:

Subject:-POSTINGS: OFFICERS
Queen's Barracks,
PERTH.
25 July 1941
Ref. No.27/6/41 HCW.
Dear Bill,
Reference your letter dated 22/7/41.
I would like to express my congratulations, on behalf of all ranks, on your safe return.

You are granted 2 months leave — against any regulations that I have ever seen — from 15/7/41 — 17/9/41.

I think it most unlikely that you will join this I.T.C., and I consider that you will probably be whisked away to some job long before your leave is up.

If you apply in about 2 months time for petrol vouchers to bring up your car, they will probably be supplied if:-

Regulations have not been altered.

There is any petrol left.

Meanwhile I have asked the R.A.F., to limit their operations with this object in view.

Should you arrive here I consider that a shooting suit and a pair of flannel-trousers will more than meet the sartorial requirements of the moment.

Yours
A.V. Holt,
Lt-Col
Comd. ITC. The Black Watch
To:- Capt. B.C. Bradford,
Empshott Lodge
Liss, Hants.

Bradford always maintained that he received 'one month's leave for escaping from the Germans and another month for escaping from the French'. He was awarded the MBE in recognition of his successful

escape from captivity. No citation was published for reasons of secu-
rity. While his account and letters give little indication that he was
doing anything other than fret at not getting home his report to MI and
the concealed messages in his letters home gives a hint that there was
another side to his time in Algiers.

Extracts from Bradford's observations to Military Intelligence
on report by Maj. Brinckman:

1. Gen. Weygand in an official speech to a large number
   of reserve officers at beginning of May maintained that
   France's defeat was largely due to Lord Gort's refusal to
   attack against the flank of the German breakthrough,
   when ordered to do so by Gen. Weygand. I have met
   many French officers who were at this gathering, and
   who believed what Gen. W. said.

2. In occupied France, people are willing to take great
   risks to help British. In unoccupied France, I should say
   80 per cent are pro-British, but are not willing to take so
   much risk to help.

3. I got into contact with <u>M. André Achiary</u> after I had
   been in Algiers for a few days. He helped me to go on
   to Oran, getting my ticket, and taking me to the station
   himself. I went to Algiers and Oran from France with
   the object of finding a way of getting the British soldiers
   interned in Marseilles away; this turned out to be impossible. When I was arrested in Oran I was very badly
   treated to begin with and put in the gaol with natives.
   When I was eventually sent back to Algiers, Achiary got
   me out of the military barracks, where I was locked up,
   and took charge of me himself, putting me in a hotel.

4. Michael Eichner, (alias M. Despax) an Austrian ex-
   officer, who works free-lance for the 2eme Bureau, and

lived at the Aletti Hotel, is a great friend of Achiary, and works in with him. I knew him and Achiary pretty well, and used to get a certain amount of useful information from him. Both he and his chief, Commandant Duriot, 2eme Bureau, left for Casablanca on about 23 June as a permanent posting. Eichner first told me of Achiary's activities, and introduced me to him. His mother and sister are in London, and are not interned.

5. Joan Tuyh is under observation by French authorities, and should not be expected to do much.

6. Escout's wireless set is worked by the chief mechanicien of Air Afrique, M. Bousson, who has every facility for keeping it in working order. He has now regained his confidence in Achiary & repaired his set which was damaged.

7. I introduced Escout to Commandant d'Aviation de Cervens (chief of 2eme Bureau de l'Air, Tunis), who is very pro-British, and supposed to be actually working the W/T set to Malta. In any case, he told me all about it & is obviously in a position to stop it, if unfriendly. He talks too much and too easily. Escout is now in touch with him.

8. M. Castay is the editor of an official paper containing news items from all countries, which circulates to all heads of govt. departments & military, naval etc. depts. daily. He is absolutely Anglophile, and tries to influence opinion by his news items as he can exclude what he doesn't like. He also started about 6 weeks ago, circulating true news items & some propaganda, secretly among his friends. He is now in touch with Escout. Under Castay, in the wireless listening centre, at least three of the operators are very Anglophile, and told me that the majority of those employed there are Anglophile.

9. Madame de Malglaive, an English lady, whose husband is naturalized British, was a Captain RASC last war, & is now serving in Nigeria, is active in many ways. She got a lot of information from Gen. Weygand and his staff, and also saw Mr Murphy (American Chargé d'Affairs) several times in connection with Gen. Weygand, being a sort of unofficial link about some matters. She is intimate with Gen. Weygand's circle. She is now in touch with her husband by trans-Sahara transport.

10. M. Fox, an Englishman, employed in a big engineering works, is a friend of de Malglaive's & worked with him for 10 years. He arranges for the letters to go to Nigeria. He is an odd position as he has no papers of any sort. His firm is now preparing all the vehicles for an expedition against the dissident parts of French W. Africa near L. Chad to take place in autumn. He says that all these vehicles will break down after 1,000 or 1,500 miles, when he has prepared them.

11. M. Mariain, who lives in small village of Chenona 65km from Algiers, is very Anglophile and would hide anyone for several days if this was of any use.

12. Mlle. Coggia, dentist at Guelma, near Constantine, can arrange to transport anyone across frontier into Tunis, if they came to her with a certain code phrase. If useful I can give you this phrase.

13. Jean Coggia, her brother, lives in Djenila Palace Hotel, Algiers, & took two messages to Springs in Tunis. He has a code with Springs.

14. M. Perret, a businessman, helped several foreigners out of the country up till January 1941. Is very friendly, & has another pro-British group. He travels a lot. The only other member of his organisation, whom I met, is a M. Bilka, a solicitor, who often goes to Morocco.

15. As an instance of number of Germans in Algiers, about 20 Germans arrive at Hotel Regence, three times a week and pass on after 2 days. There are four members of German commission at Hotel Aletti, 10 at Hotel Albert (recent arrivals), ten at Hotel Astoria, and some at Touring Hotel. Practically the whole of Hotel Albert has now been taken over by Germans (i.e. about forty out of sixty bedrooms).

16. I met a soldier who came from Brest who said that there had been 800 casualties either in the Scharnhorst or Gneisenau and that one of the ships was merely a wreck tied up to the quay.

17. Till a few weeks ago, I never heard any criticism of Petain, & even anti-Vichy people were still fond of Petain. Lately however I have heard many people describe him as an old dodderer & useless. Admiral Darlan is loathed as much as Laval & de Brinon.

18. I met the head of some important department for whole N. Africa, whose name & function I have forgotten. He went to Vichy in May, got an audience with Petain, & complained of German infiltration into N. Africa. Petain maintained there were no Germans in Africa other than 4 members of the Commission & when confronted with proof, said 'No one ever tells me anything'.

19. Large quantities of all commodities, live horses, also metals & metal ores being shipped to Marseilles & handed to Germans. Great shortage of essential foods among natives at present, so that they are the more receptive of German propaganda, which is largely done by released prisoners, who have been well treated & prepared in Germany. Britain is held up as the protector of the Jews who are loathed in N. Africa.

20. 28,000 tons of petrol was alleged to have been sent from Oran, Algiers etc. to Tripoli in May. Also 100-250 heavy army lorries (3 to 5 ton) and 150 petrol tank lorries. As Gen. Weygand's army was already short of mechanical tpt. he protested very strongly against this, & his staff were almost beside themselves at having to carry out the order.

21. The Army authorities & Navy authorities are at daggers drawn in Algiers & delight in any chance they have of pin-pricking each other.

There was, of course, much to do. Meantime Col Stephen who had been a bulwark of support for Bradford's parents during their long months of anxiety wrote to Bradford's Commanding Officer.:

O.C. 1st Black Watch [R.H.R.],
Keith
Banffshire
1 July 1941
I have just been informed that Captain B.C. Bradford, who was my Adjutant in the 1st Bn Black Watch in France, has escaped to Gibraltar.

As you know, he was taken prisoner on 12 July 1940 and escaped in the first case about 10 days later. From time to time, while I was in command of the Bn his adventures were reported by me to Higher Formation.

I had recommended this Officer as a candidate for the Staff College while he was serving in France under my Command. I trust that should he join 1st Bn Black Watch you will take this into consideration and give him a recommendation for Staff College, should you think fit. He was a first class Adjutant on active service and he has put up a very fine show in getting away from the Bosche.
Colonel CGS

Edinburgh Commanding LOTHIAN SUB AREA.

Stephen also wrote to Col Bradford on the same day:

Dear Colonel Bradford

I was so pleased to get your letter and hear the good news from Bill. He will be well looked after at Gib as we have a battalion there as you probably know.

In fact I met one of the officers from Gib a few days ago and he told me that there was a lot of 'Funny business' going on in Gib to try & rescue our officers and men who had escaped to Spain and Morocco so my hopes revived.

I had become rather despondent about Bill as I felt the French would hold him & make things uncomfortable. One cannot trust the French a yard & I trust that they are having a good hammering.

I enclose a copy of a letter addressed to the CO, 1st Bn. in case Bill is sent there.

If Bill has time & is well enough do ask him to write me a line and if he can come to Edinburgh there is always a bed ready for him.

I am moving from this address at the end of July but the New Club or better still my office 63/65 Cockburn Street will always find me.

How pleased Mrs Bradford and you must be.

Yours sincerely
C.G. Stephen

After his leave Bradford headed north to join the re-formed 51st Highland Division. After the loss of the Division at St-Valery the captured regular battalions (1st Black Watch, 1st Gordons, 2nd Seaforth) were re-raised; 152, 153 and 154 Brigades were reconstituted within 2 months and, like the fabulous phoenix, the 51st Highland Division itself rose from the ashes of St-Valery.

To bring a Division together to a level of proficiency comparable with its well-knit predecessor was not a feat that could be achieved overnight and a great deal of training went on during the remainder of 1940 and into 1941. By the autumn of 1941 Bradford joined this renascent Highland Division as Brigade Major of 154 Brigade.

In October Bradford was surprised to receive a letter from Moreau, the French naval officer who had, at one point proposed to escape from Algiers with him but who had pulled out because of the lack of an engine in L'Odetic.

My dear Bradford,

It is already a month and a half that I have been in London but it wasn't until today that I have come across your address, or at least an address which was yours.

I haven't had the chance to congratulate you on your marvellous escape but I could tell you how it looks from Algiers, you have changed the country!! For me after two attempts I succeeded in my turn and would be undeniably happy to see you again.

I have not yet succeeded in finding Le Briers but perhaps you are once more in touch with him.

I have at least found my comrade aviator Laurent whom you must have seen at Gibraltar it is a real joie to refind old friends from Alger [sic] with whom we have thought so much about you and done so much to get so far.

I ask you to accept my sincere best wishes and my best wishes for Victory

Moreau.

In November 1941, 4 months after his return home, the Red Cross, as reliably behindhand as they had been during the time of Bradford's captivity, wrote to his parents advising of a new address in Algeria to which to send letters to their imprisoned son.

*In April 1942 the 51*st *Highland Division moved from North East Scotland to Aldershot for final training and outfitting. In the third week of June 1942 the Division entrained for the ports in the Mersey, Severn and Clyde and set sail for an unknown destination. The Division was, as Salmond wrote, 'to travel far, to earn great renown, and to suffer almost 16,000 casualties before its task was done'.*[74]

Via the Cape of Good Hope they travelled, in a nine-week voyage, to Egypt. It is not the purpose of this tale to record in detail the Division's History through the next three years of war. From El Alamein to Tunis, across Sicily and then from Normandy, through Belgium and Holland, to Germany the Division fought as a constant part of the Armies under the command of General [later Field Marshal] Bernard Montgomery.

In North Africa Bradford served first as 154 Brigade Major and then as 2IC of 5th Black Watch, during which time he was awarded the MC and Mentioned in Despatches for Distinguished Service.

CITATION – THE MILITARY CROSS
Captain (Temporary Major Berenger Colborne
BRADFORD, M.B.E. (53741),
The Black Watch (Royal Highland Regiment).
Major Bradford has acted as Brigade Major to an Infantry Brigade from Alamein right up to the completion of the campaign in North Africa. Throughout this strenuous period he has never missed an action in which his Brigade has taken part.

In the distinguished part which his Brigade took in the battles of Alamein and Akarit, he played his full share, and as Brigade Major, this was of course a most important one. At the former battle, his Headquarters was heavily shelled and his Brigade Signal Office destroyed by a direct hit.

Apart from these battles, he has been noticed time and again for his courage and cheerfulness in action, and his imperturbability

under fire; and he as always set a fine example of courage and cool-
ness to the Headquarters of which he has been Chief Staff Officer.

After El Alamein the press, desperate for good news, went to town.
Richard McMillan in his account headed 'The Highlanders take
revenge' describes in some detail the tragedy of St-Valery and the
subsequent rebirth of the 51st Highland Division. In describing the
build-up to the battle of Alamein he wrote of meeting a 'Brigade
Major'. 'We found then, that not all the prisoners taken by the
Germans at St-Valery had remained in the Nazi prison cages', he
wrote, before going on to summarise Bradford's escape story.[75]

During the Desert War Bradford recalled spending hours counting
vehicles as they passed various checkpoints on their long journey west-
wards with his old friend Lorne Campbell, 7th Argylls, who was to go
on to win the VC at the battle of Wadi Akarit in Tunisia. Campbell
had also fought with the 51st Division in 1939–40. The 7th Argylls
were part of 154 Bde and had formed part of Ark Force and had thus
avoided capture at St-Valery-en-Caux. In between the vehicles the
subject of conversation was, more often than not, about favourite clar-
ets, shooting, fishing or holidays in Scotland.[76]

After the battle of Wadi Akarit Bradford found new entertainment
in disabling captured German 88mm guns. One evening he persuaded
General Montgomery to come along and have a go. 'You'll love this
Sir, It's the greatest fun,' he said. Bradford fixed the explosive in the
way he'd been shown and lit the fuse and they both retired to a nearby
ditch to take cover and wait for the bang. The explosion duly happened,
shortly followed by a large lump of breech block, weighing a hundred-
weight or so, landing in their ditch about 6ft away from Monty. He
thought he'd had enough excitement for one evening and promptly
departed leaving Bradford to complete the job on the other guns, which
he did without injury.[77]

After the conquest of Tunis Bradford sent, with two other Old
Etonians, Capt. W.J.C. Adamson and Lt J.A.H. Williamson,

a night-telegram which was duly published in the Eton College Chronicle. No doubt their Latin construe was not as well practiced as once it had been.

'Nos Carthagine deleta finibus Africanis septentrionalibus tres Duces felicitas optimas vobis hoc die mittimus.'

'Carthage having been destroyed, we three Generals,[officers] are sending best wishes to you today from the Northern boundaries of Africa.'

Bradford even took time off to drive from Tunis to Algiers in order to thank those who had helped him during his escape. In the weeks after the conquest of North Africa he achieved a reputation for throwing a good party. Part of this success lay in his ability to distil the strong Algerian wine and then using the alcohol as a base for a fruit cup.[78]

After Tunis the 51st moved on to the Sicilian Campaign. While 2IC in Sicily Bradford took over command for 3 days from Lt-Col Chick Thomson. Chick had equipped himself with a Willis Jeep which he'd had specially altered to suit him and of which he was very proud. During his three-day command Bradford managed to lose the jeep – someone stole it. Fearing Thomson's wrath at the loss of his prized possession Bradford stole another jeep and had it altered to make it as much like the missing vehicle as he could in the short time available. When he had owned up to his CO what he'd done Thomson was so horrified by this behaviour that he wouldn't have anything to do with the replacement vehicle.[79]

During this campaign Bradford moved from 2IC to become, once again, Brigadier Thomas Rennie's Brigade Major for 154 Bde. About this time he recalled getting into trouble from General Montgomery for a second time. Bradford had equipped himself with a large Humber Tourer as his staff car. There were only two such cars on the island, the other was used by Montgomery. One day he drove past a crowd that was waiting to cheer Monty. They all cheered like mad and when, some minutes later Monty drove past he found the crowd dispersing. Bradford was swiftly told to find alternative transport.[80]

The Highland Division returned to the UK in November 1943 for some well-earned leave and the commencement of training for the invasion of Europe.

Bradford was moved temporarily from the Division first as GSO1 HQ 2nd Army in January 1944 during which he was involved in strategic planning for the invasion.

There was considerable delay between the award of medals and investiture. In May 1944 Bradford went to Buckingham Palace to receive the MBE for his escape, awarded in 1941, and the MC which was awarded in 1943. As happens today, a good-news story was embellished somewhat by the press and, in so doing, some of the accuracy was lost on the way. Quite where some of the details of the following account originated will never be known but it made good copy. The statement that Bradford's MBE was for bravery in France in 1940 was not totally true as it was awarded for his escape. Bradford had been recommended for an award during the fighting in France in 1940 but nothing came of it.[81]

COLONEL ENTERED REGATTA, SAILED TO FREEDOM

A tall, black-moustached officer in the kilt of the Black Watch received two decorations, won in two continents, from the King at a recent Buckingham Palace investiture.

He was Lt-Col B. C. Bradford, of Liss, Hants, who got the MBE for bravery in France in 1940 and the MC for bravery in North Africa.

Between winning these two awards, Lieut-Colonel Bradford was captured, but the Germans could not hold him. After 3 days he escaped, and for the next 14 months was a fugitive.

He made his way through France, covering 1500 miles mostly on foot.

*Then he managed to smuggle himself on board a ship bound for
Algiers, where he was thrown into an Arab prison.*

*He got out of that too, and entered as a competitor in a sailing
boat regatta in Algiers Bay.*

*And he left all the rest behind for he sailed his little boat right out
of the race and across the Mediterranean to Gibraltar before anyone
could stop him.*

*This brought him home in time to return to North Africa and
fight right through that campaign.*

By the time of the Normandy landings Bradford was Liaison Officer
with the 1st US Army (FUSA) under General Omar Bradley.
He sailed at midnight from Plymouth on FUSA's command ship,
USS Achernar, an attack cargo ship of the Andromeda class. From
her he witnessed the landings on Omaha and Utah beaches. Bradford
went ashore at Omaha beach several times during 6 to 9 June and
by 10 June was able to move permanently with Bradley to a shore-
based HQ. Bradford had great respect for General Bradley and was
surprised that he queued for his food in the canteen just like the most
junior soldier. This was very unlike the practice in the British Army
at the time.

The Highland Division, including 5th Black Watch, had also
landed in Normandy further east at Juno beach. Some six weeks
would pass before the real breakout from the beachheads took place.
Nevertheless during the period between 6 June and late July the
5th Black Watch were in almost constant action. The eastern salient
between Caen and the coast saw some very tough fighting indeed. On
16 June Bradford wrote:

'I have heard bad news of the Bn but can't repeat it here.'

By 21 June, still with the US Army, Bradford felt that his talents were
being wasted:

'I don't feel I'm doing a full-time job. On most days I do a job which any 2nd-Lt could do.'

On 22 July Bradford acted.

> I saw the Div. Cmd. and asked him if he definitely didn't want me in his Div or thought I was not fit to command, because if so, I would much rather he said so to me, rather than tell me that he wanted me and then put forward someone else. I was very firm in what I said. I then went and saw Chick [*Lt-Col Thomson was still commanding 5th Black Watch*] who was longing to get away, as he says he is dead tired and can't go on doing this indefinitely and felt he couldn't go on commanding the Bn.

On 24 July Bradford travelled from the American beachhead to visit 5th Black Watch to discuss the handover to him of command of the battalion. He returned to the Americans just in time to be at the receiving end of an Allied bombing raid by over 1,800 bombers which, unfortunately, bombed the American as well as German positions. The raid was an early phase of Operation Cobra.

Bradford took his leave of the Americans who, from the Army Commander [Bradley] downwards were sorry to see him go. He wrote to his parents:

> Maurice Chilton (*Brig. Maurice Chilton, General Staff, 2nd Army North West Europe 1944–45*) also thanked me for my good work especially in getting that big exercise off, 'without which the invasion couldn't have taken place'.

At 16.30hrs on 26 July Bradford arrived to take over command of 5th Black Watch, a position he retained for the remainder of the North West European Campaign. On the very same day Thomas

Rennie [the 'old man' with whom Bradford had refused to escape back in 1940], now a Major-General, took command of the 51st Highland Division.

One of the young subalterns that came under Bradford's command was Lt Philip Smythe. Philip died in 1959, father of two small daughters. Nicky, the younger of these, only 18 months old at the time of her father's death, became Bradford's daughter-in-law in 1978. On her first visit to Kincardine Bradford was able to tell her about her father. 'I knew him very well,' he said, something she has never been able to say.

It was also about this date that the Allies started to make significant gains of territory. Caen was now in British hands while the Americans had taken Cherbourg. On 6 August Field Marshal Montgomery ordered a drive towards the Seine – once again the Highland Division were on the offensive and gaining ground. One of the purposes of this manoeuvre was to deny to the Germans their launch-sites for flying bombs which were targeted on London and which had, in recent weeks, been used for the first time.

Within a few weeks Bradford was awarded an immediate DSO for his part in a Battalion attack at St-Julien le Faucon. He was also wounded in the arm and leg.

CITATION – D.S.O.
Major (temporary Lieutenant-Colonel) Berenger
Colborne BRADFORD, M.B.E., M.C. (53741)
The Black Watch (Royal Highland Regiment)

On 18 August, 1944 at St-Julien le Faucon, the Battalion under Lt-Col Bradford's command was ordered to advance on a moonless night to capture a high wooded feature.

Just as the Battalion was moving up to the start line, the Commander's post received a direct hit knocking out many of the key personnel of the Battalion. Lt-Col Bradford was himself wounded before he crossed the start line, but he refused to be _evacuated and led the Battalion against determined opposition to the objective, personally bringing forward the tanks through shell fire up a steep incline to positions where they could support the infantry._

For the following 24 hours, when enemy infantry made determined attempts to infiltrate into his position, Lt-Col Bradford, although in great pain, insisted on remaining with his men repelling all attacks and carrying out local operations to clear the area of his forward defence lines, and it was not till the withdrawal of the enemy that he would consent to leave to receive proper medical attention.

Owing to severe casualties in past fighting, the Battalion under Lt-Col Bradford's command has lost most of its key personnel and a great deal of extra work descended on him. The fact that his Battalion carried out its task so brilliantly is entirely due to the able leadership and energy of Lt-Col Bradford who was at all times an inspiration and example to his Officers and men.

Bradford was again wounded, this time in the neck, on 28 August. He carried the shrapnel, deemed too dangerous to remove, for the rest of his life.

On 2 September 1944 the 51st Highland Division, commanded by Maj.-Gen. Tom Rennie, liberated St-Valery-en-Caux, a clever move made possible by Field Marshal Montgomery. At an emotional memorial service Bradford, now a 31-year-old Lt-Col, representing the 51st Highland Division, laid the wreath to honour the men who died there four years previously. Bradford wrote home on 3 September:

I believe the General and I are the only two officers still in the Division who were at St-Valery in 1940. My arm and leg are getting on well, though neither have begun to heal yet. My neck one has healed over already.

About this time Bradford, always known to be keen on his wine, did what he could to ensure that some was 'relieved' for the benefit of his Officers' Mess. At Fort St-Adresse at Le Havre which had surrendered to 5/7th Gordons, Bradford dashed up to work out how to carry the cases over the two dry moats, devoid of bridges which had been blown. His companion, RIO, Capt. Jimmy Herbertson commented that when the champagne was found it was remarkable how quickly Bradford's arm came out of his sling so that the first case could be removed.

On one occasion having inspected a cellar he sent a message back to Battalion HQ asking for transport to be sent. 'No transport available' came the unsatisfactory reply. Bradford was not to be thwarted and responded 'Dump the reserve ammunition, send transport'. It was perhaps not a wholly correct order to give in wartime but it was obeyed and the wine 'relieved'. No doubt the reserve ammunition was collected at a later date.

Bradford returned to visit the two old women who farmed at Bailleul-lès-Pernes. They had helped him on 20 June 1940 just after his escape from the Germans. 'They recognised me at once and were overjoyed to see me again. As if I had only left last week, they said 'We've got your things for you, and produced my silver flask and primus stove at once'.

By the end of the month the Division moved some 300 miles to the north-east to catch up with the retreating Germans. Between October and early December the 5th Black Watch saw a great deal of action in Holland. After a well-earned spell out of the front line the battalion returned to the fray in the Ardennes in mid-January 1945 making seven major set-piece attacks in 14 days. By February they were back in Holland and preparing to move across the border onto German soil. There followed a spell of furious fighting with the action around the German town of Goch a major feature. It was during the assault on Goch that Bradford was awarded a second immediate D.S.O.

CITATION – BAR TO THE DISTINGUISHED
SERVICE ORDER.
Lieutenant-Colonel Berenger Colbourne BRADFORD,
D.S.O.,
M.B.E., M.C. [53741]
The Black Watch [Royal Highland Regiment]
On the night of 20/21 February, a Battalion of The Black Watch,
under the command of Lt-Col B.C. Bradford, M.B.E., D.S.O.,
M.C., CARRIED out an attack round the south west of Goch
with the object of establishing itself in an area due South of the East
end of Goch and thus easing the enemy resistance in that area by
threatening to cut off his escape routes from Goch.

The plan of attack involved the capture of two farm areas to the
South of the sector to be held and then a move North to take two
further farm areas and open the road back to the centre of Goch.

After a difficult approach march on bad tracks, an attack was
carried out by the leading Company of the Battalion on the first
farm area. The timing of this attack was so perfectly co-ordinated
with the artillery concentration which preceded it, that, although
the location was strongly held, the enemy had no time to recover
from the artillery and the objective was quickly captured, many
prisoners being taken.

An attack on the second farm locality was then carried out. Here
the enemy resisted most strongly and fighting of the fiercest nature
was carried out at close quarters throughout the remainder of the
night. Lt-Col Bradford, completely ignoring the heavy artillery
and machine gun fire which swept the area, was continuously in the
forefront of the battle encouraging his men.

In the meantime, a third Company was launched against the
third objective which was again heavily contested. It was necessary
for Lt-Col Bradford to give further directions to this Company with
all possible speed. His wireless received a direct hit, wounding his
operator, so he decided to issue his orders to the Company personally.

At great personal risk, he went forward to this Company, issued his orders and directed the attack.

Daylight found the Battalion still fighting in the second and third farm areas with the fourth still held by the enemy. German S.P. guns were in the area, greatly harassing our own troops and making communications increasingly difficult. Such was the morale and fighting spirit of the Battalion however, that they continued to fight with tremendous dash and determination.

By 10.00 hours on 21 February, both the second and third farm areas were firmly held by the Battalion and the fourth was being attacked. Enemy counter-attacks were made but these were beaten off and heavy casualties inflicted, including one tank and two S.P. guns knocked out. Finally, the whole area was firmly held by the Battalion and the enemy started to withdraw. The object of the attack was fully achieved and the enemy resistance in Goch itself broken up.

This attack owed its success to the careful planning and fearless direction of Lt-Col Bradford. His determination and thrustful example was an inspiration to his Officers and men. There is no doubt that the success of the attack under the magnificent leadership of this Officer was directly responsible for the final capture of Goch.

After Goch the 5th Black Watch were involved in the Rhine crossing on 23–24 March. It was at this point that his General, Thomas Rennie, was killed by a shell. Bradford was so upset to hear the news of the death of his great friend that he could hardly bring himself to organise the attack that followed the crossing itself.

The Division fought their way north-eastwards to their last action near Bremen. On 6 May 1945 all firing ceased and the War in Europe was over. On VE day the Battalion moved to Bremerhaven.

The 5th Bn Black Watch suffered more casualties than any other unit in the 51st Highland Division. Despite this their spirit was never broken. The part played by Bradford in keeping up their morale is summed-up neatly in a letter from a fellow officer, Alec Brodie, who gained legendary status as being one of the more perforated officers in the 5th Bn. Those who knew Brodie will have fond memories of him and envisage this kind-hearted gentleman with his lop-sided face (caused by an attack of polio in his childhood) mopping his rheumy eye as he sat down to write:

Major A C C Brodie
The Black Watch
As from 59 Cadogan Square
London SW1
12 March 1945
Dear Mrs Bradford,
How very kind of you to write to me. Thank you so very much.

My wounds, though numerous, are of so little importance that I am going up to our family flat in Cadogan Square on sick leave tomorrow.

I have actually been in the Queen Elizabeth Hospital outside Birmingham where I have been looked after very competently.

The Battalion did extremely well during the 14 days before I was hit. That was entirely due to the way it was commanded – Bill thought out everything we had to do so thoroughly and explained his plans so cleverly that we did all we had to do with comparative ease, and without many casualties. Though he got very little rest, Bill was far fitter and more vigorous than I have ever known him, and he looks so much healthier than he did. He is always very cool, and, though he is often a good deal nearer the actual fighting than perhaps a C.O. should be, he never gets flustered, and keeps all around him in very high spirits. The battalion worship him. He knows how to go around the troops in drill or in dangerous places and they all have complete confidence in him.

I am apparently to go on sick leave tomorrow. I hope I shall be fit to go back to the Battalion by the end of this month. It will take

*those old hens at the War Office at least another month to send me
out. There is not much blitz about Whitehall's Krieg.*

*Please use your influence with Bill to make him answer the let-
ters I have sent him since I was hit!*

*Please also give my best regards to Colonel Bradford and let me
thank you again for your very kind letter. If you come to London in
the next few weeks would it be possible for us to meet again?*
Yours sincerely
Alexander Brodie

*While the war raged on in the Pacific there was much to be done in
Germany. German units were rounded up and disarmed and arms
and equipment disposed of; prisoners-of-war, on both sides, released;
important points guarded and assistance given to German local authorities to help them re-establish their administration. The battalion was
able to start a newsletter,* The Highland Fling, *in which the carica-
ture below appeared.*

*The 5th Bn Black Watch was disbanded in April 1946. Subsequently
Bradford held the following positions and ranks. GSO1 HQ British
Army of the Rhine 6 February 1946; T/Lt-Col commanding 42
Primary Training Centre & Depot, The Black Watch, 5 December
1946; Major 1 July 1946; Bt. Lt-Col 1947 Commanding 16th
(Welsh) Bn The Parachute Regt. (T.A.) 10 October 1948; A.A.
and Q.M.G. HQ 16th Airborne Division (T.A.) 9 April 1951;
Lt-Col 22 March 1953; Commanding 2nd Bn Black Watch, 2 April
1953; Col 28 January 1955; T/Brig. Commanding 153 (Highland)
Infantry Brigade, 1957; retiring as Hon. Brigadier on 12 June 1959.*[82]

*When Bradford took command of the 16th Paras he had never par-
achuted. He enrolled for his jumping course and completed all his 16
qualifying jumps in the same day, a fact which impressed his new command. He never had to jump again.*

Bradford married Susan (Sue) Vaughan-Lee in 1951. She had played her part in the war first with the FANY and then the ATS. Turning down an offer to work at Bletchley Park she moved from her various driving jobs to anti-aircraft and during the last year of the war saw much action from her batteries in the south-east of England.

Bill and Sue Bradford spent their honeymoon on a motoring holiday in France. Honouring his commitments they visited the de Frances at Maintenay, the de Bernard's and Nanny Cox at Nanteuil and Dr Mounicq in Arreau. A family appeared in short order with the births of four children — Robert (1952, Scotland), Margaret (1953, Germany), Andrew (1955, British Guyana) and Ronald (1958, Scotland). Before her marriage Sue had inherited Kincardine Estate and, in what time they could spare, the couple started to manage the property. The estate had become considerably run down in previous decades.

The parish of Kincardine O'Neil had been particularly badly hit by the First World War with the loss of 63 men killed in action. This represented around 21 per cent of all the men of fighting age in the parish and must have had an enormous impact on the whole fabric of the small community. Then followed the Great Depression and the Second World War. By the early 1950s the estate had received little investment for over 40 years. The farms and numerous cottages were in poor repair and of the forest only 600 of the 1,500 acres remained following war-time fellings. It was a time for reconstruction. However, one further blow was to fall. On 31 January 1953 a great gale struck and felled 95 per cent of the remaining standing timber. In those days foresters in Scotland hadn't seen a chainsaw and initially faced the daunting prospect of clearing up the mess with axes and cross-cut saws. Needless to say chainsaws quickly made an appearance. This was the same storm that flooded large areas of Holland, East Anglia and the Thames Estuary with considerable loss of life.

The Bradfords were in London at the time and so great was the devastation that it took some time for news of the loss to the forestry to

reach them. The scale of windthrow in North-East Scotland flooded the market and prices collapsed. Trying to manage the situation from London and then Germany and finally South America, following Bradford's appointment as CO of 2nd Bn Black Watch, convinced Bradford that his presence on site was going to be required. He sought postings nearer home and in 1957 took up his last army job in Dundee and was able to commute on a weekly basis from Kincardine.

By now the wind-thrown timber that could be salvaged had been cleared up and Bradford masterminded a forestry re-planting programme. Estate staff raised trees from seed and over the next 20 years they planted 1,250,000 trees. At the same time Bradford began a programme of refurbishment and modernisation of properties on the estate as well as starting an in-hand farming operation. A keen, and accurate, shot, Bradford developed an entertaining shoot and, with some excellent salmon fishing on the Dee, Kincardine was soon a destination for a great number of retired military friends, many from the Highland Division.

As a child I have fond memories of these fine men – too numerous to mention here. They all had one similar trait: modesty about their wartime endeavours. The camaraderie forged by the years at war was hugely evident but little did I know at the time that I sat amongst heroes. Nobody mentioned Brigadier Lorne Campbell's VC, or the numerous DSOs, MCs and other awards that most possessed in profusion; or others' five years of captivity. To each of them those days were history and, although it had been a great adventure, the memories too were painful. They needed to look forward.

The emotional scars of Bradford's war healed more slowly than the physical ones, however, and I remember clearly being utterly confused and disturbed by my father's nightmares in the late 1950s and 1960s. He would wake up screaming and sweating thinking he was once again shut in that underground hell-hole in Algeria.

Bradford made one further escape. He contracted Parkinson's Disease in 1971 and fought that with considerable courage for the next 25 years. He continued to shoot and fish until the 1990s. It was astonishing to note how, when a pheasant flew towards him, his tremor stopped for the second he needed to raise his gun and shoot it. Eventually dementia set in and he had to go to a nursing home. The ward which gave constant supervision was on the top floor, two stories above the ground floor. One day, in 1995 at the age of 82, when no one was looking, he made his way out of the ward to an empty room on the same floor. Carefully he opened the window, climbed out and hung from the window-ledge before dropping to the ground to attempt a parachute roll on landing.

Unfortunately his old bones were not as strong as they had been and he broke just one bone in his heel. He couldn't walk and lay on the ground. A member of staff in a white coat appeared shortly afterwards and Bradford, looking up, said, 'I'm all right, Herr Doktor'.

Bill Bradford died on 4 March 1996 and is buried in the grounds of his beloved Kincardine.

Appendix 1

In a small notebook which is considerably damaged by damp as a result of Bradford's voyage from Algiers to Gibralter, is the following message. I have tried to get it deciphered using cryptologists on the internet and approaches to MI5 and the US Foreign Service have so far proved fruitless. The message is probably more exciting as an unsolved mystery than it would be if decoded but if anyone can provide the answer I'd be delighted to hear from them. Owing to the damage some parts of the text is unclear. The asterisks refer to letters that are illegible.

Nkqol ozka rbu uk' 'u
jyegla ihyu udyyri b*[1] trkp
vauj buxuc[2] puryv[3] dk**
ykga uynk pyuw le* zdgg
zwpls lkwj s*iak iknhl
fl dkk

[1] It is unclear how many letters there are after 'b' or if this word merges with the following one.

[2] Buxuc or buuc

[3] Last letter of this workd might be 'u'

Hidden Message:

Text of concealed message in letter of 8 October 1940, see Doc. 2, reads: *'can you suggest any way of escape or help at all may try Marseilles.'*

Appendix 2

A letter from Donald Hankey to Bradford's grandmother Louisa Hardy (*née* Knight), mother of Capt. Ronald M Hardy. 1915. Hankey's essay, *The Beloved Captain*, about his uncle Ronald Hardy was a great inspiration to Bill Bradford.

Dear Mrs Hardy

I hope that you will forgive me what is perhaps 'taking the liberty' of writing to you; but I feel that I want to pay my tribute to Captain Hardy's memory, and that perhaps you will be glad to know how one who was an N.C.O. in his platoon for about 6 months regarded him. Moreover, I can safely say that I am speaking not only for myself but for every man in the platoon which he once commanded, and indeed for every man in the Company who ever came into any sort of personal contact with him.

From the time of his first joining the company until the time of his promotion to Captain, I was Captain Hardy's platoon sergeant, and it was the great change which followed his promotion which made me resign my stripes in order to go to another company. We loved him, I think, as no other officer was loved by his men. When he smiled he made every one feel more cheerful. When he was disappointed in us there was not a man who was not sorry and ashamed. There is nothing that we would not have done for him. He ruled us by the love and respect with which he inspired us. He never needed to say a harsh word. Crime in the platoon was practically unknown. Where other officers find it necessary to bully and threaten, Captain Hardy had only to express a wish. Although he seemed to take an individual interest in every man, and though he would come round the barrack rooms and himself attend to their blistered feet (in the early days of route marching) and though he was always gentle in his dealings with the men, he never suffered from his condescension. He had the prestige of an inherent nobility which effectually prevented any one from presuming on his gentleness, or treating him with anything but respect.

Somehow all this seems so laboured and so lame. What I want to say is simply that he had won the heart of every man from the roughest pit-boy to the gentleman ranker, and that every one of us was proud to be commanded by him.

It was a subject of universal regret that he did not succeed to the command of the Company. What the Company lost by his death is incalculable; but those who knew him will never forget him. He will always live in our memory as the ideal officer, a prince among men.

I am, Yours very truly

Donald W.A. Hankey.

The Beloved Captain
By
Donald Hankey

HE came in the early days, when we were still at recruit drills under the hot September sun. Tall, erect, smiling: so we first saw him, and so he remained to the end. At the start he knew as little of soldiering as we did. He used to watch us being drilled by the sergeant; but his manner of watching was peculiarly his own. He never looked bored. He was learning just as much as we were, in fact more. He was learning his job, and from the first he saw that his job was more than to give the correct orders. His job was to lead us. So he watched, and noted many things, and never found the time hang heavy on his hands. He watched our evolutions, so as to learn the correct orders; he watched for the right manner of command, the manner which secured the most prompt response to an order; and he watched every one of us for our individual characteristics. We were his men. Already he took an almost paternal interest in us. He noted the men who tried hard, but were naturally slow and awkward. He distinguished them from those who were inattentive and bored. He marked down the keen and efficient amongst us. Most of all he studied those who were subject to moods, who were sulky one day and willing the next. These were the ones who were to turn the scale. If only he could get these on his side, the battle would be won.

For a few days he just watched. Then he started work. He picked out some of the most awkward ones, and, accompanied by a corporal, marched them away by themselves. Ingenuously he explained that he did not know much himself yet; but he thought that they might get on better if they drilled by themselves a bit, and that if he helped them, and they helped him, they would soon learn. His confidence was infectious. He looked at them, and they looked at him, and the men pulled themselves together and determined to do their best. Their best surprised themselves. His patience was inexhaustible. His simplicity could not fail to be understood. His keenness and optimism carried all with them. Very soon the awkward squad found themselves awkward no longer; and soon after that they ceased to be a squad, and went back to the platoon.

Then he started to drill the platoon, with the sergeant standing by to point out his mistakes. Of course he made mistakes, and when that happened he never minded admitting it. He would explain what mistakes he had made, and try again. The result was that we began to take almost as much interest and pride in his progress as he did in ours. We were his men, and he was our leader. We felt that he was a credit to us, and we resolved to be a credit to him. There was a bond of mutual confidence and affection between us, which grew stronger and stronger as the months passed. He had a smile for almost everyone; but we thought that he had a different smile for us. We looked for it, and were never disappointed. On parade, as long as we were trying, his smile encouraged us. Off parade, if we passed him and saluted, his eyes looked straight into our own, and his smile greeted us. It was a wonderful thing, that smile of his. It was something worth living for, and worth working for. It bucked one up when one was bored or tired. It seemed to make one look at things from a different point of view, a finer point of view, his point of view. There was nothing feeble or weak about it. It was not monotonous like the smile of 'Sunny Jim.' It meant something. It meant that we were his men, and that he was proud of us, and sure that we were going to do jolly well---better than any of the other platoons. And it made us determine that we would. When we failed him, when he was disappointed in us, he did not smile. He did not rage or curse. He just looked disappointed, and that made us feel far more savage with ourselves than any amount of swearing would have done. He made us feel that we were not playing the game by him. It was not what he said. He was never very good at talking. It was just how he looked. And his look of displeasure and disappointment was a thing that we would do anything to avoid. The fact was that he had won his way into our affections. We loved him. And there isn't anything stronger than love, when all's said and done.

He was good to look on. He was big and tall, and held himself upright. His eyes looked his own height. He moved with the grace of an athlete. His skin was tanned by a wholesome outdoor life, and his eyes were clear and wide open. Physically he was a prince among men. We used to notice, as we marched along the road and passed other officers, that they always looked pleased to see him. They greeted him with a cordiality which was reserved for him. Even the general seemed to have singled him out, and cast an eye of special approval upon him. Somehow, gentle though he was, he was never familiar. He had a kind of innate nobility which marked him out as above us. He was not democratic. He was rather the justification for aristocracy. We all knew instinctively that he was our superior---a man of finer temper than ourselves, a 'toff' in his own right. I suppose that that was why he could be so humble without loss of dignity. For he was humble too, if that is the right word, and I think it is. No trouble of ours was too small for him to attend to. When we started route marches, for instance, and our feet were blistered and sore, as they often were at first, you would have thought that they were his own feet from the trouble he took. Of course after the march there was always an inspection of feet. That is the routine. But with him it was no mere routine. He came into our rooms, and if anyone had a sore foot he would kneel down on the floor and look at it as carefully as if he had been a doctor. Then he would prescribe, and the remedies were ready at hand, being borne by the sergeant. If a blister had to be lanced he would very likely lance it himself there and then, so as to make sure that it was done with a clean needle and that no dirt was allowed to get in. There was no affectation about this, no striving after effect. It was simply that he felt that our feet were pretty important, and that he knew that we were pretty careless. So he thought it best at the start to see to the matter himself. Nevertheless, there was in our eyes something almost religious about this care for our feet. It seemed to have a touch of the Christ about it, and we loved and honored him the more.

We knew that we should lose him. For one thing, we knew that he would be promoted. It was our great hope that some day he would command the company. Also we knew that he would be killed. He was so amazingly unself-conscious. For that reason we knew that he would be absolutely fearless. He would be so keen on the job in hand, and so anxious for his men, that he would forget about his own danger. So it proved. He was a captain when we went out to the front. Whenever there was a tiresome job to be done, he was there in charge. If ever there were a moment of danger, he was on the spot. If there were any particular part of the line where the shells were falling faster or the bombs dropping more thickly than in other parts, he was in it. It was not that he was conceited and imagined himself indispensable. It was just that he was so keen that the men should do their best, and act worthily of the regiment. He knew that fellows hated turning out at night for fatigue, when they were in a 'rest camp.' He knew how tiresome the long march there and back and the digging in the dark for an unknown purpose were. He knew that fellows would be inclined to grouse and shirk, so he thought that it was up to him to go and show them that he thought it was a job worth doing. And the fact that he was there put a new complexion on the matter altogether. No one would shirk if he were there. No one would grumble so much, either. What was good enough for him was good enough for us. If it were not too much trouble for him to turn out, it was not too much trouble for us. He knew, too, how trying to the nerves it is to sit in a trench and be shelled. He knew what a temptation there is to move a bit farther down the trench and herd together in a bunch at what seems the safest end. He knew, too, the folly of it, and that it was not the thing to do--not done in the best regiments. So he went along to see that it did not happen, to see that the men stuck to their posts, and conquered their nerves. And as soon as we saw him, we forgot our own anxiety. It was: 'Move a bit farther down., sir. We are all right here; but don't you go exposing of yourself.' We didn't matter. We knew it then. We were just the rank and file, bound to take risks. The company would get along all right without us. But the captain, how was the company to get on without him? To see him was to catch his point of view, to forget our personal anxieties, and only to think of the company, and the regiment, and honor.

There was not one of us but would gladly have died for him. We longed for the chance to show him that. We weren't heroes. We never dreamed about the V. C. But to save the captain we would have earned it ten times over, and never have cared a button whether we got it or not. We never got the chance, worse luck. It was all the other way. We were holding some trenches which were about as unhealthy as trenches could be. The Bosches were only a few yards away, and were well supplied with trench mortars. We hadn't got any at that time. Bombs and air torpedoes were dropping round us all day. Of course the captain was there. It seemed as if he could not keep away. A torpedo fell into the trench, and buried some of our chaps. The fellows next to them ran to dig them out. Of course he was one of the first. Then came another torpedo in the same place. That was the end.

But he lives. Somehow he lives. And we who knew him do not forget. We feel his eyes on us. We still work for that wonderful smile of his. There are not many of the old lot left now; but I think that those who went West have seen him. When they got to the other side I think they were met. Someone said: 'Well done, good and faithful servant.' And as they knelt before that gracious pierced Figure, I reckon they saw nearby the captain's smile. Anyway, in that faith let me die, if death should come my way; and so, I think, shall I die content.

Notes and Sources

1. Wood, Field Marshal Sir Evelyn; *letter* (Author's archive)
2. Bradford, Constance, *Truly a Great Victorian* (Private publication 2004)
3. Stephen, Col C.G., *History of the Black Watch 1939–41,* [BWRA 0902/6), p.1
4. David, Saul, *Churchill's Sacrifice of the Highland Division – France 1940* (Brasseys, 1994), p.3
5. Stephen, Col C.G., *ibid*, p.1
6. Mackesy, P, personal comment
7. Stephen, Col C.G., *ibid*, p.2
8. Jardine-Paterson, Noel, *Personal Diary*
9. Jardine-Paterson, Noel, *ibid*
10. Jardine-Paterson, Noel, *ibid*
11. Stephen, Col C.G., *ibid*, p.4
12. Linklater, Eric and Andro; *The Black Watch – The History of the Royal Highland Regiment* (Barrie & Jenkins, 1977), p.178
13. Fergusson, B.F.; *The Black Watch and the King's Enemies* (Collins, 1950), p.19
14. Stephen, C.G., *ibid*, p.7
15. Stephen, C.G., *ibid*, p.7
16. Jardine-Paterson, Noel, *ibid*

17. Jardine-Paterson, Noel, *ibid*
18. Jardine-Paterson, Noel, *ibid*
19. David, Saul, *ibid*, p.12
20. Stephen, C.G., *ibid*, p.14
21. Stephen, C.G., *ibid*, p.22
22. Fraser, David; *And We Shall Shock Them – The British Army in the Second World War* (Hodder & Stoughton, 1983), pp 10–11 as reported by David, Saul; *ibid*, p.16
23. For some reason Bradford states the date as 9 or 10 May, but Campbell-Preston records it as the morning of 13 May.
24. Bradford, B.C.; (Author's recorded interview, 1992)
25. Churchill, Winston S; *The Second World War – Their Finest Hour, Volume II* (Cassell & Co. Ltd, 1949), p.38
26. Lowe, Lt-Col T.A., *Armies of the World* (Daily Mail Year Book 1940)
27. Churchill, Winston S.; *ibid*, p.42
28. David, Saul; *ibid*, p.42
29. Reynaud, Paul, *In the Thick of the Fight 1930–1945* (Cassel, 1955) p.382
30. Burnaby-Atkins, Lt-Col F.; letter to author, 2007
31. Bradford, B.C.; *ibid*
32. Bradford, B.C.; *ibid*
33. Ritchie, 2nd-Lt Donald as reported by David, Saul; *ibid*, p.85
34. Bradford, B.C.; *ibid*
35. Bradford, B.C.; *ibid*
36. Mackesy, P., personal comment
37. David, Saul; *ibid*, p.170
38. Bradford, B.C.; *ibid*
39. Stephen, C.G., *ibid*, p.27
40. Burnaby-Atkins, Lt-Col F.; letter to Saul David, 1992
41. Burnaby-Atkins, Lt-Col F.; letter to author, 2007
42. Bradford, B.C.; *ibid*
43. Hunt, Leslie C.; *The Prisoners' Progress* (Hutchison & Co. Ltd, undated, but approved for publication 1941)
44. Jardine-Paterson, Noel; *ibid*
45. Hunt, Leslie C.; *ibid*
46. Hunt, Leslie C.; *ibid*

47. Jardine-Paterson, Noel; *ibid*
48. Bradford, B.C.; *ibid*
49. Mackesy, P., personal comment
50. From letter 17, Wetherby Mansions, Earl's Court Square, SW5, signature illegible (Author's archive)
51. From letter, from 1st Bn. The Black Watch, Callander, signed 'Norman' (Author's archive)
52. From letter, from *The Daily Telegraph*, Fleet Street, from Captain Hulls (Author's archive)
53. BCB's record states 'La Trouée' but this is not near the route.
54. Théry, Madame Betty (*née* de Bernard), personal conversation with author
55. A great deal more about the role of the de Bernards and Nesta Cox can be learned from Stella King's biography, *Jacqueline* (Arms and Armour Press, 1989)
56. Bradford, Lt-Col Edward A.; *personal account* (Author's archive)
57. Bradford, Lt-Col Edward A.; *ibid*
58. Bradford, Lt-Col Edward A.; *ibid*
59. Bradford, Lt-Col Edward A.; *ibid*
60. Bradford, Lt-Col Edward A.; *ibid*
61. Bradford's diary describes him as a sergeant-navigator but Sir Lewis Hodges described him as a gunner in 2005
62. Hodges, Air Chief Marshal Sir Lewis, interview with A. Bradford, 2005
63. Bradford, Lt-Col Edward A.; *ibid*
64. Bradford, B.C.; *ibid*
65. Bradford, Lt-Col Edward A.; *ibid*
66. Hodges, Air Chief Marshal Sir Lewis; *ibid*
67. Bradford, Lt-Col Edward A.; *ibid*
68. From correspondence with James, Keith, son of author James, P.S., *Conscript Heroes*.
69. Bradford, B.C.; notes (Author's archive)
70. Bradford, B.C.; notebook from 1940 (Author's archive)
71. Burn, H B; from an account contributed by his niece to BBC WW2 Peoples' War archive
72. Bradford reports the name as *L'Odetique*
73. Bradford, B.C.; personal comments

74. Salmond, J.B., *The History of the 51st. Highland Division 1939–1945* (William Blackwood & Sons Ltd, 1953) p.25

75. McMillan, R; Sunday Graphic, 14 March 1943

76. Bradford, B.C.; *ibid*

77. Bradford, B.C.; *ibid*

78. McGregor, J.; *The Spirit of Angus;* (Phillimore & Co. Ltd., 1988) p.82

79. Bradford, B.C.; *ibid*

80. Bradford, B.C.; *ibid*

81. Stephen, Col C.G.; letter to Lt-Col E.A. Bradford, 8 January 1941 (Author's archive)

82. The Officers of the Black Watch 1725-1986, 2nd Edition; RHQ The Black Watch (Royal Highland Regiment) (Samson Books Ltd) p.31

Glossary

2IC	Second-in-command
2nd-Lt	Second-Lieutenant
A/T	Anti-tank
ADC	Aide-de-Camp
Adjt	Adjutant: personal staff officer to the CO of a major unit
Bart	Baronet
Bde	Brigade: Principal tactical formation within a division. An infantry brigade is normally comprised of three infantry battalions together with supporting arms and services
BEF	British Expeditionary Force
Bn	Battalion: the basic infantry unit comprising four rifle companies and headquarters company
BOR	Battalion Operations Room
Brig.	Brigadier
Brigade Major	In the British Army the Chief of Staff of a brigade or equivalent-sized formation
Capt.	Captain
CB	Companion of the Order of the Bath
CBE	Commander of the Order of the British Empire

C-in-C	Commander-in-Chief
CO	Commanding Officer
Col	Colonel
Corps	Major tactical formation consisting of two or more divisions. Commanded by a Lieutenant General. Two or more corps constitute an army
Coy	Company
Cpl	Corporal
CQMS	Company Quartermaster Sergeant: administers company issues all stores, clothing, equipment and rations
CSM	Company Sergeant Major: Warrant Officer Class II and senior soldier in his company below commissioned rank.
cwt	Hundredweight – 112lb or a shade over 50kg.
DSO	Distinguished Service Order: after the Victoria Cross, the highest award for gallantry and leadership available to officers. Normally but by no means invariably, awarded to officers of field rank (Major and above). Since 1993 it has been awarded for leadership rather than gallantry.
Flt Lt	Flight Lieutenant
FOO	Forward Observation Officer
Free French	French individuals or units that fought against the Axis powers post June 1940.
Frs	Francs
GCB	Knight Grand Cross of the Order of the Bath
GCVO	Knight Grand Cross of the Royal Victorian Order
GOC	General Officer Commanding
GSO1	General Staff Officer, 1st Class
HE	High Explosive
HQ	Headquarters
KCSI	Knight Commander of the Order of the Star of India
L/Cpl	Lance-Corporal
LMG	Light Machine gun
Lt	Lieutenant
Lt-Gen.	Lieutenant-General
M.G.	Machine Gun
M/C	Motor Cycle

Maj.	Major
Maj.-	
Gen.	Major-General
MBE	Member of the Order of the British Empire
MC	Military Cross: Issued for gallantry in the presence of the enemy, to officers below field rank.
MI9	The department of Military Intelligence that dealt with resistance fighters and Allied troops that found themselves behind enemy lines
MT	Motor Transport
NAAFI	Navy, Army and Air Force Institutes
NCO	Non-commissioned Officer
P.C.	Post Card
pl.	Platoon
POW	Prisoner-of-War
PSM	Platoon Sergeant Major: Warrant Officer Class III
Pte	Private
RA	Royal Artillery
RE	Royal Engineers
Recce	Reconnaissance
RHR	Royal Highland Regiment
RIO	Regimental Intelligence Officer
RSM	Regimental Sergeant Major: Warrant Officer Class I
SAA	Small-arms ammunition
Sgt	Sergeant
VAD	Voluntary Aid Detachment: formed by the linking of the British Red Cross and the Order of St John of Jerusalem in 1909. Mostly they worked as auxiliary nurses but some performed a wider range of tasks including fund-raising and driving.
VC	Victoria Cross: the supreme award for gallantry in the presence of the enemy
VE	Victory in Europe

Index

Abbeville, 60, 68
Acheux-en-Vimeu, 66–7
Achiary, André, 332–3
Achilles, Theodore C., 245–6
Ailly-sur-Somme, 126–7
Air Transport Auxiliary (ATA), 33
Airaines, 99
Aisne, River, 16, 64
Aix-en-Ergny, 116
Akarit, Wadi, 340
Albert Victor, Prince, 18
Aldershot, 25, 339
Algiers, 234, 258–67, 271–90,
    291, 307, 313–9, 328,
    332–9, 341, 355, 358
Allonnes, 146
Amboise, 148–9
American 1st Army, 343–4
American Consul, 104, 220,
    226, 230, 242, 245, 250,
    262, 273, 278, 282, 287,
    296, 314

Amettes, 114–5
Amiens, 72
Ampthill, Lady, 246–8, 255
Anderson, Cpl, 90
Ardennes, 51, 347
Argyll & Sutherland
    Highlanders, 7th Bn, 72,
    108, 340
Argyll & Sutherland Highlanders,
    8th Bn, 108
Argyll and Sutherland
    Highlanders, The, 42, 169
Ark Force, 78, 82, 92, 107, 109,
    326, 340
Armentières, 40
Armistice Commission, 230,
    259, 277, 280, 282, 284,
    285, 313, 335
Arques-la-Bataille, 78
Arreau, 179, 181–2, 191, 352
Ashton, J., 295–7
ATS, 25, 352

Attiches, 30
Auch, 200, 211–2, 219, 253
Auchel, 171
Aumalle, 316
Austen, Jane, 18
Austria, Archduke Charles
  Stephen of, 326
Autun, 94
Avaray, 150

Bailleul-lès-Pernes, 115, 209, 347
Baker-Baker, 2nd-Lt H.C., 17
Barrie, Pte, 43–4
Barstow, Col. J.A., 169, 198,
  203, 273
Barthélémy, Gen. R.J.E., 163
Bazoches-en-Dunois, 146
Beagles, 16, 42–3
Beaugency, 154
Beaumetz-lès-Aire, 116, 126
Beauvin, 30
Beauvoir-Wavans, 123
Bélâbre, 166–7, 173, 202, 205,
  239–45, 247, 251, 327
Belgium, 29, 50–1, 59, 64, 171,
  208, 339
Bellac, 172
Berck-Plage, 119
Bernardi, Pte, 121–42, 257
Bernaville, 124–5
Berneuil, 125
Béthune, 101–2, 113, 208
Betting, 56
Biarritz, 230
Bielsa, 185–8
Bilka, M., 334
Billy-Berclau, 104

Binas, 148
Binet, Dr, 282, 286
Bismarck, The, 290
Bizerta, 259, 303
Black Watch, 1st Bn, 16, 20,
  23–5, 27–96, 107–11, 170,
  207–10, 241, 244, 254,
  276, 293–5, 298–9, 336–7
Black Watch, 2nd Bn, 15,
  16, 353
Black Watch, 4th Bn, 51, 52, 56,
  68, 109, 209, 326
Black Watch, 5th Bn, 339,
  342–11
Black Watch, 6th Bn, 41
Black Watch, 9th Bn, 33–4
Black Watch, The, 15–6, 26,
  108, 170, 205, 209–10,
  228, 241, 278, 283, 298–9,
  330, 343, 366–7
Blobec, 78
Blois, 15, 145, 150, 154
Boisjean, 119
Bordeaux, 100, 202–3
Botton, M, 315–28
Boulogne, 71, 117–8, 208
Bousson, M, 333
Bradford, Adela, 19, 237
Bradford, Capt. Sir Edward
  M.A., 15–6, 43, 111
Bradford, Col Sir Edward R.C.,
  16–7, 242
Bradford, Col Sir Evelyn, 15, 111
Bradford, Diana, 18, 32, 199,
  213, 241
Bradford, Felicity, 17, 18, 33,
  35, 241

Bradford, Edith M., Lady, 241,
    243, 274, 278, 304
Bradford, Lizzie, 19
Bradford, Lt-Col Edward
        Austen, 15, 19, 107,
        110, 178, 185, 202, 231,
        233, 242, 247, 254, 287,
        291–311, 337
Bradford, Margaret Louisa
        'Maggie', 18, 109,
        111, 237–8, 251–53,
        291–311, 338
Bradford, Nicola, 345
Bradley, Gen. Omar, 342–5
Brassy, 130
Bremen, 349
Bremerhaven, 349
Bresle, River, 65–6, 74, 93
Brest, 335
Bréxent-Enocq, 119
Brinckman, Major N., 275–90,
        314, 315, 319, 328, 331
Brinckman, Sir Theodore, 276
Brinton, Dorothea, 244, 291
British Army
    1st Armoured Division, 65, 72
    2nd Army, 343–4
    4th Division, 25, 27, 294
    16th Airborne Division, 353
    69th Infantry Brigade, 170
British Army of the Rhine, 352
British Cottage Hospital, 316, 319
British Expeditionary Force,
        23, 32, 41, 46, 49, 57–61,
        64–5, 71, 164, 328, 372
Brittany, 15, 224–5
Brodie, Maj. A.A.C., 349–10

Brooke, Lt-Gen. Sir Allan, 25,
        300–11
Bruay-en-Artois, 102
Buchy, 96
Budange, 46
Buingy-lès-Gamaches, 66
Burgerbraukeller, 33
Burn, Capt. H.B., 236, 258, 261,
        264–5, 269, 273, 276, 277,
        294, 304, 306–8, 368
Burnaby-Atkins, 2nd-Lt F.J.,
        68, 84, 88, 96, 99, 276,
        365, 368
Burney, Brig. G.T., 72, 91, 94

Caen, 345
Cahors, 177, 251
Cailleville, 83–8, 96
Calais, 108, 136, 163
Cambron, 68–70
Campbell, 2nd-Lt E.F.D., 24, 36,
        37, 65, 77, 96, 99, 101–5
Campbell, Maj. Lorne, 340, 353
Campbell, Mrs Ian, 253
Campbell-Preston, Capt. G.P.,
        31, 34, 39, 52–6, 70, 81,
        96, 99, 199, 366
Campbell-Preston, Frances, 199
Cape Gata, 321
Cape Matifou, 319
Carnot, 308
Cartagena, 321
Casablanca, 263, 266, 272, 334
Caskie, Revd Donald, 230,
        237–9, 248–10
Castay, M., 333
Catus, 176

Caussade, 178
Cellettes, 160
Cempuis, 130
Ceuta, 324
Ch. de Caumont, 211–2, 217,
  250, 253
Ch. d'Envalette, 201, 203, 214,
  252–6, 326–7
Ch. de Las Tronques, 194,
  196–8, 205
Ch. de Nanteuil, 15, 151–60, 352
Chamberlain, Neville, 23, 35,
  50, 254
Chambord, 150, 153
Chateâudun, 139, 143
Châteauroux, 155, 162, 165,
  166, 251
Châtillon-sur-Cher, 161
Cheetah, 19–20
Chenona, 332
Cher, River, 160–2, 168, 176, 251
Cherbourg, 27–8, 71, 345
Chilton, Brig. Maurice, 344
Chilworth, 221, 224
Churchill, Winston, 50, 58, 82,
  94, 165, 254, 278, 288, 365
Cirque de Barrosa, 185
Clarke, PSM, 91
Clarkin, Pte, 258
Clartain, Pte, 228
Clement, M. et Mme, 156–60
Cléres, 97
Clermont-Ferrand, 157
Cléry-en-Vexin, 136
Clinique des Glycines, 277, 286,
  304, 307, 313, 316, 328
Coggia, Mlle, 334

Col de Pont d'Aspet, 194
Col des Ares, 193
Colchester, 17
Cole, Felix, 262, 276, 282, 284
Compiégne, 117
Concriers, 149–50
Constantine, 334
Contres, 160
Cormainville, 146
Corsindae, 15
Couddes, 160
Courbehaye, 146
Cox, Nesta, 155–9, 352, 366
Crawley, CQMS, 73
Crouy-sur-Cosson, 153
Cugnaux, 180
Cuinchy, 113
Cummin, Revd H.W., 272, 278
Curle, Mrs, 211–4, 217–20, 250

Daladier, Édouard, 44
Dargies, 130
Dargnies, 66
Darlan, Admiral, 335
Das, 230, 258–63, 267–70
Dashiel, 284, 286
David, Saul, 20, 59, 364, 365
de Bernard, Anne Marie, 15,
  154–60, 354
de Bernard, Conte Pierre, 155–6,
  179, 352
de Brinon, Ferdinand, 335
de Castelbajac, 212
de Cervens, Commandant
  d'Aviation, 333
de Chimery, Maj., 92
de France, Mlles, 120, 352

de Gaulle, Col Charles, 117, 252
de la Pleigniere, 179
de la Taille, Capt., 165
de Malglaive, Madame, 334
de Noirmont, 211–3, 217–8, 253
Deane, Capt., 226
Demarcation Line, 148, 170
Depot 602 – see Ch. d'Envalette
Despax, M – see Eichner
Dieppe, 82
Dinant, 57
Djebel Nador, 258
Dodds, Major, 244
Domme, 176
Dorman Smith MP, Sir
    Reginald, 254, 256
Douai, 31
Douglas, Lt P.S., 24, 43
Dourges, 29
Doullens, 100, 208
Dover, 20, 24, 25, 44, 326
Drexel, Anthony J, 291–93
Drummond-Wolff, Maj.
    R.H.C., 292
Duff Cooper, Alfred, 279
Duke of Wellington's Regiment,
    The, 92
Duke, Col J.P., 294
Dundas, Maj. W.F., 61–8, 76–7,
    82–4, 88–90, 96, 101–3
Dundee, 353
Dunkirk, 60, 66, 71, 136, 163
Durham Light Infantry, The,
    178–9
Duriot, Commandant,
    280–85, 333
Dyle, River, 51

Eauline, River, 77
Ecault, 117
Egypt, 339
Eichner, Michael & Mrs, 263–4,
    267, 280–85, 333
El Alamein, 90, 339–40
Elphinstone, Lt Hon. J.A., 90,
    96, 99, 298
Elser, George, 33–4
Envermeu, 76–7
Epône, 137
Escout, M., 333
Etain, 60–3
Etaples, 117–8
Eton College, 15, 17, 44, 70,
    235, 340–1

Fabian, 183, 190
Fall Rot, Operation, 72
FANY, 352
Farquharson, L/Cpl, 85–7
Fecamp, 78
Fergusson, 2nd-Lt B.E., 17, 364
Figuere, 232–3
Filièvres, 121
Finnebre, Pompe, 32
Fitch, Capt. Freddie, 171, 177,
    178, 179, 181–90, 191, 224,
    227–34, 248–9, 258, 264,
    285, 289, 303
Flavacourt, 133
Fleselles, 126
Fontainebleau, 63–4
Fontaine-le-Dun, 82–3, 95
Foret d'Arques, 77
Foret de Boulogne, 153
Formerie, 98

Fort St-Adresse, 347
Fort St-Jean, 226–37, 257–8, 263
Fortune, Maj.-Gen. V., 42, 69, 75, 77, 109
Fox, Mr, 334
France, The State, 23, 24, 79, 117, 147, 184, 203, 210, 217, 234, 332
Free France, 149, 157
Free French, 117, 296, 306, 313, 328, 372
French Army
  1st Army, 57, 60
  2nd Army, 61
  3rd Army, 60
  6th Army, 73
  7th Army, 57, 73
  9th Army, 57–61, 63
  9th Corps, 81
  10th Army, 73
  12th Brigade, 35
  21st Division, 40
  22nd Division, 165
  31st Infantry Division, 70
  87th African Division, 161
  Chasseurs Portées, 70, 83
  Groupement Cuirasse, 70
French Army, The, 50–1, 52–3, 57–60, 66, 70, 74, 83, 90–4, 99, 192, 197
French Artillery, 47, 52, 64
French Cavalry, 47, 65, 83, 88
French Navy, 165
French Foreign Legion, 230, 235, 262, 280
Fressenville, 69
Frévent, 101, 121
Frieres, 70

Gamaches, 66
Gamelin, Gen. M.G., 35, 58–9
Gardiner, L/Cpl, 87, 95, 115, 207–8
Gardnor-Beard, Anne-Marie – see de Bernard
Gardnor-Beard, Beatrice (Betty), 155, 157–8, 368
Gardnor-Beard, Billy, 15, 154, 160
Gargenville, 136
Garrow, Capt. Ian, 171, 173, 202, 205, 217, 218, 225, 236, 247, 251
Garrow, Mrs M., 252
Gauthier d'Annous, Baronne, 179, 196–9
Genneville, 81
German Army, 24, 39, 48–9, 52, 60–104
German Army 7th Panzer Division, 73–4, 107, 108
German Army Group A, 66
Germany, 24, 45, 57, 71, 94, 112, 117, 169, 222, 335, 339, 352, 353
Gibraltar, 229, 278, 305, 320, 321–29, 330, 336–9, 342, 359
Gilbert, M., 152
Gimont, 216
Giradot, Freda, 224
Gisors, 63
Glandon, 173
Glasgow, 190, 252, 330
Glasgow Highlanders – see Highland Light Infantry
Gneisenau, The, 335
Goch, 348–9

Gordon Highlanders
  1st Bn, 41, 71, 337
  5th Bn, 56–7, 69–72, 83, 87
  5th/7th Bn, 346
  6th Bn, 41
Gordon Highlanders, The,
    90, 109
Gorges, 125
Gort, Gen. The Lord, 41,
    328, 332
Goupillières, 138
Gradelet, Col, 210, 221
Grand Bois de Cambron, 68–71
Grant, Maj. J.M., 48
Grant-Duff, Capt. N.A.M., 95,
    208–9, 275
Gratens, 180
Grosenwald, 54
Grosrouve, 139
Guelma, 334
Guerville, 65
Guetteville-les-Grès, 83,
    85–8, 96
Guichard, 232–3
Guiry-en-Vexin, 134–6
Gwynne, Erskine, 280

Hamilton, Cmdr Harry, 325–7
Hankey, Donald, 16, 357–63
Hardy, (false name of Bradford),
    266, 268
Hardy, Capt. Ronnie, 16, 358–63
Hardy, Louisa, 18, 358
Hardy, Pte, 121–6
Hartbuch Wood, 49
Hasciari, 277, 281, 284
Hassler, Maj.-Gen. J.L.F., 166
Havernas, 126

Henin-Leitard, 28
Hennequet, Henriette, 34–5
Herbertson, Capt. Jimmy, 347
Herly, 116
Hesdin, 120
Highland Division
    152 Brigade, 41, 47–50, 65,
        68–9, 337
    153 Brigade, 50, 57,
        65–70, 337
    154 Brigade, 27, 50, 59, 63,
        65, 70, 78, 108, 209, 338,
        339, 341
    51st, 41, 46–7, 51, 57–94,
        100, 111, 254, 295, 300,
        326, 337–49, 355, 365–6
Highland Infantry Bde – 153
    (Highland) Infantry
    Brigade, 351
Highland Light Infantry, 9th Bn,
    170, 205
Hinges, 113
Hodges, Pilot Officer Lewis
    'Bob', 106, 222–3, 225,
    235, 368
Hogg, Lt Martin, 171, 178,
    179–181, 191, 192
Holland, 33, 45, 50, 57, 339,
    347, 352
Holt, Lt-Col. Vesey, 330–1, 336
Honeyman, Lt-Col. G E B, 9,
    50, 61, 64, 69–70, 76, 78,
    83–4, 96, 99, 109, 112
Hopwood, Capt. J.A., 91–2
Hornburg, 46
Hotel Albert, Algiers, 335
Hotel Aletti, Algiers, 263, 264,
    279, 280, 285, 332–3, 335

Hotel Astoria, Algiers, 336
Hotel Djenila Palace,
    Algiers, 334
Hotel Regence, Algiers, 335
Hotel Royale, Algiers, 273–4,
    291, 294, 299
Hotel Splendide, Marseilles, 231
Hotel St-George, Algiers, 261
Hotel Touring, Algiers, 335
Houdent, 73
Houdetot, 84
Howie, Lt, 96
Huisseau-sur-Cosson, 154
Hunt, 2nd-Lt Leslie, 97–8, 365
Hunter, Capt. C., 228
Huppé, M. et Mme, 136

Incheville, 66
India, 17–9, 220, 307, 369
Indre, River, 157, 168, 242,
    244, 251
Irham, Major, 303–12
Italy, 79, 204, 218, 222, 235

Jacob, Claude, 302–5
Jardine-Paterson, Lt R.N., 24,
    26, 30–1, 34, 37–40, 84,
    96, 98, 100, 104, 364–6
Johnson, Maj.-Gen. D.G., 25
Josnes, 148

Ken, Loch, 17
Kensington Regiment (Princess
    Louise's) 1st Bn, 46, 78, 92
Kincardine & Kincardine Estate,
    15, 345, 352–4
King Edward VII, 18

King George V, 18
King George VI, 25, 343
King's Royal Rifle Corps, 16
Kleist, General, 60
Knight, Edward, 18
Knight, Montagu, 18
Knight, Thomas, 18
Koe, Patrick, 233
Kolhapur, 19–20

La Barthe-de-Neste, 181
La Bassée, 30, 104, 106, 208
La Rue, 161
La Tremblée, 132–3
La Tuileries, 74
Labradie, M, 182
Lainville, 137
Lalandelle, 132
Lalanne, M., 277
Lascoux, 195
Lattainville, 134
Laval, Pierre, 335
Le Briers, Todo, 314–29, 338
Le Havre, 41, 78–82, 92–4, 107,
    108, 326, 347
Le Plan d'Aragnouet, 183
Le-Dorat, 172
Le Mans, 28
Lefaux, 117–9
Legrand, M. et Mme, 191
Lens, 27, 31
Les Chabries, 222
Les Heaumes, 150
Les Sicaudières, 162
Lez, River, 195
Libya, 293, 336
Lignières-Châtelain, 98

Lille, 37, 39–42, 136
Lillers, 209
Limoges, 173, 202
Lisbon, 217, 244, 246, 253
L'Isle-Jourdain, 216, 220
L'Odetic, 315–29, 338
Loire et Cher, 176
Loire, River, 15, 134, 138, 143, 146, 148–52, 155, 251
Longwy, 57
Loos, Battle of, 34–5
Lothians and Border Horse, 1st Bn, 54
Lubbock, Maj. Alan, 243, 244, 247, 291–2
Luftwaffe, 74, 76, 84, 207
Luscan, 193
Lussac-les-Eglises, 172
Luxembourg, 46
Lye, 162

MacGregor, C.S.M., 26
MacGuffin, Bill, 286
Mackesy, Piers, 14, 364–5
Mackintosh, Pte, 121
Mackintosh-Walker, Col R., 104, 208, 226
Macpherson, Capt. R., 328
Madrid, 186, 237, 242–4, 247, 291, 293
Maginot Line, 29, 35, 40, 46–50, 53, 59, 61, 63, 94
Mailleul, 40
Maintenay, 119, 352
Malines, 274
Maps, 46, 66, 76, 82, 114, 123, 126, 138, 143, 145, 148,

151–7, 166, 171–3, 176, 179, 181, 182, 321
Mariain, M., 334
Marseilles, 79, 104, 163, 166, 178, 196, 200, 203, 220, 225–37, 242–9, 256, 259, 268, 276, 285, 291–93, 299, 303, 306, 313, 328, 332, 335, 356
Martigny, 78
Martin, Lt-Gen. H.J.J., 163–4
Matthewson, Provost Sergeant Stewart, 56, 70, 76, 87–8, 99
May, Miss, 261–2
McCreadie, Pte, 91–2
McGowan, Pte, 91–2
McKay, Pte, 121–42, 257
McMillan, Richard, 340–1, 367
McNaughton, RSM, 56
McPhail, Capt. M. (Padre), 76
Méhers, 160
Melville, Lt C.L., 27, 37
Mer, 146
Mers-el-Kebir, 166, 236
Metz, 35, 37, 46, 60, 61
Meuse, River, 51, 57
Mezieres, 57
Miannay, 66–9
Military Intelligence, 237, 262–72, 280, 295, 303–12, 328–36
Milly-sur-Thérain, 132
Milne, Maj. G.H., 10, 90, 96
Monaghan, Pte, 228
Mona's Queen, RMS, 28, 71
Moneville, 91

Monferran-Savès, 200–26,
    246–7, 251–6, 327
Montauban, 178
Montgarri, 195
Montgomery, Gen. Bernard,
    339–45, 346
Monti, Mr & Mrs, 215–24,
    234, 235
Montmédy, 63, 94
Montréjeau, 181, 192
Moon, Lt J.R.P., 24, 56, 65,
    83–4
Moreau, Lt. Jean de Vaisseau,
    314–5, 338–9
Morocco, 299, 308, 313, 322–3,
    336, 337
Moulis, 179, 196–7
Mounicq, Dr P., 179, 181–4,
    189, 353
Mourot, Lt J., 164–5, 166
Moyenneville, 66
Munich, 23, 33
Murphy, Mr, 334

Namps-au-Val, 128, 130
Namur, 51, 57
Neufchâtel-en-Bray, 63
Nicolas, Lt, 163
Niemiec, Commandant,
    279, 308
Noble, Maj. N., 36, 73–5
Norfolk Regiment – see Royal
    Norfolk Regiment
Normandy, 339, 343
North Africa, 229, 257, 260–89,
    293, 301, 303, 310, 336,
    339–41, 343

North Sea, The, 57
Northumberland Regt – see
    Royal Northumberland
Noyen-sur-Sarthe, 27–8

Offranville, 82
Omaha Beach, 343
Operation Catapult, 165
Oran, 233, 237, 265–71, 273,
    277, 291–2, 299, 332, 335
Orle, River, 195
Ostenga, 232–3
Ouville-la-Rivière, 81–2

Pacy-sur-Eure, 61, 64
Parachute Regiment, The; 16th
    (Welsh) Bn, 353
Parcé-sur-Sarthe, 28–9
Paris, 37, 58, 61, 63, 79, 94, 99,
    148, 168–9, 228, 233, 236,
    249, 280, 326
Penn, Arthur, 305
Pernois, 126
Péronville, 148
Perpignan, 171, 191, 196, 203,
    221, 227, 230, 233
Perret, M, 334
Petain, Marshal Philippe, 65,
    100, 117–8, 285, 303,
    305, 335
Pic de La Munia, 184
Pic de Troumouse, 184
Pic, Lt, 170
Poigny-la-Forêt, 141
Poland, 24, 259
Port d'Orle, 195
Port de Barroude, 184

Port de la Hourquette, 195
Port Pichard, 152
Portugal, 104, 188, 253
Pradère-les-Bourguets, 222
Prévillers, 131
Price, Pte, 228
Prince of Wales' Volunteers,
    The, 42
Prunay-le-Gillion, 143
Pyrenees, 179–90, 198, 214–5, 221,
    237, 241, 254, 306

Quakers, 178, 205, 213
Queen Elizabeth, 25, 33, 213,
    295–9, 306
Queen Victoria, 18
Queen's Own Cameron
    Highlanders, 4th Bn, 70,
    81, 121, 227
Queen's Own Cameron
    Highlanders, The, 16,
    42, 108
Quoeux, 123

Radinghem, 116
Raikes, Lt, 171
Rambouillet, 141
Rangiport, 137
Red Cross, The, 169, 198,
    203, 219, 222, 223, 241,
    242, 246, 254, 300, 304,
    338, 370
Reims, 72
Rémeling, 56
Rennie, Maj. T, 90, 104, 207,
    223, 226, 251, 341, 345,
    346, 349

Revelles, 127
Reynaud, Paul, 44, 58–9, 65,
    100, 117, 365
Rhine, River, 349
Rifle Brigade, The, 16, 108
Ritchie, 2nd Lt D., 365
Ritchie, Maj.-Gen. N.W., 300–1
Rogel, Lt, 163, 166
Rogers, Sgt, 90
Rommel, Gen.-Lt Erwin, 72, 107
Ronbaisc, 121
Roney-Dougal, Col, 103
Rothois, 131
Rotterdam, 58
Rouen, 65, 75, 78, 97–8
Royal Air Force, The, 158, 204,
    220, 233, 259, 289, 332
Royal Army Medical Corps,
    87, 380
Royal Artillery
    17th Field Regiment, 41, 78
    23rd Field Regiment, 41
    51st Anti-tank Regiment, 78
    75th Field Regiment, 78
    76th Field Regiment, 41
    77th Field Regiment, 41
Royal Artillery, The, 52, 81, 370
Royal Engineers
    26th Field Company, 41
    236th Field Company, 78
    237th Field Company, 78
    238th Field Company, 41
    239th Field Company, 78
Royal Engineers, The, 46, 75, 370
Royal Fusiliers, The, 42
Royal Military College,
    Sandhurst, 15

Royal Navy, 44, 92, 165
Royal Norfolk Regiment
    1st Bn, 37
    7th Bn, 46
Royal Norfolk Regiment, The,
    171, 303
Royal Northumberland
    Fusiliers, 7th Bn, 46, 68,
    234, 276–7
Royal Scots Fusiliers, 6th Bn,
    46, 78
Royal Scots Fusiliers, The, 46, 75
Royle, PSM, 84
Rudellat, Yvonne, 157–8
Russell, Lt S., 95–6
Russell, Maj. O.G.H., 95–6
Russell, Pte, 43

Saar, 35, 42, 46, 50, 52, 57, 61,
    76, 80–1, 92, 105, 110,
    166, 208
Salamanca Barracks, 25
Salardú, 195
Salignac-Eyvigues, 175–7
Salmond, J.B., 93, 339, 367
Sandford, Lt. R.U.E.A, 24, 39,
    65, 83, 91–2, 107, 109, 163
Sandhurst – see Royal Military
    College
Saragossa, 187
Sarlat-la-Canéda, 176
Sarrancolin, 181, 191
Savignies, 132
Sayonara, 326
Scharnhorst, The, 335
Scheldt, River, 58
Seaforth Highlanders

2nd Bn, 16, 41–2, 48, 337
    4th Bn, 64, 70
    6th Bn, 41–2
Seaforth Highlanders, The, 16,
    91, 108
Seclin, 104
Sedan, 51, 57
Ségur-le-Château, 175
Seine, River, 136, 138, 233, 345
Sellar, Dr, 171, 177, 178, 181, 191
Sentelie, 130
Séris, 149–51
Seysses, 180
Sharp, Cpl, 76
Sicily, 339, 341
Sierra Nevada, 321–2
Sixe, M., 31
Smythe, Lt Philip, 345
Solignac, 173
Sologne Resistance, 159
Somme, 60, 64, 65–72, 92,
    109–10, 126, 127
Spain, 104, 106, 121, 168, 169,
    171, 178, 179, 182, 184–8,
    193, 194–9, 208, 226–30,
    249, 251, 254, 258, 299,
    321, 337
Special Operatins Executive
    (SOE), 159, 233
St-Aignan, 170
St-Gaudens, 181
St-Girons, 194, 196, 200–3, 206
St-Josse, 119
St-Julien le Faucon, 345
St-Lary-Soulan, 182, 190
St-Laurent-des-Bois, 148
St-Laurent-de-Neste, 181

St-Léger-en-Yvelines, 141, 257
St-Léger-lès-Domart, 97, 100
St-Malo, 251
St-Nicholas-d'Aliermont, 77
St-Pierre-le-Viger, 82, 86
St-Pol-sur-Ternoise, 100–1,
    208–9
St-Rémy-au-Bois, 119
St-Saveur, 127
St-Valery-en-Caux, 47, 81, 85,
    88–97, 107–12, 163, 207–9,
    237, 254, 276, 299, 312,
    326–8, 337, 340, 346
St-Valery-sur-Somme, 60, 66–8
St-Yrieix-la-Perche, 173
Staff College, 294, 336
Stanley Clarke, Brig. A.C.L., 44,
    78, 108–10
Stephen, Lt-Col. C.G., 20–30,
    48–50, 61, 92, 207–10,
    273–5, 293–4, 298–306,
    336–7, 365, 367
Stephen, Mary, 298–9
Stettin, 222
Stewart, Maj. Duncan, 328
Strangforth, Ronnie, 301
Sudan, 20, 307
Surreaux, M., 168, 241–4
Switzerland, 57, 207

Taft, Orray, 262
Tait, Piper, 91
Tammai, 171
Tangier, 234, 267, 272, 275,
    279, 308
Telfer-Smollett, Lt A.D., 95–6,
    207–9, 275

Théry, Frédéric, 159
Thiers, 263, 264
Thomas, M., 314–7
Thomson, Lt-Col. Chick,
    341, 344
Toeuffles, 66–7
Toucoing, 37
Toulon, 166
Toulouse, 171, 178–80, 182,
    196–7, 199, 200, 205, 213,
    218–25, 253
Tour, Brig. & Mrs Wyndham,
    244, 291
Tours, 145–6, 165, 243
Trie Château, 134
Tripoli, 336
Tunis, 276, 286, 313, 333, 339,
    340–1
Tunisia, 286, 340
Tuyh, Joan, 333

USA, 180, 242, 244, 326
USS Augusta, 343
Utah Beach, 343

Va la Don, M., 150
Valines, 66
Vallière, 148
Vaqueira, 195
Vaquier, Liason Agent Pierre, 79
Varenne, River, 78–9
Varennes, 62–3
Vaughan-Lee, Susan, 352
Vaux-en-Amiénois, 126
Velennes, 130
Verdun, 62–3
Veules-Les-Roses, 92

Vichy, 117, 229, 235, 236, 283, 284, 296, 305–8, 335
Vignacourt, 125
Villentrois, 162
Villepoix, 132
Villers-sur-Trie, 134
Villiers-le-Màhieu, 138
Vismes, 73
Voluntary Aid Detachment, 224–5
Voves, 145

Waldeshare Park, 25
Walker, Capt. D.H., 74, 87, 90, 96, 99
Walton, Mr, 267
Wanchy, 77
War Office, 111, 169, 210, 241, 243, 247, 252, 273, 293–7, 300, 305–11, 330, 351

Wardlaw, CSM, 73
Warren, T., 272–5
Wauchope, Gen. Sir Arthur, 34–5, 241, 305
Wavell, Gen. Sir Archibald, 278
Weygand, Marshall Maxime, 59, 65, 305, 332, 334, 336
Whittaker, Winthrop, 170–2
Willeman, 120–3, 209
Winkelman, General, 58
Woincourt, 70
Woippy, 35
Wood, Kitty, 111
Wright, D.H.C., 326
Wy-dit-Joli-Villages, 137

Yacht Club, Algiers, 315–6
Yerville, 97
Young, 2nd-Lt M.H.C., 17
Ypres, 16–7